Slightly Bonkers Jamie

For Lucy
from Jamie

# Slightly
## Bonkers
### Jamie

Jamie Summers

First published in Great Britain in 2020 by A. J. P. Summers

Edited, designed and produced by Tandem Publishing Ltd
http://tandempublishing.yolasite.com/

ISBN: 978-1-5272-6110-5
10 9 8 7 6 5 4 3 2 1

A CIP catalogue record for this book is available from the British Library.

Printed and bound in Great Britain by CPI Group (UK) Ltd, Croydon CR0 4YY.

# Contents

# INTRODUCTION

Everyone has a story, and this is mine.

The title for the book comes courtesy of Joseph Boulter, son of Adam and Beth, brother of Hannah and Benjamin. He was aged six and needed to distinguish between the two Jamies he knew, as to who it was who was coming round for tea. The epithet has stuck and strikes me as pretty accurate.

Who among us can say that they are 'normal'? Perhaps we all desire to be called normal, not to offend anyone, not to stand out as different, but if I'm honest that's just not me. Or probably you for that matter. There is a much-quoted 'statistic' that one in four people will have a mental health problem at some stage in their lives. Personally, I think the true figure is much nearer one in one. Okay, I'm not saying you might be deemed schizophrenic (one in a hundred of us apparently), or bi-polar / manic depressive (one in two hundred they say), but moments of deep despair or uncharacteristic elation are commoner than you think. Trouble is that so many of us are acting out parts in our personal plays so as not to upset our friends, hiding our true emotions in the quest to stay on the right side of sanity.

What I want to explain to you over the ensuing pages is my own journey – some of the ups and downs, the traumas, the joys I've been given.

There are many people out there, not least members of my own family, who dismiss me out of hand. He's mad, he's not well, he's 'not normal' they would say. Others will mock the afflictions of a poor little rich kid – a spoilt brat, I've got no time for him, what he does or what his opinions might be.

They know who they are and are welcome to their opinions. In my defence can I bring people like St Francis and Jean Vanier to the table, likewise born with silver spoons in their mouths? It wasn't their fault that they were 'well born', it's what you do with the blessing that is important.

My tribe may be the few gifted with private education leading to Ivy League universities and consequent comfortable lives, but my heart is with the many less fortunate. There is no 'them and us' in society, there is only 'us'.

# 1

# DEATH'S DOOR

"Michael, you've got to help me" – my little, soft, croaky voice is calling my GP at his Knightsbridge practice from the pay telephone on Bluebell Ward at Springfield. The phone is right by the disgusting toilets never cleaned, by the open bathroom with shower-curtained cubicles to preserve a tad of modesty in this mixed male and female ward. The baths too are in a disgraceful state, chipped and stained.

It is 14th December 1991 and I am under attack from the powers that be, masquerading as carers in the psychiatric system. I am not sectioned but nevertheless I shouldn't be seeking help from my home doctor … he is out of the equation; one is in the hands of the consultants and registrars, they are in charge, in control of one's destiny.

I explain pitifully over the phone to Michael that I feel desperately weak, is there anything that he can do. "Okay, Jamie," he says, "I'm going to get a second medical opinion…" Praise the Lord, thank you Michael – he has effectively saved my life.

That evening I am prostrate on my bed in the allocated ward, partially curtained off from others. I am in very poor shape – despite being a fit and active 37-year-old, my body systems are being broken down – my white blood cell count has "gone bananas" according to one of the nurses, my frame is pole-axed, stupefied into a taut contortion. And yet the visiting consultant (my two have gone on holiday) wishes to continue me on the current levels of medication – indeed, my wife and middle sister were keen that my drug levels be increased, a fact I learned some time later when I accessed my medical records. Wow, am I lucky to be still alive. This visiting shrink called Dr Vince had increased my daily dose of Droperidol liquid from 30mg to 80mg two days previously. As stated, I am in serious trouble; death is just around the corner – had I died, cause of death would be attributed to the trauma of my mental illness. Poppy-cock – it would have been caused by criminal overdosing of dangerous drugs, done in whose name? Done in by the demons of the psychiatric profession. Makes me angry even now, over twenty-eight years later.

Okay, back to that telephone call to Michael – with the massive doses of Chlorpromazine (1000g), 80mg of Drop-eridol and over 800mg of lithium carbonate going daily into my body, it goes into a deep sedated state with only minutes of sanity and awareness when the effects briefly wear off before the next onslaught from the drugs trolley. I had to choose one of those brief interludes in which to makes this call – thank God Michael was there.

So that evening, and it's almost like an annunciation, this vision soon to become my saviour stands by my bed and gently asks me questions, takes my pulse and so on. She is I know not who, nor where she has come from. She has been sent via Michael Gormley to deliver a second opinion on my treatment. She tells the attendant nurse, "You are not to give this man any more drugs." For some reason her statement has to be obeyed – she has more clout than my consultants. Unfortunately records are sketchy but Michael now believes he would have telephoned Mark Collins at Springfield and this lady would have been on the staff there. My life is saved – thank you madam.

Slowly my body begins to recover its status – free from

the onslaught of pharmacology. I agree to continue the Pria-del, the branded lithium carbonate, because taking that will please my wife and anyway you shouldn't suddenly withdraw it completely – there are dangerous complications from so doing. Someone told me liquid Droperidol had been with-drawn from use soon after but an internet search reveals it is still out there to be used in doses of up to 2.5mg ... not 80mg!

By 28ᵗʰ December I am sufficiently awake again to start making a stand on behalf of my fellow patients. Aha, I know who I can write to ... Virginia Bottomley. It so happened that her husband, Peter, was a long-time friend of one of my brothers-in-law. Stephen Fry memorably discovered her name is an anagram of 'I'm an evil Tory bigot'. Anyroads, Virginia was Secretary of State for Health and I felt writing to her about the woeful conditions in Springfield might yield results. A lengthy correspondence ensued with her and later with Dr Enid Vincent of the Wandsworth Health Authority, all of which got me nowhere.

Some of the letters exchanged I have included at the end of the book in Appendix 1. In them I railed against the megadosing and polypharmacy practised by my consultant psychiatrist, Greville Gundy, and his underlings. Just a quick comment on Dr Gundy: I understood from friends he was an alcoholic but he retained his registration with the GMC until his death – I found him a ridiculous figure.

At the beginning of this chapter I omitted to mention how I got myself into this predicament. So here we go now. Eight years into our marriage the relationship had deterio-rated. My wife felt that I was a changed character after the manic moments that I will describe in Chapter 6. Me, I was ever hopeful that things could be turned around or at least improved – so how to do that? I had finally given up smok-ing dope and now just relied on nicotine and the odd bit of alcohol as my chosen stimulants. Bakery production and profits were languishing, she was finding life with me not what she wanted anymore – her previously stated message of, "If it happens again I'm leaving you" hung over the situation. Daughter C, it has to be said, was proving a more difficult child and was playing up at her nursery. My wife S found this hard and I doubt I was much help either. Continuing the lithium had given me a) the hand tremors and shaking that comes with this stuff and b) a sort of lackadaisical air, a blandness of emotion that is another side effect. Can you imagine the embarrassment of hardly being able to hold a cup of tea? No wonder my golf chipping skills were declining.

So how to recreate a bit of spark? Stupidly, I thought that as we'd enjoyed smoking weed together in times past, perhaps a little more would do the trick. A friend had some Thai sticks that he said were top quality and so I bought one. Okay, better try this out myself before I smoke a joint with S.

Error, gross error. Halfway down the joint I was on a 'high' once again and the high stuck. Round I go to friends Rupert and Simi on the Earlsfield Road who said nothing, bless them, as I toured their flower beds removing all the black plant tags which I then proceeded to show to the sun in my odd attempt to cleanse the blackness and bring them to the light. Whether Simi reattached them all I am not sure. Rupert, I remember, came with me for a rushed appointment with a social worker at nearby St John's clinic – a rather charming young girl who made arrangements for me to return, on a voluntary basis, to Springfield that evening. Michael Gormley had visited and written out a prescription note.

Anyhow, with my GP's prescription (as usual in dreadful doctor's handwriting) in my pocket and a packed bag of clothes, cigarettes and sundries, S drives me to the door of my allotted ward, Bluebell this time. It is clearly curtains for the marriage – I have sinned again, albeit unwittingly and with the brain cells in disarray in cannabis country perhaps not entirely my fault. Excuses, excuses but pathetically the attempt to rescue the ailing marriage has withered.

As S departs I enjoy, well undertake, one final fling of freedom. Leaving the bag at the foot of the stairs to Bluebell I head off for an extraordinary circuit of the Springfield site, crawling through bramble thickets, along ditches – my hands and knees become scratched and sore but I have achieved my objective in 'securing' the area by circumnavigating it. Only for the last few minutes am I spotted on the CCTV cameras and met by a couple of burly security guards.

They bustle me into the ward where for some reason I continue the wild encircling, round the main sitting area and into the dining area along the tops of radiators and window sills before being restrained and calmed. The story then continues as per the letters to Virginia Bottomley in Appendix 1 but you can see why I accepted my 'clinical condition' had changed on admission in the exchange with Enid Vincent. My behaviour had been bizarre.

So here we are on the upstairs ward of Bluebell with Crocus Ward underneath. Radiators are all on full pelt, it's almost suffocatingly hot – the carpets and linoleum floors are grubby. Life for us patients revolves around the drugs trolley, assembling for the awful meals and very occasional chats with nursing staff. I won't dwell on the depressing surroundings here – it's already stated in those letters to Mrs Bottomley but squalid it was.

Because I am one of the better-off ones on the ward and like to think I have a caring generous side I make frequent forays down Glenburnie Road to local Tooting Bec stores. Here I stock up with cigarettes (most of us lunatics like a smoke – nicotine is also a recognised antidote to anti-psychotic medicines), fruit, chocolate and other goodies that I dish out liberally to my fellow inpatients.

Ward rounds were meant to happen once a week but were often summarily cancelled. These are events where a consultant and up to ten others, nurses, students and social workers, all sit and stare at the patient, gauging their medical condition. If you wanted release, and most of us did, best to act normal and respectful to these 'professionals'. Your life is in their hands. Remember that nice young social worker on admission day? Well, at Ward Round No. 1 there she was again – so as is my wont I gave her a friendly peck on the cheek in greeting. Oops, this is destined to be written up as 'inappropriate sexual conduct' in the notes. Honestly!

Before my medication levels are increased to obscene levels there is a period of relative calm. Friends come to visit which is always nice. Rupert Johnson and Bill Bradby dropped by – Janie Hill and son Roland I introduced to the three ever-so-friendly sheep that were kept in a pen near the kitchen garden. In those days the grounds were unencumbered by the 9 holes of the London Golf Course – I helped out by weeding a couple of flower beds and played some tennis with a friendly nurse. These days the site is much reduced – no sheep, no tennis court and saddest of all no church, merely an all faiths' 'sanctuary room'.

I need to tell you about the church at Springfield. It means a lot to me. Currently it operates as a gym space, all padded pillars and mats for children, but back in 1992, indeed since 1840, it was St Peter and St Paul's Church. It becomes my refuge in this time of trouble. Here is an extract from a letter I wrote to its vicar some four years later:

In that little church, even at that kneeling window when its doors were shut I experienced wonders unimaginable to most. One time I was moved out of the blue from sitting in Bluebell Ward, drawn across the grass and paths ... not knowing a reason ... and there you were, saying some last words over some unfortunate's coffin to an audience of maybe six or seven (oh how the world forgets us) and there I saw that man or woman's Spirit ascend. The Power, the indescribable tingling, exhilarates.

All sorts of thoughts were oppressing my thinking at this time – some no doubt of a demonic nature. It seems even just one joint had affected my brain cells. There was one visit from S (which I do not recall), none from the children and it became clear that I wasn't welcome back at the family home. The onslaught of neuroleptic drugs was now being increased – I remember one Sunday lunch I was picked up from the hospital by Andrew and Carole who drove me up to their Primrose Hill home. Andrew's mother Oriel was there, no doubt thinking this slobbering shaking shambles of a relative was seriously mentally ill. That's what people assume; it's the illness not the side effects of the medication. At least I was fed a decent meal, something not available at Springfield – oh, perhaps in the staff canteen, but not for the nutters. I wonder what was going through the mind of my sister, now apparently in cahoots with my wife, as she dropped her little brother back at Springfield?

But once the salvation described at the beginning of this chapter had occurred my brain began its return to normality. My previous visits to the bin had lasted about three weeks each (more on them later) – this last one lasted twice as long because I wasn't welcome back in my own house. I languished on the ward, busying myself writing letters, trying to be good to fellow patients and becoming involved with the Patients' Council, a small advocacy outfit sticking up for the battered beleaguered inmates.

Let's have a break now from mental ailments. Let's look at my genetic inheritance and see where I came from.

# 2

# My parents

John David Summers. Born 18/8/1916. Died 20/1/2008.
Frances Evelyn Adelaide Patrick. Born 24/1/1919.
Died 6/9/1969.

The first two years of a child's life are so important – this was apparent to Aristotle and philosophers down the ages. Without warm, enveloping love in early years one's subsequent journeys in life will be beset by difficulties. Poor Dad got off to a rotten start – his father Alfred Spencer Mason Summers, a Captain in the 19th Royal Hussars had been seconded into the fledgling Royal Flying Corps, 60th Squadron.  At the age of thirty he

was shot down in his Beatty-Wright biplane over Beaulen-court on the Somme. He died of his wounds as a Prisoner of War on 15th September 1916, just one month after my father was born. Dad's mother, Mimi, of whom he seldom spoke and rarely met, somehow blamed him for the death of her husband. Probate records show that she received the lion's share of Alfred's estate, some £81,624 (£5 million today), but I am led to believe that once he knew a son and heir was safely delivered Alfred added various codicils to his will. And it seems these codicils were enough to sour and blight the mother's relationship with her son.

I only met her once, on a golfing trip up to Scotland with Dad; I remember a white house under a hill outside Peebles and being fed porridge with salt – yuk. She remarried in August 1918 Bache (pronounced Beach) Hay and moved to rural Northamptonshire – at least Dad was treated kindly by his stepfather and enjoyed the hunting and riding around North Berwick. Bache, by all accounts, was a dapper bon viveur, good at golf and entertaining. Life between the wars was easy for the moneyed middle classes – but remember that so many of their peers had perished in the trenches. World War I decimated the officer corps, mostly garnered from the public schools – they were the first to show their heads above the trenches, leading their men and were thus the first to be felled in the barrage of bullets.

From Farnborough prep school in Kent, Dad went to Eton, gaining a stack of School Certificates and on to Christ Church, Oxford where he read Agriculture. Member of the Bullingdon Club in 1937 and 1938 (before its excesses of later years perpetrated by the likes of George Osborne, David Cameron and Boris), a Polo Blue and a Divot, the second Oxford golf squad. He was appalled when his mother, without his knowledge, decided to have the Summers family pile (Emral Hall near Wrexham) pulled down and its contents sold in a fire sale in 1936. He rushed up to the sale, rescuing some pieces of furniture – the grander bits of the mansion, a Jacobean plaster ceiling, ornate windows and so on were bought by Clough Williams Ellis and now embellish the 'Town Hall' of Portmeirion, North Wales.

Dad was always aggrieved that he was thus unable to inherit Emral Hall – even though it was hardly part of the Summers family heritage. The land had belonged to the aristocratic Puleston family from the 13th century until 1904 when it was bought by the Summers family. John Summers & Sons, the steelworks at Shotton in Flintshire, was the source of our wealth – I'm the eldest son of the eldest son etc. of the entrepreneurial founder, John Summers, who started with a factory in Stalybridge in 1852 after buying a nail-making machine for £40 at the Great Exhibition the year before. Amazingly, the plant is still going, producing zinc and plastic-coated coils of sheet steel. Privatised in 1967, it became part of the British Steel Corporation, then Corus, then Tata from India and was most recently acquired by Jingye, a Chinese concern.

It irked my father that he had these 'trade' roots – he would much rather be seen as 'landed gentry'. Sad really – it doesn't matter a jot to most of us, nor should it. Do your best, whatever your background. Anyway, Dad joined the Life Guards after Oxford, rising to become a Major, and during the war a Lieutenant Colonel. He met Mum when he was point-to-pointing in his early twenties and soon realised she was quite a catch. They were married the day war was declared in a hurried ceremony in Mayfair followed by a reception at the Dorchester Hotel on Park Lane.

As an intelligence officer with the Life Guards he had an interesting war. When Hitler moved into Czechoslovakia on the night of 15th March 1939, Dad was the only person on duty in the Cabinet War Rooms. He chose not to wake Neville Chamberlain until the following morning to break the news. He was later in charge of all the Commonwealth cavalry arriving in Haifa (Palestine) where he spent most of the time refreshing his polo skills. He saw some action at El Alamein, more outside Fallujah in Iraq where the Life Guards came under fire from German Stuka dive bombers and later with Monty's Third Army pushing up from Sicily through Italy under the overall command of General Mark Clark, the American in charge.

His final hurrah came at the end of the war when alone with his batman and Jeep he was sent to halt the Russian Army advancing south towards the Middle Eastern oilfields that Britain wished to keep sweet for themselves. Somewhere near Batumi in modern day Georgia on the borders of Turkey and Armenia near Mount Arafat, Dad stopped the Russians single-handedly with orders from Churchill, Eisenhower and that devious rogue Stalin. Bravo.

Throughout his life he remained Major Summers (one comes down an officer notch on decommissioning) – Signor Majore when in Portugal. He bought a farm, Little Barrow, between Moreton-in-Marsh and Stow-on-the-Wold

in Gloucestershire shortly after the war and 'gentle-
man-farmed' its 600 acres. Local politics and administration
were his forte – he tried and failed to become the Conservative candidate locally and at St Albans but became Chairman of Gloucestershire County Council and the North
Cotswolds Rural District Council. For many years he ran
the Moreton Show and was District Commissioner for the
Heythrop Pony Club.

This is a gilded existence is it not, and position and power
came with a golden education and money in the bank. However, all that glisters is not gold – wealthy he may have been
but wise he was not. Zero emotional intelligence plagued
his first marriage. In the Palestine days, Mum would often
retreat to their Cairo flat in Gezira with deep depression.
Dad was unable to understand her moods – perhaps the
result of his abandonment as an infant – unable to help,
ineffectual. Where Mum found her solace I am not sure,
because Dad destroyed the letters she had written to him,
keeping his own to her, which show banality but not 'being
alongside'.

Theirs was not quite an 'open' marriage but infidelity
abounded. Mum apparently with an Akers-Douglas and
a Smith-Bingham in their early years together, Dad with

a host of local ladies throughout the thirty years of marriage. What upset me most was when gearing up to divorce Mum in 1969 he chose to set up a separate life in London and Sandwich, Kent with the woman who was to become his second wife. This was stupid and cruel – he could have waited. It eventually led to Mum's suicide.

And his behaviour then was weird – so ashamed was he of Mum's demise that none of his children was allowed to attend her rushed funeral at Barton Cemetery, Oxford. The word 'suicide' was never mentioned – it was a heart attack apparently. The family home was sold within weeks, a wonderful house designed by a Mr Griffin, the architect, with much input from Mum. We had moved 'inland' from the Fosse

Way in 1960 towards the River Evenlode as dogs were getting run over tragically on the increasingly busy main road. The Little Barrow house was just a hundred yards from the Roman highway.

Can you imagine the trauma of losing your mother in your early teenage years, having to suppress the truth of the reason, not attending the funeral and dispatched to school just a few days after the death? It never seemed to bother me at the time but when one thinks about it…

Marriage number 2 was not a success for Dad. Moving to a small mews house in London off Pont Street and carting half of his country house English furniture out to a villa on the Vale do Lobo golf course in the Algarve. His infidelities continued in the Portuguese heat and soon he had captured the heart of the course manager's wife, Betsy.

Divorce from second wife Helga cost him dear – financially, anyway. The London house was sold (I had moved out / been moved out at the age of eighteen to my own flat), he and Betsy moved to Vilamoura initially, but when shots were fired in the communist putsch of 1973 they ran scared back to the safety of England. Having spotted a cottage in *Country Life* magazine on Romney Marsh, they bought it sight unseen and were to spend the rest of their lives among the sheep and drainage ditches.

Marriage number three lasted over thirty years and I guess was happy enough, she painting Kent scenes and still lifes in oils, he pottering around in his vegetable patch, helping at the local Citizens Advice Bureau, occasionally entertaining friends. Visits were fleetingly made to grandchildren – they once drove out to Italy, stayed one hour for lunch, then drove home. To be honest, our paths did not cross much over his last thirty years. Losses at Lloyd's took their toll – he was one of the first to sign up to the draconian Lloyd's Hardship Committee, chaired by the fragrant Mary Archer, and I believe had to survive on a gratuity of £14,000 per annum with Lloyd's taking ownership of all he had left.

He got to 91½ years old – the last couple of years tormented by the cruel ravages of dementia. What can one say? A good organiser, yet prone to damaging interference in his children's lives. A good gardener, providing us with ample fruit and vegetables. A supporter of responsible agricultural techniques: crop rotation, using no pesticides or artificial fertilisers – indeed an early member of the Soil Association, the arbiters of the organic movement founded by Lady Eve Balfour. Kitten seemed to be his favourite child, his cine camera concentrated on her, and fittingly she was kindest to him in his final years. At the end there was little left but a tired cold cottage. Betsy, although many years younger than him, did not survive him long herself and they are buried side by side at the south-eastern corner of the ancient Old Romney church where he always felt that Thomas à Becket was interred in 1170. He was a keen advocate of saving the Romney Marsh churches for posterity.

By contrast, Mum had a better start in life. It is only fairly recently that I have been able to piece together much of her history via snippets from sisters and strange coincidences. It has been a fascinating journey to learn more about her sterling work, indeed starring role during the war. She remains, in my view, one of the unsung heroines of our island story – her mental frailties clouding my siblings' memories of their mother. Is it that canard, that label 'mentally ill', that distorts people's recollections of others? But look at Winston Churchill and his 'black dog' depression – he done all right, eh. His dark moods and his stirring rhetoric were well portrayed by Gary Oldman in the film *Our Darkest Hour*. Without

him (and as you will learn soon, my maternal grandfather) where would the United Kingdom stand today? As a vassal state of a Third Reich Nazi Empire or as a Soviet satellite? Mum's parents met in a house outside Rugby. The Mulliners' country pile had been commandeered by the authorities during World War I as a rest and rehabilitation hospital and home for officers (and I hope men) of the Royal Flying Corps. Like Dad's father Alfred, Mum's father Mark had been seconded to the RFC from a cavalry regiment, in his case the 16th Queen's Lancers. The daughter of this house outside Rugby, my grandmother Mary, was enlisted as a nurse. When Mark Patrick arrived wounded from the front, love blossomed.

Mum's father Mark deserves a biography of his own, so apologies for giving him only a synopsis here. Eton and Christ Church like Dad and myself, but scholastically in a different league. There was a scandal during his time at Oxford which meant he had to leave before graduation – suffice to say the incident which caused this will possibly remain forever 'remaindered' or 'redacted', certainly for a hundred years. Nevertheless, he soon entered our country's Diplomatic Service, passing out top in the Civil Service exams.

A spell followed in the embassy at The Hague, the Netherlands and at the age of twenty-nine he was our man in Switzerland, head of the legation in Berne. Promotion soon followed, and at age thirty-two he become 1st Secretary in Moscow, under the Ambassador, Sir Anthony Evey. By now he was married to 'Gran' but she chose not to accompany him to Russia. I have a picture of Mark shaking hands with Joseph Vissarionovich Stalin at an embassy reception, Trotsky lurking in the background.

In his time there he wrote a book excoriating Bolshevism – *Hammer and Sickle*. Worth another look I can assure you … indeed Columbia University of New York recently discovered its existence and I understand the CIA would like it republished because its advice holds good to this day. Its message might not appeal to Mr Putin, or even to Mr Corbyn, and sadly communism survived in the USSR for decades after the book's publication.

Sadly too, Mark had to return to the United Kingdom to divorce his misbehaving wife. He was able to name as 'co-respondents' all his fellow officers in the 16th The Queen's Lancers, his cavalry regiment. In other words she had slept with *all* of his mates in his absence – disgraceful in my book. People say it was the times, morals were looser – the roaring twenties with cocktails, cocaine and the Charleston were her métier and milieu. Mark packed in the Diplomatic Service as a career at this stage and stood for election down in Tavistock, Devon as the Conservative candidate.

Success – he was elected as their Member of Parliament. His father, Colin Grant Patrick, had made money in the London property market, owning at one time bits of Oxford Street and Berkeley Square. Mark, therefore, had a London house in North Audley Street and later one in Thurloe Square, South Kensington, in addition to a house on the edge of Dartmoor outside Tavistock, with stables for his horses and my mother's ponies. He was quickly recognised as a rising

star in the party, soon becoming PPS (Parliamentary Private Secretary) to Sir Samuel Hoare, initially at the India Office but following him to the Foreign Office. His best friends in the House of Commons were Anthony Eden and Rab Butler.

Aghast at Hitler's policies in Germany and unnerved by Messrs Halifax and Chamberlain seeking peace with this evil, Mark started the 'Eden Group' to counteract their appeasement ideas. Round to his house he invited Hoare, Churchill, Eden, Duff Cooper, Harold Nicolson and young Harold Macmillan, where they conspired to thwart the appeasers. Thank God they did. I would like to think also that he contributed to the 'Kindertransport' set up by his boss, Sir Samuel Hoare, to rescue young Jews from the continent.

Mum at this time was attending point-to-points (where she met my father), 'coming out' in London but also, at the age of seventeen, teaching at a cookery school in Seer Green, Beaconsfield. I imagine she divided her time between mother in London and father in Tavistock – she was only fourteen when they divorced. Where she went to school I know not.

So as war breaks out, Mum and Dad make plans for Palestine. She writes to the Bible Lands Society (Embrace, they are called today) offering her services to refugees in Syria. They move to a small house near Ladrun, between John the Baptist's home village of Ein Karem and the airport at Lod. Mum commences further work as Secretary / PA to Colonel Bryant, the Chief of Police in Jerusalem and is recruited for MI6 work there, as well as in Ankara, Turkey and Cairo in Egypt. The offices of their Jerusalem work were close to Jaffa Gate – the site of David's tomb and the Judaeo-Christian church of Christ Church. It is the highest point in the Old City.

On my first visit to Israel in early 1992 when visiting the Christ Church museum adjacent to the church, dedicated to the memory of Michael Solomon Alexander, the first Jewish man to become Anglican Bishop of Jerusalem, I was astonished to discover that all the descriptive cards of the exhibits were in my mother's distinctive handwriting. Wow.

I was staying in the annexe of the American Colony Hotel (where rooms were just about affordable at the time). I later discover that my parents' second home in Palestine was a flat in the main building there – and would you believe it, perhaps the very flat that was loaned to Tony Blair when he became 'Middle East Peace Envoy' in 2007.

My mother's primary job in Palestine, however, was running the Rest and Rehabilitation Centre for all the Allied officers fighting in the Middle East. This was in the grounds of the beautiful Church of the Multiplication of the Loaves and Fishes at Tabgha on the north shore of Lake Galilee – it is now a German-run convent. When I first came there in 1992 I had no idea of its connection to my mother, her life and times were shrouded, scattered in the belongings and memories of my sisters. So here is Mum, aged just twenty, cooking and cleaning for scores of bruised and battered men

– I think there was just one other woman to help her. I learnt many years later that she travelled about in a Buick convertible with a Boxer dog and a donkey called Percy who both sat on the back seat of the car! After the war Percy was retired to the famous Brook Animal Hospital in Cairo and when Mum visited once, he sensed her presence and rushed to the gates to greet her.

My eldest sister Anne was born in Cairo on 18th July 1941. It must have been galling for both parents to send her back to England. There to be cared for, for the duration of the war, by Ada, Mum's grandmother who lived outside Rugby. One's country or one's kin – where do one's priorities lie? Anne went with her nanny in a flying boat back to England from Cairo before she turned one, and I'm sure she was well looked after. Around this time Mum was suffering mentally – post-natal depression no doubt. Added to her woes was the news that her father had died back in London on 7th January 1942. He had enlisted in the 16th Lancers once again but succumbed to the wounds he had received in World War I, having been shot in the stomach 'going over

the top'. General Mark Clark sent her a kind letter offering condolences – he was Commander of the US Fifth Army and had heard Mark Patrick speak about communism and Russia some years before.

At the end of the war Mum devoted her time to breeding and training horses, gardening, entertaining and us children, albeit with the help of nannies and governesses. We had dogs, Kay the greyhound, Freckie the English Setter, chickens (so often viciously slaughtered by foxes) and some of the best show and eventing horses in the country. Their names will live on – Lady Astor (champion Dartmoor pony), Xanthos, who was sold to Anneli Drummond-Hay, plus gems such as Cashla, Mervyn, First Knight, Merlin and Satnar, the elegant Akhal-Teke horse who spent his later years at Cliveden with Bronwen, the real Lady Astor. Mum's best friends were her horsey ones. Mary Rose Williams over near Northleach and another who I thought was such fun, Van de Vater as he styled himself. Irish and probably bisexual – I discovered the other day that he employed Norman Scott on his farm in Ireland – notorious as Jeremy Thorpe's 'little bunny' in the infamous court case of May 1979.

From North Rye House, our second home in the Cotswolds, Mum started the Evenlode Riding Club in a covered riding school by Broadwell village. She gave her time to design and organise the gardens at the Moreton-in-Marsh hospital and we were always dropping off old magazines for the patients there. A very talented cook she was too, using Elizabeth David and Katie Stewart recipes, hosting elaborate dinner parties and yummy picnics when we went to one-day horse events around the local area. I can taste them now … hard-boiled eggs with Aromat, jellied consommé, cheese and chutney sandwiches…

I think there were absences when things became too much and Mum would spend time at the Priory, I believe even undergoing the dreaded ECT (electro-convulsive 'therapy') but these I don't recall, or have I blanked them from my memory? Sure, she had some wacky ideas at times: "Toothpaste gives you cancer" ... I've been frugal with the stuff ever since. A florid imagination – sadly lost is the marvellous typed letter that she sent all of us children when divorce loomed and her hopes for a new life near Loulé in Portugal with a donkey and cart beckoned. Another dream was a place on the Thames near London with a boat to use on the river – we even attended a weekend course together down near Chichester on navigation techniques. I was always on her side – even as a child mocked by my father for this, as per A. A. Milne's poem ...

> James James
> Morrison Morrison
> Weatherby George Dupree
> Took great
> Care of his Mother
> Though he was only three

... my father would taunt, only half-joking.

Towards the end she asked me, "You know your father is stupid don't you?" "Yes," I replied. Sister Kitten once showed me a book that Mum had written notes inside, thinking this encapsulated her madness – but it was a complex theological narrative that would have confounded any mortal and to me it was perfectly understandable that she had struggled. Many people scribble in books, anyway.

So matters came to a head in the summer of '69 – Dad was often away with his new lady in Sandwich Bay but had returned to Gloucestershire. At a scrambled eggs and chives supper one evening at the kitchen table Mum actually threw a glass at him and he made notes and a little diagram of the incident. Perhaps he thought this might aid his legal case. On the fateful final day I'd been at Adlestrop, playing in a cricket match, and returned to find the door to their bedroom locked. Lady Mary Rose Williams, her best friend, and I got a ladder and climbed up through an open window from the garden. We found her slumped over her basin, unconscious, with bottles and pills scattered around. It was obvious to me what she'd done. Research in recent years has uncovered the likelihood of suicidal thoughts as a side effect of anti-depressant medicines – was that a trigger in Mum's case? Who knows.

Anyway, an ambulance came, took Mum to Moreton-in-Marsh cottage hospital and they pumped her stomach, but it was apparently too late. Dad insisted that Kitten and I carried on as normal that evening – there was a party at Little Barrow, our old house, given for Francis Mander by his parents Sir Charles and Lady Mander. Another of those extraordinary coincidences occurred – Sir Charles' god-daughter was staying there, and I remember her descending the stairs to the hall. We didn't meet again until our paths crossed in the mental health world in 1992. Kitten had been dining that evening with the Aizlewood family at Brookend House, Chastleton and was taken aside by father Peter to be told of Mum's demise. Kitten and I were duly ferried back home when it became clear that Mum had died.

I remember eating baked beans on toast on returning to our kitchen – somehow not crying. Dad was grief-stricken, failing to understand what he'd done wrong, perched on the bottom step of the small flight of stairs that led to their bedroom. Ros Hammond-Maude, Mark Patrick's only other daughter, had committed suicide in 1963 – Mark would have been horrified to learn that both Ros and now Eve had taken their own lives.

So that's my parents' story. We shall return now to their son's sorry saga of mental troubles. Brace yourselves.

# 3

# MASQUERADE

Published in August 1979, Kit Williams' fabulous book, with his naïve realist paintings woven around a story containing clues as to the whereabouts of a buried jewelled hare, set my and many other hearts soaring. I got my copy in the summer of 1980 and the quest to find this hidden treasure began to take over my life.

When not baking loaves and cakes for a little shop on local Webb's Road called The Tangled Web I was poring over Ordnance Survey maps both 1 inch and 2½ inches to the mile – convinced that various of Kit's paintings were corresponding to the road layouts in Plymouth and elsewhere. Massive amounts of marijuana were fuelling these ideas – one night in November I set off from Battersea following the brightest street lights and those in the sky heading I knew not where. "Follow the yellow brick road," I was thinking. I walked for miles and miles through the streets of south-west London via Putney and Barnes, through Surbiton (I recall passing St James' church there), Isleworth where I was stumped by a lack of river crossing and on to Hampton Court. At one stage I saw a house resembling one featured in Kit's book.

House-mates came to rescue the knackered walker the following morning. That lunchtime I was musing on where else the *Masquerade* hare might be – perhaps it was buried at the corner of Jamie's Wood (between Little Barrow and Heath Barn, which we knew as Ludlow). It was there in the mid-seventies that Mary Rose Chichester and I had once

camped. Did I lose the silver hair bracelet that she once gave me at that very spot that night?

Perhaps the finest family heirloom I have is an oil painting by Raoul Millais (grandson of John Everett) of my mother riding Cyclone just there, with the Ludlow farm buildings in the background.

At half past two in the afternoon, Christopher P-B (my GP's partner) arrives hot foot – alerted, indeed startled, into action by my sister Carole's emergency call to their practice. He is reassured that little brother Jamie is not climbing the walls as she has claimed and does not need immediate sectioning. I do promise to call in soon and talk to the nursing sisters back at the Priory. Big sister Anne asserts that Carole was merely trying to 'pull me back from the edge', but that is not how it felt to me. My judgement may well have been clouded, even distorted, by the dope-smoking – who knows?

Throughout this book I will occasionally insert verbatim passages from my GP's notes which give clarity and veracity to things. Here is Michael's entry for 17th November 1980:

'High again for the last few days. Trying to find the mystery rabbit in Tim Williams' *Masquerade*'.

Let us not embarrass him by using 'sic' but this should read 'hare' and 'Kit', not 'rabbit' and 'Tim'.

Sisters Camille, Renée and Margaret Mahoney at the Priory had been kind and caring to us patients there. One of those Holy Spirit moments had happened towards the end of my first stay, which I talk about in Chapter 8. Camille and I, on Sunday, 10th February 1980, are conversing in a room off the 'Treatment' corridor when we both hear the sound of rushing footsteps accompanied by whispering noises. We dash out to see what is going on – but there is no one to be seen. 'Tellement étranges ces ésprits,' I record. In English that is 'So strange these spirits'. There are definitely ghosts and such out there but they rarely bother me.

A few days before that long walk I had gone by train and

taxi to Buckland Abbey, Sir Francis Drake's house, near Buckland Monachorum in Devon. To me the picture of the girl swimming in the *Masquerade* book held the key to the puzzle and somewhere in the woods below the old Cistercian monastery on the River Tavy I was sure the golden hare was buried. I had even taken the prongs of a garden fork in my Colombian bag with which to dig it up.

In fact in all of his paintings I was seeing relevant villages and features – Kit's Hill was near Horrabridge, Great Mister, Maristow (Mary's toe), Buckfastleigh, Buckland, Fishacre Wood, Pennycomequick – all these names were saying you are on the right track. A 'buck' can be a male hare.

In the grounds of the Abbey there was some drainage work in progress – heaps of soil, planks, plastic tubing, ditches and wheelbarrows. This appeared to me to be a precise mock-up of the swimming page in the book and I photographed the area from all angles in the dusk with a Polaroid-type camera I had brought with me. In my delusional state it seemed that someone had deliberately created this montage for my benefit. Trudging down through the woods to my chosen spot, however, revealed no new insight, just seeing a beautiful kingfisher.

Back to Plymouth I went, empty-handed – briefly searched by police who fortunately missed the bag of weed that I carried, but who advised me to take the milk train back to London. Desperate for clues I was; even castaway mailbag tags at the station seemed to have messages for me.

The *Masquerade* hare was eventually unearthed in Ampthill Park, Bedfordshire where Kit and Bamber Gascoigne had buried it – I was nowhere near. The book spawned many other literary treasure hunts but Kit Williams' was the first – he is a formidable carpenter, jeweller and craftsman as well as being perhaps my favourite artist. From the Portal Gallery in Grafton Street I used to occasionally buy similar artwork – one by James Grainger of a vicar juggling hedgehogs, several sheep by Jerzy Marek and one by Barry Castle, but sadly I was unable to afford a Kit Williams original.

Better to have searched and lost than never to have searched at all. I had such fun with all those maps, tracing paper, felt-tip pens and wild madcap theories. Dryden put it succinctly – "there is a pleasure sure in being mad which none but madmen know." Up until the late autumn that year had passed relatively serenely. I'd attended outpatient clinics both at the Priory with Desmond Kelly, and with Anthony Fry at Guy's. I even experimented with acupuncture, seeing a Dr Phoenix Mann in Harley Street. Useless for mania as it turned out but his name alone was inspiring.

The comedown from the massive 'high' that had hit me in December and January took probably until the end of February to quieten, judging from the entries in my diary. Time is one of the great healers. I had stayed some three weeks at the Priory which had cost me £3,000 – gulp. Despite the nursing staff's best endeavours BUPA chose not to pay for my treatment. But I felt sufficiently happy with the time at the Priory – the food is pretty good, croissants for breakfast etc. – that I decided to donate a present which I gather still adorns Inner Court at the hospital.

Mum had left me two parcels of land in her will. One was a 2/9th share of a small parade of shops in Fulham (more about that later), the other was a 5-acre field with a clapboard bungalow where she stipulated that George Moreton, now in his dotage, be allowed to spend the remainder of his days. Of course, Mum. Not long after, Dad went behind my back, without my permission, to make enquires at a local estate agent with a view to selling this inheritance – I understand Mr Moreton had heard about these machinations, indeed he had allegedly received threatening letters from John Drury & Sons (land agents in Moreton-in-Marsh) and was understandably distressed.

Sadly, this was just one example of the interference into his children's financial lives that my father sometimes undertook. I must have internally harboured this 1977 intrusion into my affairs because the meddling muddled my thinking three years later on the night of my friend Mary Rose's funeral. Towards the end of Chapter 8, in the diary entry for 25th January 1980, you will learn more of my starting a bonfire to purge elements of my father's influence from my life. A cathartic conflagration in the garden it was.

George Moreton was our long-standing groom. He had a wonderful way with horses, was as strong as an ox, yet as I have learned just now had beautiful handwriting. Totally deaf, he used to shout his sentences without realising. A classic countryman, he lived with his agoraphobic wife, first in a cottage by Little Barrow and then up in this bungalow on the edge of Stow-on-the-Wold. I gather he had only once in his life been as far as Cheltenham, just twelve miles distant.

On 23rd February 1980 I had driven the Morris down to Stow and loaded it up with some of the heavy staddle stones stored in a dilapidated barn close to the bungalow. Mr Moreton, at age eighty-three, was able to pick up these blocks of limestone as if they were made of polystyrene, such was his strength.

Anyway, one of these 'mushrooms' I presented three days later to the Priory. I had been allowed home fully on 15th February after several brief home visits and welcomed my freedom. Fellow patient (and friend from school and Christ Church) Harry Percy kindly gave Sue Gernaey (a friend from the New Forest) and me a tour of Syon House and its upper corridors. He explained how German bombing raids in the Blitz had often ended their runs over Syon Park where they would discard any unused bombs. Miraculously, all but one missed the 1760 house, the incendiary one that fell on the roof was extinguished by his nanny! Poor Harry died at the age of forty-two in 1995, despite a dalliance with Naomi Campbell's mother – I fear as a consequence of huge consumption of prescription anti-depressant medications. Another friend, Luke Montagu, likewise burdened or blessed with stately home responsibilities, might well agree with my peroration. He heads up, with James Davies, the excellent Council for Evidence-Based Psychiatry (www.cepuk.org) who challenge the mores of the Royal College of Psychiatrists and their often blinkered medical model approach.

This period towards the close of 1980 was turbulent if not quite as dramatic as the year's opening. When 'fired up' and frenzied, my mind moves in mysterious ways. Too much concentration on 'the world' with its mass media, profusion of advertisements, signage and so on becomes confusing. When the signs come from God, however, life becomes more placid. One such sign was delivered on the day I dropped the mushroom at the Priory. Kitty Barrell, who I had dated for several months in 1979 and who lived at my house when I set off for Nepal, had given me a silver cross and chain, purchased down in Lyme Regis, Dorset.

This is how it came about:

26<sup>th</sup> February 1980

My dear Jamie,

I agree it is extraordinary the way people and events link to form patterns around one. On Friday afternoon I said goodbye to Julian and boarded my train early – the carriage was empty: then an attractive dark haired girl was struggling to put an enormous red suitcase on the rack – I helped. We sat down, faced each other and immediately I heard myself say 'but, you are Lizza, I was at your wedding on October 5<sup>th</sup>!' I had not seen her before or since. She had been Martin's girlfriend for a couple of years and after they parted she almost immediately got engaged to Sebastian. Martin took me to her wedding. It was a weird meeting because I felt I knew her as Martin had often spoken of her, and she likewise had heard about me from his friends. We talked and talked in a by now packed carriage; starting strangers and ending friends!

When she got out, I was alone again until two youths settled in. The one opposite me wore a striking silver cross on a black t shirt. I couldn't help it, I kept staring at it and thinking about Lizza & why we should suddenly be face to face and then I realised why I was staring – the significance was obvious. You had written of a silver cross in your black notebook and there it was on a black t shirt. So here is yours now: it is given in friendship – you were evidently meant to have one.

See you soon

All love

K

These days I wear this simple silver cross all the time. There were times, however, when it seemed wise to keep one's Christianity hidden. Like when a new director arrived at Hammersmith & Fulham MIND … "You're not another one of those bloody Christians are you?"

Yes, actually!

He had spent time as a mental health nurse in the NHS – perhaps their training is awry? Or their outlook? Let's take another break from mental health issues shall we…

# 4

# THE EARLY YEARS

I always thought my family nickname was 'Mouse', for I was small and scurried about a lot. But apparently I was known as 'The Blessing'. Primogeniture, or at least the patrilineal version, meant much to my father, and after three daughters the sought-after son arrived.

At 7.45 a.m. on 13th July 1954 on the labour ward of Nuffield House, Guy's Hospital, London EC3 with Nurse Burchmore attending and John Blakeley in charge, Andrew James Patrick Summers is born. 8lbs 12 ounces, 19 inches long, chest circumference 14 inches and head 14½ inches – all this meticulously recorded by Mum. I love her description of the previous day... "Waked early, then shopped at Selfridges and went to the hairdressers at 11.30am. David picked me up and we took the Bentley to Nelson's to be serviced and repaired – We lunched at Fortnum's with Mummy." That night she and her mother saw *Night People* with Gregory Peck in it before dining with Dad at 'Le Perroquet' Restaurant in Leicester Square. "I had crab cocktail ~ Omelette ~ Strawberries" says Mum. As I have mentioned before I come from a rich background; few at the time drove Bentleys or lunched at Fortnum & Mason. Some post-war rationing was still in place, Churchill was our Prime Minister meeting President Eisenhower at the time, the Methodists were doubting Billy Graham's theology and Lord

Brookeborough over in Ulster was issuing warnings to the IRA that civil and religious liberty would be defended with all the resources at our disposal.

People were singing the tunes from hit musicals like *South Pacific* and queuing to see *The Boyfriend* in the theatre. The gloom of the long war years was finally lifting. Mum was allowed to spend a few days recuperating in Room D8 at the hospital, saying prayers in the charming chapel and attending a Choral Communion on 25th July at the close-by Southwark Cathedral – set to become my default church many years later.

I was christened at Bourton-on-the-Hill parish church on 12th September – there is a splendid photograph of me that day being cradled by sister Anne and surrounded by all my other sisters and cousins. Kitten, two and a half at the time, looking suitably miffed. Indeed apparently she developed a psychosomatic illness later that day after polishing the pews in the church – yes, Kitten, time to take second place for a while. My godparents were Barbara Shakerley, Pauline Rankin, Peter Thin and Arthur Budgett. The last two were decidedly horsey – Peter the starter at Cheltenham Race-course and Arthur the trainer of Derby winners Morston and Blakeney.

Jean Vanier has written: "The capacity to love develops in the very first months of a child's life through the relationship with their mother. One needs the experience of a first love that is unconditional. If the small child is wounded by rejection or the absence of this first love it is likely to lack self-confidence and have great difficulty in later life."

So, I was ever so fortunate with my predicament. First memories are the bull pen on the farm, lupins at the foot of the garden; the tortoise in the sunken garden and the somewhat dark oak-panelled rooms of our Jacobean mansion. Perhaps my care was often undertaken by nannies and food prepared by a cook in a distant kitchen. Horses played a major part in our lives – I remember the clever stone 'mounting block' in the stable yard close to our very own petrol pumps, which fuelled tractors for the farm and exotic vehicles like the aforementioned Bentley and later ones such as the splendid Humber Super Snipe with its fold-down wooden tables for back seat passengers.

I was plonked on various animals, dressed like Little Lord Fauntleroy when winning a rosette at the Oddington show in the leading rein class atop Lady Astor, that pesky Dartmoor pony. There was a rotund Thelwell-like brown pony called Robin who was my first mount – an easier ride than most in

our stables. I think he came from the Sheldon family over in Evenlode – lovely parents of Sally, Caroline and Jamie.

They, along with many other local 'posh' children, attended the school set up by Dad in Bourton-on-the-Hill. Pilgrim Cottage was a tiny terraced house with effectively two class-rooms where Mrs Holder taught her charges their times tables, a bit of French and how to write and read. At the back was a sloping garden which seemed quite large at the time – we were always careful with two of our fellow learn-ers who were haemophiliacs. Robin and Susan Aizlewood from Chastleton, Tim and Julie Robinson our doctor's chil-dren from Stow-on-the-Wold, the Sheldon clan, naughty Edward Studd from Lower Swell, Deidre Ward from near the Four Shires Stone and several others got a marvellous start to their education.

Mrs Holder lived in a large house at the top of the village where we would assemble once a year for a pageant with games and dancing around. Clearly cakes and biscuits and copious quantities of orange squash would have been involved too. Our teacher, who had been in the S.O.E. (Special Operations Executive) during the war, was wise and kind. Many of us gathered in the village hall in the nineties to thank her personally at a get-together organised by Julie.

Sometimes Kitten and I would be dropped in the morning at the top road where a footpath descended to Pilgrim Cottage – in autumn it was such fun kicking the fallen leaves. I guess I stayed from the age of four to the age of seven in this Laurie Lee-like Cotswold idyll. I love that bit in *Cider With Rosie* when on his first day at his first school he is told, "Now you just wait there for the present." He waited all day and no present came his way, poor mite.

In 1960 we moved into North Rye House which I adored. The building work had cost some £100,000 and taken some two years. We rented a temporary place in Donnington where Kitten lost a handkerchief, nicked and buried by a large dog, an Airedale Terrier I believe, at the crossroads. I remember sheds for bantams, their tiny eggs, and sneakily drinking the dregs from the thrown-out bottles of alcohol. More months were spent at Pond House in Broadwell and even some nights in a caravan parked next to the building site. On moving-in day we sank a horseshoe into the mortar near the kitchen corner window – for good luck.

My playmate sister Kitten – I hope I gave as good as I got because she treated me pretty poorly, much like Clare Balding's treatment of her little brother, Richard – disappeared off to big school, Ladymede near Aylesbury, leaving me to fend for myself. So no more hair being elastic-banded and scissored off, no more snails to eat nor blame to be attached to me for her misdemeanours. Funny that I missed her really.

The best days at North Rye (I had wanted it called Star

House but lost the family competition) were summer days with friends over, like Robin Aizlewood and Tim Robinson, to dam the little stream and ford close to the house, to ride bikes all around – Kitten's little blue one was a superior vehicle to my cumbersome and heavy red and cream one – to play in the hay barn, consume quantities of strawberries, gooseberries and raspberries sitting in the kitchen garden fruit cage or to make early examples of crop circles in the wheat fields (not appreciated by grown-ups). We had a big bell outside the back door which was rung to summon children in for elevenses or lunch or tea or whatever. I have fond memories of clumps of primroses in Crowthorne Wood, gathering sticky buds and catkins in spring. Less attractive to a sensitive soul were the dead crows and assorted vermin arranged on wooden scaffolding at the woods corner by farmworkers Len and Roy – not sure why they did that.

My first pet was a grey rabbit called Brackie – given I think to compensate for the loss of Kitten. I was a useless guardian for poor Brackie but enjoyed feeding him with that silver-fronded plant that rabbits like, plus the odd carrot etc. I'm sure he was found a good home nearby – my next pet didn't appear until I was thirteen or fourteen, a long-haired miniature dachshund, Bettina or Tiggy. Still too young to be a responsible dog-owner so sister Anne took her to Elsenham in Essex.

Home life was great – such a finely designed house. An 'island' in the kitchen, a hatch through to the dining room with its elegant floor-to-ceiling bay window, a green baize door from the backstairs, beautifully carved wooden fireplace surrounds, a trompe-l'œil set of books concealing the television in the sitting room – the list goes on, our own playroom beyond Mum's flower-arranging room, with its archaic huge radio with tunings for Hilversum and distant stations and crackly reception on the short-wave band. *Listen with Mother* was a regular feature after lunch. Happy days. I used to stage complicated battles with my toy soldiers and fort, little artillery guns firing bits of matches at exposed troops. Kitten's friends visiting and sitting on the sofa in the playroom. Libby Butler often, and Claerwen, who I thought was gorgeous. Her nice brother Martin, who was kind to me at big school later, was one of Kitten's first boyfriends and became a policeman.

Outside, we had a kidney-shaped swimming pool. My blow-up boat got ruined by some of Carole's boisterous friends attending her 21$^{st}$ birthday party – it was hardly used, as heating the thing cost more than housing a racehorse, said Dad. There was an 'En-Tout-Cas' tennis court between the fledgling arboretum (where Brackie lived) and the riding school and barn behind the hedge. One passed by the stables and manure heaps to get there. Dad was a crafty wily player using spin to confound opponents but there were plenty of tennis afternoons with local ladies. Best for me was the green board at the back right where I spent hours practising forehands and backhands. I also constructed a little golf course around the flower beds and streams, sinking plastic pots into the lawns with bamboo flagsticks.

Given an airgun one Christmas I used to shoot tin cans off the walls – once I wounded a sparrow and had to finish its life soon after. Oh dear, I shan't do that again, I vowed. And I haven't. Horses need to be exercised – mostly done by Mum and my sisters I have to admit. But when we had Pony Club Camp on our land I played my part – we all did gymkhana-type things, learnt how to make currycombs from bits of straw, cleaned our mounts' tackle with saddle soap, enjoyed sugar buns and squash at appropriate moments. I took a shine to long-haired lovely A (who later become Jeffrey Archer's mistress) but had my first fondle among some hay bales with Alice P. Another early and innocent 'girlfriend' was Dinah Nabarro, daughter of the famous local MP Sir Gerald. In a slightly more serious vein was

Carey Graham, met at local dances, whose sister Juliet (now a teacher at Kitebrook, near Chastleton) remembers the liaison with amusement.

Holidays abroad were rarer in those days – I always wanted to go to Butlin's but it was never on the cards. We went far and wide eventing – Kitten was a good rider and joined Anne and Lavinia (Mini) Morrell in the Heythrop team. Stoneleigh and Kidderminster come to mind and many places nearer us. Lovely picnics as I've said, and I enjoyed my role as the little 'chef d'équipe' finding out how our rivals were doing, the VWH, the Quorn, the Pytchley etc. Amanda Sivewright on Ripalong always won the dressage for a rival team but one could usually catch them in the cross-country section.

One year we went to St Malo for a beach holiday which was great fun – I remember winning pots of Dijon mustard in some beach game I hardly understood. Not long after the Brittany trip I was sent on a less enjoyable 'exchange visit' to the St Lager family, dropped initially at their St Cloud house outside Paris but travelling to the Chateau de Chauval, their place at St Germain les Vergnes in the Dordogne. Boy, was I homesick aged nearly ten, trying to cope with the ultra-annoying daughter of the house. At least I enjoyed her brother Christian's company. Lowlight was becoming ill and having a suppository inserted by Madame St Lager (those French customs eh?) but I did like eating little fromage frais

'petit suisses' that one unwrapped and ate with white sugar. My elder sisters had enjoyed 'exchanges' with the Taittinger family – yup, them of the champagne dynasty. As I keep reiterating we were indeed a fortunate family. But every year, and this is just fantastic, we were taken skiing, usually just after Christmas.

Train journeys through France to Switzerland and sometimes Austria… Mum and Dad travelling first class, Kitten and I second class – this once caused terrible problems when the train divided at Landquart or was it Chur and they lost us for hours. But wow, what fun. At age four, I was in Arosa, Switzerland, perhaps just skating on trip number one – staying at a lovely hotel where the doorman had a pet red squirrel called Hansi. Apologies again for coming across as a spoiled brat but that's the way it was – not my choice and I'm not going to deny my history.

In subsequent years we visited Verbier, Wengen at least twice, Klosters, Kitzbühel and St Moritz. It was the days of wooden skis, strap-on leather bindings for your lace-up boots, inadequate jodhpur-type trousers, polo necks and anoraks. Mittens never quite kept out the cold of January in the Alps but the hot chocolate and mille-feuille pastries at

teatime were a lovely treat. Mum preferred the rum-soaked babas I recall.

Our parents were nervous skiers – Dad on hugely long early metal efforts, Mum all in black, stem-turning her way slowly down the slopes. Yours truly got the hang of this great sport early on and Kitten still skis neatly – the pistes were not groomed back in the fifties and sixties and judging from Dad's cine films the whole business was a bit of a lottery.

We used to stay in some wonderful hotels. The Swiss are the world's best hoteliers I reckon. At the Hotel Regina in Wengen one year I managed to get Jean-Claude Killy's autograph as the French team were there for the Lauberhorn race. Possibly the best hotel was the Schweizerhof in the main square of St Moritz where there were baskets of fruit in each corridor of rooms and sumptuous meals.

That year in St Moritz was the most difficult for Dad because Harold Wilson had restricted the export of money to £50 per person. Somehow by pre-paying a package we just about managed. In the evenings we would play bridge, vingt-et-un using Dad's metal tin of plastic counters, and Mum would enjoy her Dubonnet with ice and lemon, Dad his Amontillado sherry.

Kitten and I would go to ski-school in the mornings but preferred the afternoons when we were allowed to ski with Mum and Dad. Some years of course, like 1963, you didn't have to travel far to enjoy winter sports – Stow-on-the-Wold, the highest spot in Gloucestershire, would suffice. In the back garden and field of our other doctor, Dr King (who I found a bit frightening) was a rope-tow so one could ski and toboggan there. On the lake below Adlestrop Church, with its Jane Austen connections, we would skate on the thick ice.

Let's go to big school now shall we.

# 5

# COTHILL AND ETON

At the age of seven years and two months I am bundled off to Cothill prep school near Abingdon – it's an hour's drive from home, the Headmaster George Pike married to Gabrielle who was Chairman of the Women's Institute. GLSP was an affable Major in the Scots Guards whose father had run the school before him.

The first two weeks are awful – lots of blubbing and missing the securities of home. I am weighed and measured, 3 stone 7 pounds, 3 foot 7 inches. Consequently every day I queue up with some of the other small fry for a tablespoon of barley malt – yum, dished out by Matron. Once the homesickness wears off life becomes more tolerable. It's dormitories for six or eight boys with enamel jugs and basins at the foot of the iron beds.

But here is the start of my Christian journey – that very first term I am reading my Bible under the bedclothes with a torch after 'lights out'. It is Matthew's account of the Crucifixion and I am crying for Jesus. On Sundays, we march crocodile style to Dry Sandford Church in the neighbouring village, in our maroon caps and grey trousers. On Sunday afternoons there was usually a walk in the woods, towards and into a disused quarry where we got up to all sorts of dangerous activities in those pre Health & Safety days. The school adjoined an SSSI (Site of Special Scientific Interest);

there we would stomp along the paths singing, "Onward Christian soldiers, marching as to war, with the cross of Jesus going on before…" I still love those old hymns, such powerful words and great tunes.

Lessons in our first year were given by Mrs Hall in all subject areas, then it was Mr Jackson for Maths, Mr Liversege for Geography (I still have some of the notebooks), Mr Swinbank for French, George Pike for Scripture, Mr Lachlan for Latin. At morning break we got that ⅓ pint of milk that Mrs Thatcher 'the milk snatcher' so memorably stopped, a sticky bun or a rock cake. We did PE, jumps and stretchings in the school yard, home to the urinal and endless games of stump cricket. 'Batty Tank', our groundsman George Fairbrother's rain butt was there by the carpentry room where one Christmas I made my parents a box with sliding partitions but measured poorly so LPs didn't quite fit vertically.

We made 'dens' in the hedgerow between the golf course and the football pitch from branches, leaves and cardboard boxes. Secret hiding places where you and your friends could consume the sherbet fountains, penny chews and

wine gums from your tuck box. The golf course circled the bleak swimming pool (unheated), 9 shortish holes, but it's where I honed my game and in my last year won the cup. Fawcett once went round in 28 shots which I presume is still the course record. We had cricket nets, a long jump pit and a grass running track round the cricket pitch.

Everyone knew each other by their surname or nickname. If you had a brother at school you would be surname major (ma), surname minor (mi) or occasionally minimus (min). There was Johnson, Foxwell, Rivière, Barnard, Meiner-zhagen and Molesworth (I made that one up!), Jonks Sey-mour-Williams, Dixon, Palmer ma, Hamilton and Clowes. Older than us were Gough ma and mi, Milne ma and mi (mi always seemed to beat ma, well done, Chris!). In my year too were Weld-Forester, Porter mi and Goodrich. Younger than us were Leanse, Oppé, Gruson and Alacouzos – the 'squits'. We hung our coats and hats on named pegs, we ragged in the dorms with pillow fights (six strokes of the swishy cane if caught), in the summer terms we were dunked in cold baths before breakfast, we ate meagre portions of burnt porridge (cooked slow all night), powdered scrambled egg, something we knew as 'hedgehog' which may have been rolled pork belly, tiny portions of butter to go with our toast.

If you had worked hard you might be awarded your V badge which meant a special 'treat' afternoon with decent grub. We once got a half-day holiday when we drew at football with Horris Hill who were fearsomely good at the game and usually beat us 10-0 or something.

Highlights included old boy Robin Dixon bringing his Innsbruck Winter Olympics Gold Medal bobsleigh to the squash court, school plays like *Elijah* (written and produced by Mr Armitage), *The Pirates of Penzance* with Scott singing 'I Am the Very Model of a Modern Major General' rather well. Films were often shown, I remember *North West Frontier*, the story of the Hindu / Muslim slaughters as the British left India to its own devices. We learnt how to waltz with Mr Williams. There were holiday camping trips organised – the first outside Redruth in Cornwall, then with Mr Armitage again and Fatty Malim (later disgraced as a paedophile when he was Headmaster of Brambletye Prep School and eventually jailed for 6 years, but he never touched me) up to the Norfolk Broads.

Ping pong, chess, what else? Racing our toy cars up and down the ground floor corridors, writing letters home at old-fashioned desks in the main classroom every Sunday where we were assembled to hear the news of JFK's assassination. George Pike wrote the definitive account of his school, *The Cothill Story*, in 1991. Its motto was 'Dum Spiro Spero' ('While I breathe, I hope') – he was kind to mention me a few times in the book, the last being this:

Jamie Summers wrote a 'Vale' when he left, beginning 'I came in tears, I leave in tears', with a concluding verse, 'And now I have to leave my friends, / And leave the school. I make amends / To those who helped on my way, / Whether at work, or rest, or play.'

Happy days and a good enough education to get me over 63 per cent in the Common Entrance Examination, the minimum required to get me into the next boarding school for Michaelmas Term 1967. Dad gave me a watch with stopwatch capabilities for doing well at work – bribery of sorts but perhaps it worked.

My first term at 'school' (as we arrogantly call it these days) was a bit terrifying – some senior boys looked so adult, some even with beards. I was in RHP for one term as Bud Hill's house couldn't squeeze me in. Stevie Norman and I were the new boys – he came first in 'trials' that year and I was third. R. H. Parry was a Welshman who could 'speed read'; slowly we learnt how to cope at this strange school with its ancient ways, difficult dress (the little white ties in particular with the stiff collars and studs to deal with) and 'fagging'.

"Boy up", the prefects would shout at the tops of their voices and the two lowest years' intake would scurry to the source. Last one there would have to do an errand – we also had to cook and serve the senior boys' tea … poaching eggs, making toast etc., which ate into the time of one's own meal. Tidying their rooms was also part of the slavery – two small boys for each senior in the 'library', as the house prefects were known. On moving to BJWH in my second term this rigmarole worsened – the senior boys there were, in my opinion, brutish, cruel and snobbish. One called King was the worst offender.

They were allowed to cane younger boys and did so. 'Birching' – caning with birch twigs – was just coming to an end but Anthony Chenevix-Trench, poor man, had been a prisoner of the Japanese in World War II, and as Headmaster had a prurient interest in corporal punishment. 'Pop tanning' was still in vogue, caning by Eton Society or Pop boys (the self-electing school prefect body) – by the time I reached that exalted status the practice was over, although one of our peers, Chris Mackenzie, I recall, was keen to reinstate it.

You 'messed' (ate tea) with people in your year. My fellow eaters were Philip Remnant and Julian Hill. Philip's parents had a herd of Jersey cows, and birds to shoot, so we had an ample supply of the best double cream and hung pheasants outside his window. Each boy in the school had his own room, varying in size but all with beds that folded up onto the wall and each with a coal fireplace.

We were learning our hierarchical place in this school society. Lessons were taken in classrooms scattered over the large site – woe betide you if you arrived late. Each subject would have ten or twelve divisions for each year with up to twenty boys (no girls of course until later years when a few masters' daughters joined in) in each class. For the first two years one had a 'classical tutor' then a 'modern tutor' where groups of about six people would chat informally with a teacher. My classical tutor was bright and keen, Jeremy Greenstock, who went on to be Britain's Ambassador to the United Nations between 1998 and 2003.

Indeed we were blessed with probably the best teachers in the country, along with a few rubbish ones. Those that stood out in my time were Dave Lowther, a gritty but solid man from Durham who inspired us in the human geography field – 'Slob' Card (TSBC) and Al Simpson (ALS) for their sensible knowledge of that impossible subject, Economics. The great late lamented History teacher who regrettably never taught me was Michael Kidson with his stick and Cocker Spaniel. Tom Wheare, who directed the house plays for m'tutor, RHH (Robert Hardy) who was my housemaster now, Bud Hill having retired at the end of my second year. *Luther*, *The Marowitz Hamlet* and best of all *Toad of Toad Hall*. I played Ratty, the water vole, in the play by A. A. Milne based on Kenneth Grahame's novel *The Wind in the Willows*. Tom took some of us up to London to watch Chelsea play Blackpool and Arsenal play Leicester I think, and always offered a kind and welcoming sofa for a chat – he went on to be Headmaster of Bryanston. Jerry Nicholls too we liked, good at football and later Headmaster of Stowe.

The facilities and opportunities available were just astonishing. This was costing £300 per term in those days – nowadays it's over £25,000 a year and out of bounds to virtually everyone unless one is clever enough to gain a King's Scholarship to get into College where the education is free. But then again in our day the 'tugs' of College were considered a bit weird – one called Dyer must have been high on the autistic spectrum; he memorised bus timetables and came fourth in the World Maths Olympiad when aged fourteen. Hope he's okay these days.

Allied to the excellent education was a grounding in social responsibility and Christian ethics. Every Thursday, certainly from the third year onwards, I and some others were mini-bussed into Slough for the Thursday Club – a knees-up befriending afternoon doing the hokey cokey with learning disabilities people. Others did old people's gardening – all good stuff and better than the alternative which was square-bashing with the Corps, first reserves for the British Army. Keep away Ruskies, the toffs of Eton will sort you out if you dare to invade.

I move to discuss briefly a difficult area – many of you will think that public schools are a hotbed of homosexuality with predatory paedophile pedagogues and older boys grooming younger ones. One quickly learned which masters to steer clear of... Messrs Foreman and Mosley spring to mind. Granted, the absence of the fairer sex may have predicated some of the goings-on – there was some 'fiddling around' between boys but these are difficult years – things are happening in the nether regions, hormones are developing. Very few became gay as a result – I can think of just three or four boys out of the 1,200 present.

Bullying was more commonplace – sadly, I partook too. We were cruel to poor Peter Hogg and would often strap him to his bed and upturn him to the wall. He became so used to our cruelty that as we entered his room he would say,

"All right, strap me down." Peter, I do apologise for my part in your mistreatment and I hope you have had a better life since those schooldays.

Physical bullying is one thing, mental bullying quite another. Sticks and stones may break my bones but it's words that truly hurt me. Only when I read Dave Profumo's account in his book *Bringing the House Down* did I learn of the invidious actions of a boy in my year targeting new boy Dave who had been kept in the dark concerning his father's indiscretions with Christine Keeler. Whether that was a wise decision by his parents is another matter. Personally, I think not. Dave was highly intelligent and I'm sure would have been robust enough to counter his oppressor's jibes.

Being good at work and good at games gave one an easy life at school – those who didn't quite fit in were often at risk of being excluded. However, because of the plethora of opportunities available to all, most found a niche – even the allegedly somewhat thick Prince Harry was apparently excellent in the Art Schools and has gone on to be a credit to his late mother. His contributions to the mental health debate have been inspirational.

Oh pampered youth, you mollycoddled 'middle class morons', as a colleague once deemed me – cosseted upper class bigots we might have been, but at least most of us turned out to be better individuals than you might assume. Noblesse oblige, the notion of privilege entailing responsibility was part and parcel of a country gentleman's ethics, even my father's. There was really no one particularly famous in my year group – Noel Malcolm KS (King's Scholar) went on to become a political and foreign affairs journalist at the *Spectator* and the *Daily Telegraph*. Nicky Gumbel, Holy Trinity Brompton vicar and developer of the Alpha course you may have heard of – boy done good after an iffy start as a barrister, bringing 20 million people to Christ. Justin Welby was in the year below. He is quoted as saying, "my career at Eton was only distinguished by its mediocrity." Perhaps there are other 'sleepers' who I have forgotten – certainly we had our share of aristocrats, even princes. Zere Yacob of Ethiopia wasn't the brightest spark but was the grandson of Haile Selassie. Hope he's okay too.

We were also blessed with some great vicars giving us daily prayers and Sunday services in Lower and College chapels. Peter Pilkington led the squad with Roger Royle (Radio 2 etc.) close at heel. Canon Roger I met again at Southwark Cathedral in the mid-nineties and he agreed to become Patron of a charity I chaired many years later. He evokes my type of Christianity – fun, humorous (he's always extracting the Michael from the Methodists) but borne of personal suffering matched with a care for those in need.

You tended to mix with your year group and many have remained close friends to this day. Rupert Johnson, Jamie Dallas, Jimmy Chute, Simon Ball and Sam Mitchell-Innes I see but others have faded away as friends often do. I have pretty much lost contact with Kim Beddall and John L-P and I see little these days of Philip Remnant, once my best friend. As one rose up the school more responsibilities and privileges came one's way. For some reason I was good enough at Latin declamation to win prizes, good results at A levels and 'trials' led to election to the swots' group, Sixth Form Select as an Oppidan Scholar. This allowed me to change the flat white collar to a stick-up collar with dickie-bow white tie – election to Pop allowed one to sport coloured silk waistcoats. Very dapper.

My last term I recall being able to bring my car to school – HUL805K, a 700cc red Mini bought by my Trustees for me for £702. In my capacity as secretary of the Keynes and Political societies I was able to invite captains of industry (one I asked to speak was Sir Richard Summers from the family steelworks) and leading politicians and trade union-ists. Jack Jones came, as did Jeremy Thorpe and Sir Robert

Carr. Guest speakers were treated to dinner with the Head-master and assorted others before being introduced by me and speaking in Upper School, a magnificent oak-lined upper chamber close to the chapel.

My best subjects were Geography and Economics – perhaps the most inspirational speaker, giving his talk in the newish and comfortable Farrer Theatre, was Teddy Goldsmith, brother of Jimmy, uncle of Zak. Founder of the *Ecologist* magazine, to which I was an early subscriber and the Green Party, likewise. His book *Blueprint for Survival* must be worth another look. We also enjoyed a week in the Arts School (next to the Farrer Theatre) experimenting with whatever came to hand – a nice change from academic pursuits. What a rounded education it was, with seminars on world religions and apartheid. Films and plays, concerts from Barclay James Harvest, dances with girls from Heathfield, doing Scottish reels with the Caledonian Society and good stomping jazz from the Dixieland Jazz Band comprising masters (ORS Bull on trumpet) and boys.

I knuckled down, revising for the Oxbridge entrance exams in the tucked-away Provost's Library – they suit me, these dusty places smelling of old leather-bound books.

These words I am writing in one such. Enough of this soporific stuff now … let's get back to cracking that nut. More madness, well mad times anyway, came after a ten year gap of relative normality.

# 6

# MARRIAGE, MADNESS AND MARIJUANA

We come to my penultimate bout of 'madness', perhaps the one with the most unusual and potentially disturbing thoughts and actions. Bear with me while I try and explain my thinking.

Trouble is, I haven't kept any diaries from this time so we are going to have to rely on memories apart from several verbatim extracts from my GP's medical notes which are illuminating. These will give us more precision, accurate timelines and also my doctors' perspective.

The eighties are nearly over, I have married a solicitor's daughter from Southend at the age of twenty-nine in the Christopher Wren-style church by the river near Battersea Bridge with its beautiful galleried interior and friendly vicar. We have the reception in a marquee in the garden of a Searcys house up by Wimbledon Common. It is 10th December 1983, cold but clear.

The wedding cake we have made ourselves – it is a three-tiered number topped with a model of my new grey Morris Minor split-screen convertible (actually one month older than me) PAC 632. Organic fizzy white pretends to be champagne, most of the canapés, sweetmeats etc. I have produced in the bakery at our home. There are hundreds of little Parma ham and gruyère croissants and anchovy ones, sausage rolls, mini quiche Lorraines and profiteroles – Searcys have added to the fare with smoked salmon rolled in brown bread. An Oxford friend has brought along cocaine, some of which we snort in a downstairs loo – the day had certainly started out with strong joints. Speeches are given by my best man Minnow Powell, me and an old Southend friend of S's who has 'given her away'.

We leave the festivities, crank-handle starting the Morris (which behaves better on the whole than its yellow predecessor) and tootle down to the Carlton Tower Hotel before starting the honeymoon proper the following day – in Mexico, Belize and Guatemala, although cheekily I hadn't told S where we were going. Bakery duties I had assigned to my helper Danny Levitas in our absence.

Life continued in a haze of clouded, nigh-repressed emotions. Our first daughter arrived in May 1988 after several years of far-flung holidays, long-distance walks in England and many theatre visits. S's sister was by now married to *The Times'* theatre critic. I particularly enjoyed anything done by the National Theatre of Brent with Patrick Barlow and Jim Broadbent.

Cut the chase to just after P's birth. I did have a mental wobble after S's parents had come to stay for a couple of weeks in the immediate aftermath – I was working at the bakery (in a converted one-room cottage at the end of our garden), catering for two elderly relatives while learning the ropes of fatherhood. S found breastfeeding sore and painful, her parents found me rude, crude and different I imagine. Because of the lack of this year's diary I cannot verify my movements but S informs me that, "You vanished on the night of 21st June. You returned the following evening, very distracted. You were convinced the television was talking to you, you put the plugs in both the baths and turned the taps on full. I telephoned Michael Gormley and he came round at about 10 p.m., taking me and P to stay with him. We also stayed with Rupert and Simi, and James and Annabel before returning home." I cannot recollect nor confirm where I went that night but will fess up to believing messages for me can seemingly emanate from television – this has happened on several occasions. Goodness knows why I filled the baths, but many thanks, Michael, for taking S and P to safety. His medical notes at the time verify S's account:

"Called by wife who can't cope any longer. Had first baby 4 weeks ago. Jamie overactive and overprotective to P, but not a support to her. He disappeared on a walkabout yesterday on the day of her birthday and returned today covered in blisters on feet. He talks of a new clean-up campaign in Wandsworth and to ask Maggie Thatcher or Prince Charles about it. Δ Hypomania. Wife to take baby and move to friends for rest. Jamie to start Lithium 400mgs qds."

Then with P nearly two and S pregnant again – and with her hormones all over the shop it seemed to me – I lost my marbles once more. It is early May 1990, the bakery I have closed temporarily for a thorough spring clean. My smaller gas oven I start to disassemble and, this it's hard to describe, but the dial went to mark 12; removing that, I found 11 notches, then 10 cogs then 9 holes in each burner, 8 rack levels and so on and so on. With the parts all away, they

are wire brushed and cleaned before reassembly – the dust particles and metal filaments are so numerous. To me they are redolent of the millions of Jews gassed at Auschwitz, Birkenau, Dachau, Buchenwald, Sobibór. I break down.

The grout between the tiles on the walls has grown grubby over the ten years this bakehouse has been in operation. Scrubbing the joints with bleach doesn't do the trick, and so ridiculously I paint the grout with white gloss. There are hundreds of white crosses therefore, which then become super messy when I attempt to remove the paint. Lordy be. My cleaning efforts continue through the night – sleep deprived again. On the mute black and white television I have on a shelf there is a programme being shown that seems to relate to my activities ... a tiled room with a large table is on the screen with mops and brushes all around. This sort of vision, this sort of message affects us nutters, affirming our follies. There may be other signs that we see on the street or hear on the radio. "Does it all add up to you?" goes the 'Living by Numbers' song from New Musik.

I begin to get obsessed by colours – anything black becomes symbolic of evil. The white crosses in the bakery have got to me ... white is good, yellow and gold are good – purple is royal. Green for go, red beware danger. Now, this sort of thinking can get very confusing – there is so much printed material in our world, so many adverts and road signs that are going to make living out this stuff extremely awkward.

Another trait is ensuring arrangements are 'just so'. So combinations of clothing, placement of bits of furniture, items on tables are regularly moved round to create the perfect pattern. I have seen this in others over the years so it can't be just me with my cannabis psychosis ways. Association of words with deeds (which paraphrases the Gospel of James, does it not?) further complicates the thoughts of those in hypomanic states – I once wrote in an article that never got published: "Kick an empty Sony cardboard box and the Japanese economy will stumble." All this echoes my thoughts at the time.

I restarted production of loaves, buns and croissants. The bakehouse was cleaner now. But I remember that core supplies were low, the recipe for the fruit cakes I had to change for lack of some crucial ingredients. As ever, I'd smoked up a storm. S had returned to work training accountants in maths, an au pair looked after P while I worked. Things went pear-shaped when I set out in the white Honda bakery van to deliver the morning's output to the local shops, restaurants and delicatessens that I supplied. The traffic felt oppressive, it was a battle to get around, everything seemed to be conspiring against my delivery plans. 3-point turns to avoid jams, round the back-streets etc. With just a couple of bread crates remaining in the back of the van, full of granary rolls for Pollyanna's restaurant I recall, I stop the van by some wooden posts embedded at the junction of two little streets close to the crossroads of Battersea Rise and St John's Road. The sun is streaming in as I open the van's side sliding door – it appears to be blessing my buns.

There is a double gate to a garden just there. I fall to my knees, praying, but also reaching under these gates inscribing areas with whatever I had in my hand. Why I do not know. For some reason I bang with my fist on the little glass panel to the side of the nursery door nearby where P now goes – was I sensing she was in danger? The glass breaks. I seem to recall shouting P's name too. Nobody answers, probably quite rightly, and the children are apparently moved upstairs out of possible harm's way. During the night I'd been sorting through the black-typed pages of the nursery's invoices – perhaps that had influenced my confused mind? (Some time later I apologise as best I can for this obscure behaviour in a letter and pay for the glass replacement.)

Next I'm on Battersea Rise heading up towards the Common – on the opposite side of the road is Edwardes' furniture place, on my side there is a flower shop and I fall to my knees again, reaching inside this shop. Aha, the police (well two of them anyway) now arrive, alerted perhaps by the nursery staff and sit on me before bundling me into their van. There follows a good cop / bad cop routine – one talks kindly to me while the other has me in a brutal half-Nelson hold which hurts. A while later I'm shoved into a spartan cell in Battersea Police Station near the river.

Enquiries are made – my GP is called. Apparently police called round at S's place of work to tell her that I had been arrested, had thrown something through the nursery window and that I was naked when arrested – what absolute baloney. I was 'apprehended' not arrested, it was my fist that had broken the glass and I was certainly not naked; dishevelled yes, because I'd been scrabbling around on the pavements. In the basement cell I tell them about the open-doored van still left with some bread crates inside and abandoned on the corner – no problem they say. Little bits of light come in through the slits of windows high up, in the open loo I wash my hands. No refreshments are offered – merely short stares through the door peep-hole. About an hour later I am taken, on my GP's recommendation, back to the Priory in Roehampton. This time, I'm on a trolley being held down by four or five burly nurses and a syringe of sedatives is injected into a buttock by another. Because the police have brought me in I'm on some sort of 'section' and have lost my rights. I am allowed to exercise in nearby Richmond Park, however, where one afternoon I walk round the entire acreage. Encircling places to sort of make them 'safe' is another theme of those deemed mentally ill and I was no exception.

A room on Lower Court is found before I get moved a day or so later. My wife comes in with golf magazines and can't fathom why I decline them (they had black and red script on the cover). Understandably she is concerned, confused and a tad frightened one suspects. At least my access to cannabis is now curtailed, but the thought processes are still weird. I make friends with the current crop of patients until about four days into my incarceration news comes through that I am to be moved (in an ambulance would you believe, as these are the rules for sectioned people) to an NHS hospital called Springfield.

S has contacted Graham Millar, now my sole remaining Trustee after Desmond Reid has died. He advises there isn't the cash around to pay out large sums for Jamie's inpatient stay at the Priory. You will learn more about this man later but let's stick to this for now. So, from the relative salubriousness of the Priory it's all change to the squalid surrounds of Springfield, Crocus Ward, for me and ten or so others. The quality of food plummeted, the prescription level of Largactil probably soared, but as ever I met plenty of interesting people.

I hated being 'sectioned' and soon fought successfully for release from strictures. However, be warned, being a voluntary patient doesn't mean you can escape at will … the men in white coats would soon come after you and detain you. Gradually I was granted more home leave, where I would roll another joint despite beginning to become aware of its link with my condition. "Red rag to a bull," one of the nurses presciently called marijuana.

Within three weeks I was back home once more although the writing was on the wall in terms of my marriage – "If it happens again I am leaving you," says S. Okay, not perhaps the words of a loving caring wife but perfectly reasonable you may think. She remembers her words as being, "You need to seek medical help and sort out your finances otherwise I am leaving you," but I heard the aforementioned phrase. Our second child C arrives in September 1990 but marital relations have soured to frostiness. My intake of dope continues and sadly becomes more secretive as is so often the case with burgeoning addiction. Actually it's more accurate to say habit-forming. Work in the bakery becomes less enticing, S had kindly 'nursed' me through a bout of mumps and I loved the company of P and C. P and I had definitely bonded, things with C were more strained (her temperament was fiery) but improving all the time. We cruised along as a bruised family of four, albeit with continued help from a succession of au pairs, for another year and a half.

A word on the equating of a marijuana high with a manic high. Dead similar I assert – a semi-euphoric happiness (à la 'soma' in Aldous Huxley's *Brave New World*), an intensification of music, generosity of spirit, largesse i.e. the danger of spending too much money but fortunately I was relatively wealthy; a flurry of ideas and half-finished madcap schemes. The last I am possibly still guilty of. I may finish your sentences for you but something I've started may have been put on the back-burner. All the above are termed hypomanic symptoms of illness but what would Jesus think? I like to think he would support the open-heartedness of those in trouble – of course, marijuana was around in his day; it's even been found on Phoenician ships 600 years before he appeared – did he imbibe one wonders?

Another break now from mental troubles – let's go to Oxford … obviously not Cambridge, eh! And while we're at it, have some sporting reminiscences. 'Tis good to amalgamate the two subjects, Oxford and sport, because sport, be it frisbee or golf, dominated my time there.

# 7

# OXFORD AND THIS
# SPORTING LIFE

Like father and one grandfather the hallowed path of my education led to Christ Church, Oxford from Eton College. My paternal grandfather had gone to Trinity College, Cambridge from Eton, somewhat spoiling the symmetry. Eton / Christ Church is quite a well-trodden route for the country's elite – thirteen Prime Ministers I think. Not that I thought of myself as elite … it was just the guided gilded route, somehow mapped out for me from birth, but I was fortunate to avoid the cavalry regiments that my antecedents had felt obliged to join.

My trust fund, to which I had very limited access, paid for the university fees and for the 'battels' that soon mounted up at the college's buttery (bar) in the antechamber before entering the dining hall. This was where we took breakfast and supper, now made famous as Harry Potter's Hogwarts hall. Terms were now just eight weeks long.

Whenever I am asked, "What did you read at Oxford?" I tend to reply, "Drugs and frisbee" – in fact it was Geography with which I started. Sam Mitchell-Innes and I joined I think three non-Etonians in Mr Parker's rooms between Peck and Tom quads. He was our Tutor, an expert on Russian physical geography. The Geography schools I visited but once – Theresa May the following year will have been a more regular attender I imagine. One lecture that first year, one tutorial, one essay of limited quality on ecology and no weekend field trips, which caused great difficulties towards the end of year one.

The reason that I couldn't go out on Saturday Geography field trips was because I was always absent playing golf for the university. My place in the side was much due to owning a car and we often squashed four of us plus clubs and clothes into my Mini. At ghastly hours for students, from 5.30 a.m. onwards we would assemble in Oriel Square to head off to some of the greatest golf courses in the country – Sunningdale and The Berkshire, Little Aston, Burnham and Berrow, Hollinwell outside Nottingham, Royal St George's in Kent. This is the crème de la crème of UK golf courses – we were so lucky. The members gave us board and lodging, very keen always to beat these boys, often trying to get us a bit drunk at lunchtime with wines, port and kummel so as to clock up more points in the afternoon singles matches.

My first year I often partnered Robert Mitchell but leading up to the annual match against the Tabs (Cambridge) at Ganton in Yorkshire, my foursomes partner became Etienne de Villiers. Etienne was a smart South African on a Rhodes scholarship, older than most of us and already married to Nina. We lost our match narrowly but the following day I managed to overcome Charlie Travers and his catapult-style swing. Overall we lost, but lifelong friendships were forged. In the two terms, Michaelmas and Hilary before the Blues match, I had managed to play golf every single day … whether at Huntercombe on the way to Henley where we were only required to pay 50p, at Southfields in the middle of Oxford where every Wednesday there was a medal competition, or traipsing a little further to play at Sunningdale where I was a member on the youth rate of £30 per year. I gave up membership there when the rate soared to £60 in my twenties! It must be over £3,000 these days. But not really a decision I regret despite the two superb courses – many of the members were not my cup of tea. Gambling was rife, along with haughtiness.

My second year's match was at Hoylake on the Wirral peninsula outside Liverpool with its tricky internal out-of-bounds area – the drive off the first tee being a bit of a nightmare with out of bounds all the way up the right-hand side. Once again I had played virtually every day – no wonder I was a reasonable player. Robert was Captain now and I was his number 2, Secretary (although secretarial duties I apologise for neglecting so badly). My foursomes partner was Minnow Powell, best friend and later to be best man. We lost our game – my father commenting that Minnow hadn't put me on a single green with any of his second shots. So what: chipping and putting were my strong suits – but you should see me now, that's all gone. Again, the following day, despite Cambridge being overall winners I beat John Cross 2 and 1. He was a far better golfer than me, a lovely man but perhaps overcome with nerves on that day.

After the match and the evening dinner and festivities, we bundled Cliff Weight naked through the revolving doors of the clubhouse and chucked him into a bunker by the 18th. Good stuff, but sadly some members never forgave us for destroying their doors, despite us paying for a replacement. A combined squad then toured Scotland – Prestwick, Troon and Muirfield I seem to recall, although the hospitality we received was so good the golf seemed secondary. Great fun, great people – Barry, Robert, John and Tom all came up north. By this time the Mini had been traded in for a superb G reg BMW 2002 which was more capacious and less capricious and went like the clappers – RWF830G once covered the sixty-odd miles between Kensington and Christ Church in thirty-nine minutes. These days it takes you that long to get to the middle of Oxford from its ring road.

Life was sweet – a flat on Ebury Street, an allowance, a girlfriend in London and Hampshire (same girl!), parties all over the country in fine houses (I was deemed an eligible bachelor and thus on Peter Townend's list of 'Debs' Delights'), starting my dope-smoking days and happy as Larry. Small wonder I wasn't attending my lectures, I was rarely in the city of dreaming spires.

When the time came for Honour Moderations in Geography at the end of year one in the Examination Schools I relied on A level knowledge to see me through. Stalled though, by the requirement to hand in one's 'practical notebook' of field work done – perhaps a piece on bunker sand on heathland courses would do but no, in the end, and it was late being sent in, I shamefully cobbled together something using Sam's notes. It wasn't good enough and I was awarded the first ever 'Pass' grade in Honour Mods Geography and obliged to change course for Year 2. I chose Politics and Economics, tutored in Economics by Peter Oppenheimer (who was never in his Blue Boar Quad rooms, always on the BBC up in town) and Peter Pultzer for Politics. I chose not to include the usual Philosophy section as that's a subject I've never had time for and certainly then it was beyond my limited brain.

The gallivanting lifestyle continued, however, for the next two terms and in March 1976 I was summoned into the rooms of the Dean, Henry Chadwick. Kindly he said it was probably better if I went and got a job rather than continue not attending lectures and rarely tutorials. There was no 'sending down' and I class it as 'retirement'. Had I wasted my time there? – yes, academically. I was too immature to grasp what opportunity there was, indeed to realise that I was actually quite clever. Hedonism had dwarfed the learning.

Highlights included hitting 9 irons from Peck Quad lawns, past the library corner through a surprisingly narrow gap, over some rooms and into Tom Quad, just short of Mercury Pond. Simon Foster and I shared lovely rooms, one got two bedrooms and basins and a shared oak-panelled sitting room on the north side of Peck Quad – reader, I led him astray. We played loud music to visiting tourists … 'Good Vibrations' from The Beach Boys. We spent hours playing frisbee in this most elegant Oxford Quad. Once we drove the Mini all the way up to Glenshee in the Cairngorms for a bit of skiing. Rain had closed all the lifts so we walked up to the first station, skied down for twenty minutes and drove back to Oxford.

Punting was the main summer term activity and not once were we overtaken. The Cherwell Boat House up past the Victoria Arms pub was our default route – taking it more slowly, and trailing bottles of white wine behind when we had female company. I lost my virginity with CK in a single bed that first year – all over rather quickly. It was my impression she was part of a set that wasn't my style – Jasper Guinness and John Jermyn doing heroin and cocaine. I started smoking cigarettes at this time to allay worries about those exams and soon was pre-rolling joints in one of those clever rolling machines to take up to London.

Climbing back into Christ Church in the middle of the night – the main Tom Tower doors only opened for a few minutes on the hour – wasn't easy but I found a route behind the Meadows building over into the Dean's garden (where Lewis Carroll had been inspired to write those *Alice in Wonderland* books, suffused with laudanum which 'helped' create those crazy characters, The White Rabbit, The Red Queen, Tweedledum and Tweedledee, the March Hare and so on). From there easy peasy back to my rooms in Peck Quad.

Parking was and is an Oxford dilemma. I got so many tickets I eventually went to the Police Station and attempted to cut a deal – no dice, and they pursued me for months afterwards, a lady used to come to my flat door in London seeking yet more payments.

Food was mostly toast and marmalade as I installed a fridge and kettle in the second year rooms I shared with Rory MacNamara (also led astray and sadly no longer alive – his diet being mostly cigarettes). We enjoyed bottles of port and 1972 Pommard, Pimm's too kept us going. Food in the Hall was only fair; I usually missed breakfast and one had to put a gown on for supper. Socialising when in Oxford was generally with my golfing mates – Vincent's Club some-times, nice pubs like the Turl or the Blue Boar Inn or when one wanted to impress the ladies there was The Elizabeth on the High Street for blanquette de veau or good lunches up at the Cherwell Boat House. Pubs on the Thames further afield were The Rose Revived at Standlake and the Trout Inn at Wolvercote, just north of Oxford.

Cricket I'd played at school – mostly 3rd XI stuff with 'Strawberry', but once the ever-bubbly Johnny Barclay, later Captain of Sussex and England 'A' and President of the MCC was one short for the 'Twenty Two', Eton's 2nd XI. He burst into Al Simpson's Economics 'div' (class), disturbing Piers and I who were doing *The Times* crossword at the back and told me to leave at once to play in the 22 that afternoon. Thus I became an Eton Rambler, eligible to wear their splendid maroon, green and gold tie.

More cricket followed down the years – I became one of the 'Bounders', an eclectic squad originating from the Oxford Polytechnic days of Dave Higgins. Beg their pardon, it's now known as Oxford Brookes University, which perhaps punches above its weight. They certainly claim to be among the top institutions. Some great fun I had from the late nineties up to my 60th birthday, turning up for their Saturday and Sunday matches in the country, Surrey mostly, and often on the Bank of England's ground close to the Priory. Some were indeed 'bounders', cads and worse, but Dave was always desperate to win and selected many 'ringers' to his squad. One year we were undefeated and he paid for all our air tickets to tour the Cayman Islands as a reward – extraordinary place, banking haven for Putin and other super-rich. We were outplayed by their over 40s squad and their supporters' sledging – "Don't you like batting, son?", as one returned to the sidelines ignominiously out for 0. Other tours went to Holland, Majorca, Estonia, Latvia and Malta where I got a 'Man of the Match' frosted glass for a gritty 47 or something. Me and Dave used to open the batting – he was a slow scorer in the main but in one match we thrived, with a partnership well over 100. My best was an 86 I think, but on pitch three at the Bank of England with one very short boundary.

Spike Neilson, a half-Maori Kiwi masseur, was a good player and kind to boot. He loved his golf too, plus the lunch banquet down at Royal St George's. Speno Collard always bowled menacingly and well but we tended to rely on the ringers (good cricketers drafted into the side on a one-off basis) for runs. Before I turned sixty, I migrated to another London-based side, the LJs – full of Wandsworth businessmen and no ringers. Good friends Rob, Nick and others played with a more friendly ethos – latterly I made the teas for their games which were always on dodgy pitches on Wandsworth Common – it was an easy journey from my flat at the time.

At prep school I once took 8 for 8 in the under-ten match versus Summer Fields school in Oxford. My off-spinners never spun much and in later years I bowled medium pace rubbish and fielded very badly but it's a fine game, particularly on a lovely summer's day on a leafy village green. Those Australians with their nasty sledging tactics have ruined it for the amateurs and the young.

Golf is / was my best sport although skiing comes close. After a couple of lessons from David King at Tadmarton Heath near Banbury, where Dad was a member, I was up and running. He recorded my early achievements – whacking the ball 47 yards aged six and 107 yards at age seven. I imagine Tiger Woods was knocking it 300 yards at the same age. I don't recall my first clubs but I soon graduated to Patty Berg woods, named after a top US lady professional and a variety of irons (it was mashies, niblicks, mashie-niblicks, cleeks and jiggers in those days) down to the heavy Ray Mills half-moon lead, well it resembled lead, putter. The course at Cothill helped; at Eton we bicycled with pencil bags over our shoulders to the slightly unfriendly Datchet G.C. My grandmother's second husband was Derek Savile who occasionally took me to play at Swinley, and she owned Bay House in Sandwich Bay and then a flat there in 'The Dunes', so Princes and St George's became part of my life.

It's a funny place, Sandwich Bay, an enclave of private houses reached by toll road from Sandwich town or Ancient Highway from Deal. As children we went fairly often in the summer holidays to stay with Gran who I found forbidding – boiled eggs on the kitchen formica table. The pebble beach there was always covered in tar, globules of oil from passing tankers. But there was a large sandpit and grassy area where the local children gathered to play with tennis courts behind. Peter Breeden and I used to practise golf there. His gentle parents had a flat in a block with Colin Cowdrey's family before building an ultramodern house in the Bay called 'The Lighthouse'. It was always a joy to be with David and June, both good cooks and kind people.

Princes G.C. was more rough and ready than St George's and we played thousands of holes there. Three rounds a day was commonplace. In later years, the latter more famous links became our golfing home. The old pro Albert Whiting handing over to grumpy son Cyril, the fabulous Sunday lunches (with Dover sole 20p extra but big fish they were then) which were de rigeur for local gentry. The catering there is still legendary. The sea air, the larks high in the sky, bee orchids and wild asparagus. What a great place – is this where St Augustine landed bearing his Roman Christianity, which eventually overwhelmed the Celtic Christianity of St Columba and St Patrick? Or did he land in Pegwell Bay at the far end of Princes?

My name doesn't appear on many trophies or winners' boards but in a glass case at Sandwich is a silver hip flask inscribed with Dad's and my names for the Fathers and Sons tournament of was it 1963? We played a couple of times in the West Hill G.C. event of the same name but with limited success. If only I had the shoulder turn of my early years nowadays – I guess I never quite fulfilled my potential.

Peter and I in 1973 drove out in the Mini to Switzerland and France to compete against assorted francophones who luckily were behind the British curve in golfing prowess. We won the foursomes at Évian-les-Bains and then my 77 and 70 round the narrow tree-lined course was good enough to become that year's Champion Amateur de Savoie et Haute-Savoie. A few days later at Crans-sur-Sierre, I added the Swiss Junior Prize to my tally. We pitched a tent up in the hills and cooked our supper on a Primus stove – an early culinary failure I remember was trying to stew aubergine cubes – they don't soften, you need to fry them in slices.

Much later Peter and I partnered each other sometimes in the Halford Hewitt, played every year at Deal and Sandwich where 640 public school golfers assemble. Intense rivalries develop but everyone wants to beat the Etonians. My greatest triumph in that tournament came in 1989 when after

one round with Anthony Clegg I then played with the truly excellent player, Bruce 'Jeeps' Critchley and we beat all-comers. *Golf World* once called him the finest striker of a 1-iron in golf – he played Walker Cup games against the Americans – and it was a privilege to cruise along in his wake. Eton recently have done well in this festival but we paved the way in the late eighties. Several times in the eighties I proved myself as a player by winning twice both the Spring and Summer meetings of the Old Etonians at The Berkshire (Red and Blue courses) and at Royal St George's respectively.

One summer there we stayed with John and Julia Pender at Tilmanstone. Their house guests cleaned up the silverware in the Summer meeting. What a delightful man – sadly missed by all who knew him, godfather to David Cameron's brother Alex who spoke well at John's memorial service. "Continue with vigour," was his rallying cry. Bless you, sir.

In my baking years, certainly from 1984 to 1992, I joined the nearby red-shirted course, Wimbledon Common – funnily enough the venue for the very first Oxford / Cambridge tussle. Without the finesse of its neighbour Royal Wimbledon (and with lesser fees) it was fun and unfussy to play. Pretty much every Tuesday, Thursday and Saturday afternoons (sometimes still stoned I have to admit) I would be

up there. Plenty of friends were happy to join me for social golf, unfazed by the relaxed atmosphere. Jeff Jukes, the pro, I once took to play down at Sandwich as I did the wonderful Dan Maskell, the BBC tennis commentator, who was a regular at Wimbledon Common, often close to scoring under his age. Because the track had more than its share of short holes and several reachable par 4s it wasn't difficult to score a 65 – indeed my handicap at one stage got down to 2, as the 'Standard Scratch Score' there was 67 I think to the par of 68.

An interesting anecdote I would like to share with you at this stage. Asked to represent the Old Etonians in a match against the boys at Sunningdale one year I found myself playing in a foursome or greensome match against Eric Anderson, who was the current Head Master. This was the man selected in an advertising campaign "No one forgets a good teacher" by Tony Blair who had been taught by him at Fettes. Well, when this man learned quite early on in the round that I was merely a baker, it was my impression that he chose to ignore me and talked only to the others for the rest of the match. Okay, his prerogative I suppose, but how you treat others in life, particularly those you deem of lesser importance than you, will come back to haunt you.

I garnered many pewter tankards in the mid-week medal competitions, once won the Whiffen Cup (knock-out singles) but failed miserably in the big Club Championship where I was expected to at least challenge the best players. Now here comes an admission – in a gorse bush to the left of the 17th, our 8th hole that day, I improved my lie ... six inches to the left gave me the chance to swing a 9-iron. This I trust is the only time I have cheated at this game and it did me no favours. I clocked up a dismal 79 or 80 to trail in well down the field. Serves you right, Jamie. Do not do that again.

The competitive urge has abated as I age and these days

I'm happiest hacking around in friendly twos or fours with dogs enjoying the outing as much as us. Joining Swinley Forest has been special. Overheard at Lahinch G.C. in Ireland … "If God played golf he'd play at Swinley." Not being part of the English Golf Union it avoids all the unnecessary rules and regulations prevalent nowadays – joyously one can invent one's own handicap so now I play off 12 (but only on a good day). Nerves have hit my chipping badly – please don't ask me to float a half wedge over a bunker, but sometimes I give the bigger clubs an effective thwack.

For many years a group of us Londoners travelled in late spring to Scotland, Ireland and once to Austria to compete for the Derval Cup. We were all trying to get our name etched onto this little cup as that year's winner. Golf inspires great camaraderie and encourages etiquette, the good manners essential to a sport's success. Respect both your opponent and your partner if you have one. Do not fidget while someone takes a shot, stand out of eye-shot and walk with your mates, not ploughing your own furrow. Above all, look for your opponents' balls when they are in the rough and all will be well, all will be well, as Julian of Norwich affirms.

These days my golf game is poor indeed but occasional visits to the wilds of Sandwich and the ever-improving Swinley – thanks go to secretary George Ritchie for that – have lifted the spirits. Being a member of two clubs was not cheap and although Sandwich would have soon become free when I hit fifty years of membership I recently resigned, unable to justify the huge fees when playing there so little. Apparently Royal St George's have now changed the rules and this concession no longer applies, which I find mean-spirited. But it was always good to be able to invite friends and relatives to both these lovely courses which feature in lists of the world's top 100. Generous Andrew Ingram, my brother-in-law who sadly succumbed to Motor Neurone Disease, loved to join me at both places to exercise our dogs

– greyhounds and lurchers haring around in elliptical loops, sometimes through bunkers. His second son is now a Swinley member. There is also the yearly Oxford colleges day at Frilford Heath where I and others turn up to grind out a few points for Christ Church before an evening dinner in another college's dining hall. Always an enjoyable day.

Tennis I played okay from age ten to eighteen but skiing needs more of a mention. Oh, the beauty of those snow-covered pine trees and fpeaks of the European Alps – on sunny days at least. When you are in cloud and you can't tell your up from your down my skiing technique fails me and I resort to stem turns. So, the spoiled brat started at an early age, and as is so often with sport, the earlier one starts the more proficient one becomes over the years.

P and C plus friends I would take in February half-term to Ellmau in Austria first off, Andorra la Vella, one year over to Lake Louise and Sunshine Valley by Banff in Canada and then a succession of years at Rauris near Zell am See

in Austria. The Rauriserhof Hotel served us so well with its indoor tennis courts, excellent food, breakfast, tea and supper, three bowling alleys and a superb covered swimming pool. Austrians are second only to the Swiss in their hotel skills methinks. Rauris has a floodlit evening toboggan run down a special track which gave us much hilarity and not a little danger. C loves the sport, sadly P doesn't but what hey, I have introduced them to the delights of downhill – langlaufing I've never tried nor shall.

Over the years I have skied in some unusual places – Scotland for those wet twenty minutes, Israel up on Mount Hermon on the Syrian border being shouted at by the Israeli Defence Force when straying too near the Quneitra Syrian side, Bolivia at 17,785 feet above sea level on the Chacaltaya glacier which has now melted, India at little Gulmarg by Srinigar and so many places in France, Switzerland, Italy and Austria.

Kitty Barrell (now Mrs Alain Adam), once told me I ski like a swan which is kind – not super speedy and these days anxious not to fall over as getting up is a strain on the old muscles. Like golf, it's a sport that one can enjoy well into one's eighties. I broke my leg once in Verbier, in crusty stuff just off the piste below Attelas and above Les Ruinettes – avoiding another skier I double somersaulted, hearing a snap on the second circle. Blood-wagon down to Dr Eggar's surgery in the village – I remember Dad was charged £17 for the anaesthetic alone, but I was back at school within days, fortunately with a ground floor room in Angelo's, Robert Hardy's house in Common Lane. Thirteen weeks in plaster and crutches before the leg reappears all skinny and hairy.

I was very average at football – three years running in the 3rd XI, did some squash, fives and rackets. As I've said before I am grateful for all those opportunities, oft denied or unavailable to those in other schools. Once I played 5-a-side rugby and once I ran a mile, four times round the athletics track – boy was that an ordeal.

So we leave the sporting arena, and the sybaritic life of my university days. Before we look at softer matters like music and travel we must return to the ravages of the mind and my very first bout of insanity.

Brace yourselves again.

# 8

# JANUARY 1980

A huge month in the history of the world. The Soviet Union had invaded Afghanistan on the night of 24th December 1979 (which would have been Mum's 60th birthday) and were destined to remain for ten years. This upset me greatly because I'd been travelling through that fine country in March and June 1979, spending time in Herat, Kabul and Mazar-i-Sharif, and had grown fond of its people. The Soviet juggernaut's progress was stalled by snow at the Salang Tunnel but by early January their initial 30,000 troops were heading down towards Kabul.

Other big news concerned Paul McCartney, detained at Narita Airport, Tokyo for possession of half a pound of marijuana on 16th January and fortunate to be released from custody on Friday 25th. Marijuana had been playing a leading role in my own life since the early '70s and by now was beginning to affect my brain cells in a negative way. Friends had noticed a change in my demeanour over the previous month or so – over-enthusiastic thoughts about starting up a little food company called Mange 2, imagining I was soon going to become a leading amateur golfer, and (as so often in my life) falling in love quickly in mid-December on re-acquaintance with Cha Weychan. I had wooed her with a message squirted on my bathroom mirror with shaving foam reading: "All you need is Love".

In my exuberance I had assured her that one day she would become editor of *The Times* – she was at the time editing a small travel magazine.

Such grandiose thinking is called hypomania by psychiatrists and allied with reckless spending deemed a characteristic of manic depression or bi-polar disorder as it is called these days. In my case, however, was it an intrinsic madness or one brought on by smoking dope? Cannabis psychosis in other words. I shall endeavour to educate you over the ensuing pages but in the meantime let's take this month's happenings day by day ... well, chronologically at least.

On the 1st I drove down to Rye in East Sussex in my rickety yellow Morris Minor Convertible (1956 split-screen version) – a far cry from some of my earlier vehicles but full of character. Dad and his third wife, Betsy, had moved to Old Romney from Portugal some years previously and I used to stay with them when playing in the Presidents' Putter, the annual get-together of Oxford and Cambridge ex-golfing Blues. This year, as so often, the ground at the Rye links was frozen solid, making golf somewhat tricky as the ball would go gdoing gdoing as if bouncing on tarmac before gathering enough hoar frost on it to then stop rapidly.

In my overconfident state I'd been playing some pretty good golf in recent weeks – the diary records a 72 on Boxing Day and a 71 on New Year's Eve round the Old Course at Sunningdale. A lesson from Clive Clark, who had likened my wristy swing to that of the South African Bobby Cole, further boosted my confidence and I felt ready to conquer all-comers at Rye. My weapons at the time included a 3-wood, handmade by Lambert Topping, a famous club maker, the head of which I had painted pink and green with a heart shape on top reading T.L.C. (Tender Loving Care). I must have got this idea off Jamie Warman, a Cambridge golfer who had painted his driver white.

Anyroads, my self-assurance came to an abrupt end in the

first round when I succumbed 4 and 3 to John Wilkes who coped with the difficult conditions far better than I did. Things hadn't gone very well the previous day either, when David Baxter and I teamed up as Christ Church, Oxford people in the Croome Shield foursomes to score a disappointing 85. So it was back to London before the weekend, no silverware to cherish and polish, merely a bruised ego. Better golf followed on Saturday and Sunday with a 73 and a 71 round the New Course at Sunningdale, which is a darn sight more difficult than the Old. Also recorded is production for that little food company … thirty heart-shaped (theme developing here) salmon fishcakes of which I'd managed to sell sixteen by 9 p.m., the rest heading for the freezer.

Earlier that Sunday evening I had planted out about 500 bulbs in the Belgravia garden of my friend Mary Rose Howard née Chichester. She had been an on / off girlfriend

(mostly on) over my Oxford years and after, before marrying Greville, a successful city financier, perhaps a bit on the 'rebound' from yours truly. She was now dueña of a lovely maisonette in Chesham Place and drove a Range Rover but as ever a joy to be with.

Then it's a long-planned skiing break, leaving the Morris behind, travelling through the night – train to Dover, ferry to Calais, train to Paris. There spending much of the day with my friend Didier Rousseau who I had met on my South American travels back in 1978. We played frisbee on the concourse of the new Richard Rogers designed 'Beaubourg' and probably smoked a bit of weed before I caught more 'Corail' trains to the Swiss border and on to Zurich. I arrived at Klosters Platz at 11.30 p.m. I seem to recall staying a few nights in the Hotel Bündnerhof before being generously offered a room with the Fatorini family nearby.

It was ostensibly a 'family holiday' that I was joining. Sisters Carole and Kitten, along with husbands Andrew and Mickey had rented a smart apartment across from the Bündnerhof but there wasn't room for me. Andrew was a very proficient skier, had skied for Oxford, and knew his way around the Klosters slopes. The snow was excellent and he kindly guided us off-piste into the powder snow. I still try to mirror his technique whenever I dare to venture off the pistes these days. Their children were also present although I'm not sure the younger son was yet skiing.

One evening that week I was dining in their rented flat when sister Carole, who would have been preparing the evening meal, started behaving impatiently towards me, eventually throwing a glass at me (which missed) and accusing me of talking nonsense to her children. Big sister Anne staunchly defends her sibling by saying she was simply protecting them from my 'druggy influence'. I remember retaliating to Carole by saying that she should 'give' more, which would have riled her.

Many of you will have difficult relationships with members of your families – sibling rivalries, petty jealousies, whatever. Anyway, it became obvious to me that in order to defuse this tension it would be better if I departed earlier than the planned 19th January. So a week before, on the 12th, I told Andrew at the base of the Gotschnagrat cable-car station that I would be heading back to England after Kitten's birthday on the 14th. Sorted. So it was back to Paris on the 15th, arriving at Didier's flat near Les Halles at midnight. The following day was spent gently in the suburbs with new friend Marie, who I had met on the Corail train the previous week – no hanky-panky for sure as Cha was my chosen one at that time, but I do make friends easily, then as now. A large metal 'mouli-legumes' was purchased, to prove useful for making soups – more bric-a-brac for the kitchen but vital in those days before liquidisers and other blitzers were on the market.

Once again, I travel through the night from the Gare du Nord and arrive back at my house off Lavender Hill at 7 a.m. on the morning of Thursday the 17th. Walk down to my friend's place off Abbeville Road, Steve Morris (yes, Morris) my trusty car mechanic, where I collect the mended Morris – drive back to Altenburg Gardens and start preparing things for more Mange 2 production, the fledgling food business I was starting up. Then at 10.30 a.m. the phone rings and my easy life is about to end. Forever.

It is Georgie Chichester on the line, Mary Rose's elder sister. "Mary Rose is dying," she tells me – she had been knocked unconscious falling from her horse on frosty ground on the morning of Saturday 12th riding hatless near their weekend cottage at Hullavington near Swindon. And had been in a coma ever since then at a hospital outside Bristol, apparently the best brain injury hospital in the region. Her husband Greville and her mother and father stayed at her bedside throughout. She was new to riding and not fond of hunting.

I break down into a physical and mental heap on my kitchen floor before going out walking. I need to pray, so I try to enter churches but they are locked ... the sixth, in Clapham Old Town, is open but full of scaffolding and the builders have perched their coffee mugs on the altar – so I go out onto the Common screaming and wailing to pull the adorable Mary Rose through. In the evening Georgie rings again to say that her heart is beating more strongly and that she has passed urine ... so back I go onto Clapham Common and ask for miracles. I had offered to help in any way but Georgie said, "Pray from where you are."

The following morning, ignoring Georgie's advice, I drove down to Lymington and appeared unexpected and unannounced at noon at the family home bringing six of my heart-shaped fishcakes. Mary Rose is still living, contrary to what a friend had told me that morning, "Oh, she died – didn't you hear?" Georgie and I drove across Beaulieu Heath to their granny's house where just before lunch Lady Chichester rings to say, "It is finished." The life support machine has been switched off. At least I was in the arms of her two sisters, Coral and Georgie, when this human tragedy and travesty reached its denouement. I share their grief for some five hours before returning to London.

The following morning I'm up early again, driving to Heathrow to pick up Cha Weychan flying in from Bulgaria. For some reason there is a confusion over flight numbers and terminals and we do not meet but manage to talk later on the phone. The afternoon is spent baking bread – kneading by hand is therapeutic is it not? And then it's off to dine with friends, James and Annabel Dallas who were living on Bucharest Road in Wandsworth. I accepted their offer of a bed for the night but I could not sleep, or rather, it felt as if God did not want me to sleep. So I left quietly at midnight, lighting a candle in their spare room and returned home some two miles east. Not very wise really to leave a burning candle but I was keeping Mary Rose's memory aflame.

I packed all I might need for a couple of days on the road. "Where on earth are you going?" asks Minnow Powell, one of my house-mates. "West," I replied. On go the Adidas sneakers (60,000 miles and still going strong), I light another candle at my house and one in the ashtray of the Morris. Off we go, following our fortunes, doing His will on earth. At about 2.30 a.m. nature calls at the Heston Services on the M4. There I pick up two Welsh hitch-hikers who'd been trying for a lift for four or five hours. What a charitable nation we are. I tell them I'm not sure where we are going, but Bristol seems a possibility. Avebury, let's go to Avebury we decide – so we pull into Membury services. I spot a man with a friendly face to ask, "Excuse me, could you help, we're trying to get to Avebury?" "Oh, I live there," he says, "got a 17th century cottage right in the village." We follow his directions where we stop to listen, to walk round the circle, to touch the stones, to feel the brilliant stars. There seemed to be a real ethereal power at this ancient site. Moles were pushing up their pyramids as we walked around. Avebury Church was dream-like, its stained glass windows sentinels of salvation.

We drove on through Bath to central Bristol. Ritchie, one of the hikers, knew of a splendid all-night café where we had coffee and breakfast. A man with a limp comes up to me and says, "Can I help you at all?" I asked where was the best hospital if one had a serious accident – "Oh, just across the road from here, the Bristol Royal Infirmary." My first taste of hospital enquiry desks follows. Mary Rose wasn't there but we discovered where she was and are asked to return after 10 a.m. My friends leave – it's now 7.45 a.m. on a Sunday morning and I clamber up Sion Hill, Clifton to the Camera Obscura to witness a spectacular dawn. Flocks of birds floated above the Avon Gorge and the frost was thawing. It became obvious what my mission was – to say to Mary Rose, "Arise and walk."

Cha's mother lived close by so I phoned and went round with the Sunday papers to be fed fine coffee and good conversation. At about 10, Wanda drove me up to Frenchay Hospital in North Bristol. I was then at the last gate, telling the fat man behind the enquiry desk my story. It was not his responsibility to allow me access to her bedside so he passed the buck to a Dr Briggs. Via telephone he tells me that I cannot see the body as he has already started the post-mortem on Mary Rose … "We don't usually work on a Sunday, but we've had such a backlog. We've had a lot of experience here with death and I can assure you that we are acting in your best interests." Clinico / scientifico / anti-emotion syndrome, I wrote in my diary.

Wanda drives me back to Clifton. We say goodbye and because the sun is so warm that January morning I fold down the Morris' top. The candle in the ashtray still burns in the gusty conditions and finally snuffs out on Sion Hill between the obelisk and the church where they queue to hear the vicar preach on a Sunday.

By now I am writing up a sort of diary in an A5 black-covered notebook. So here are the entries for the next couple of days, pretty much verbatim. I called these days 'The New Dawn'.

The story from Sunday 20th January:

Wanda tells me the way to Lymington from Bristol – Bath / Warminster / Salisbury. The sun is hot that day and I am crying tears of happiness because God has brought me home some 800 miles, through the French train strike and Paris, all the way to Mary Rose's side when her soul ascended to heaven. And he had shown me at that final gate at Frenchay Hospital that men often have jaded, faithless and unloving personalities.

So me and Morris trundle off through Bristol, through that beautiful city of Bath to Warminster. Nature called in

Warminster. I found a little café on the High Street – there was a nice old lady behind the counter and a poacher too; then a country yokel came up to the bar where I was. On glancing down at his jacket pocket I said to him, "Do you realise that you are carrying exactly the same things in your pocket as I am?" We were too … one of those digital clock / calculators covered in cloth material, the same silver felt tip pen, Silk Cut, matches etc. He works on Lord Bath's estate & has a beautiful silver cross too which I lack at the moment but my body is my cross. Well, yet again, Morris won't start so he helps me give her the customary push and we're off again… "See you on the Judgement Day", I shout to the farmworker.

Morris then sets me off on the road to Salisbury, all along the chalk escarpment, past the White Horse, past stone age settlements, tumuli etc. Salisbury Cathedral was looking miraculous as we climbed the hill heading out to Southampton. Across Salisbury Plain, with those rather worrying signs saying – 'BEWARE TANKS CROSSING' – I prefer cows myself! Then via Cadnam to Beaulieu where most of the Chichester family were clearing out a copse at a ruined cottage on the river & having a bit of a picnic. I help for five hours or so, cutting, stacking, burning etc. And by no means do I tell anyone there about my week's mission as it could easily upset people. God tells me what to say and when to say it.

So at about 6 p.m. I return towards London, stopping off to see Sir John Chichester who was looking after the house and taking the incessant clichéd telephone calls. Well, they're not all clichéd but many are. Sir John understands & even Susannah, their ten-year-old whippet, she knows. I give two hitch-hikers a ride from Brockenhurst to Chandler's Ford and the Morris reaches London in good shape in time for supper chez nous at Altenburg Gardens.

Then I go to bed, having done the best I could – and sleep like one of those logs.

Monday 21st January

I return my salopettes to Alpine Sports – the queue-barger woman. Then have a long rap with Tom Bovingdon up in Harrods' Olympic Way about golf nets, people and ancient ledgers.

To Basil Street... Doc 15 mins late. Supertramp's 'Child of Vision' playing as we near Guy's Hospital, (my birth-place 13/7/1954) Keats House – for my appointment with Anthony Fry. He's ½ hour late as well. Prescribes lithium carbonate, "Slow down kid!" Say goodbye to Michael & hop into Buttercup. I am introduced to Revelations 14 – the references to the Lamb, Syon (Zion) Hill etc. Amanda F-H comes for tea – fresh-baked bread and chai. Colour selections for the jersey she is machine-knitting for me – has to dash off to see her knitters. Take loaf of bread to Bishop's.

9.30 p.m. arrive at Gail's house at Leatherhead Golf Course – snacks from the kitchen. Gail understands but the new boyfriend was in a right old bolsh. Morris stalled 200 yards up the road. A fine household of people.

Back to town at about 2.30 a.m. ...

It's getting manic isn't it? Trauma combined with sleep deprivation, not good for the brain cells. I clearly thought Supertramp's lyrics were talking about me... "Child of Vision, won't you listen?" Anthony Fry was a psychiatrist friend of my GP Michael Gormley – if only I had listened to him and slowed down. But when one is manic it's hard to get off the roller-coaster – it's an adrenaline surge gathering momentum.

Gail Bishop was a friend who I'd met on my travels in Colombia back in 1978. She, Tessa Cormack and I had rented rooms on a farm up in the hills above San Agustín (see Chapter 10). I had talked to her on the phone for two hours during the night and arranged to visit.

Goodness me, the following morning I am up at 4.30 a.m. (two hours sleep) heading to Heathrow again, this time bent on a day trip to Paris. The yellow Morris is having none of this and conks out at a petrol station in West Kensington. Take a taxi ride to Terminal 1 (£6.50 in those days!) and board the 6.40 a.m. British Airways flight to Charles de Gaulle, the new airport for Paris. I call the place a 'tubular monstrosity' in my diary. Bus into town and it's another day with Didier. We go shopping in the afternoon in Samaritaine and I purchase a cornucopia of stuff … three frisbees, dried fruits, olive oil, Greek wine, an M. C. Escher book, stickers, peppercorns and taramasalata. We tour the remarkable quartier around St Estèphe before I head back to Heathrow from Orly Airport, this time on a most agreeable Kuwait Airlines plane. Two of my house-mates, Patrick Sumner and Sue Phipps, are having a drinks party on my return, then it's out to supper with Kim Beddall and Françine Preston in Fulham. Thankfully the Morris is back working now. What an exhausting day – tiring enough just writing about it.

Wednesday 23rd I note that I 'scored' more marijuana in the morning – it's going to be many years before I correlate this Jamaican 'Weed of Wisdom' with mental woes. At 2 p.m. I have my second meeting with gentle Anthony Fry over at Guy's Hospital. On my way back home I buy my third combination of Sony Walkman (very early version, the 121) and Sony headphones – a bit of a pioneer here, before it became supercool to wander the streets tuned into a Walkman, let alone a mobile phone. I'd been using this cassette machine and headset for skiing – sometimes rolling a joint on a chair lift and smoking it before reaching the top while listening to Blondie or whoever. What an idiot – I don't think dope helps one's skiing one iota.

That evening I'd travelled to Perivale to meet an American friend, Maggie Lapiner who was working in a pub. We had a lovely time cruising around town and she came to stay the night down in Battersea.

The following morning Maggie and I head down to

Heathrow again because I have gifts to give to Gail Bishop who is flying out to Kenya via Moscow. She is already through security and in the departure lounge of Terminal 2 but, and this wouldn't be possible these days, she is 'paged' and able to return from 'air-side' to the main concourse.

An extraordinary event then occurs – one of those special enlightening moments when the Holy Spirit flows and surges through one's being. Boy, I am blessed to have these feelings. This is how I recorded it in the diary:

> Maggie and I were standing at the iron gates in front of the departure channel when, from nowhere it seemed, six sisters or nuns were buzzing around us, like little hummingbirds. A most beautiful moment it was; then Gail appears through the doors to receive her gift – the Sony Walkman & headphones, three cassettes, two candles and a card saying 'Go as you are' – all wrapped in a sheet of *The Times* in a Raven Records bag. We buy some more Duracells, then Gail has to go.

Raven Records was a small independent record store on the Fulham Road, owned and run by an old school friend, Simon Craven. Some of you may remember the idiosyncratic adverts for his shop, on screen at the Odeon, Fulham Road … "Only 378 yards from this cinema," or some such.

Maggie heads back to Perivale, I to Sunningdale for thirteen holes with Peter Breeden who I hope will become my co-founder of Mange 2 foods. He plays better golf than me that day. We have been golfing friends for many years down at Sandwich, competing together in Switzerland, Savoie and sundry places – sharing an interest in perhaps opening a restaurant but now discussing setting up this company. I have organised solicitors Allen & Overy to draft the necessary papers and am due at their offices in the City of London at 4 p.m. The meeting had been combined with one finally closing matters on my mother's estate.

The wretched Morris lets me down again by stopping on a

roundabout by the Compleat Angler at Runnymede. A gracious push-start later and I arrive at Cheapside half an hour late. An amusing incident had happened in Knightsbridge when I chanced to pull alongside Ted Molt the broadcaster who himself had owned one of these jalopies. Several luminaries greet me at Allen & Overy and I am handed a cheque for £360 and the company memoranda for Mange 2.

There is an orange fireball of a sunset over Buckingham Palace as I return up the Mall. Then it's supper out with friends again, Franny Newton and others in Gastein Road, Hammersmith. Home after midnight. But sleep is short once again.

Friday 25th January – a huge day in my life encompassing all the emotions. It starts with a vision.

At 3 a.m., I am out on the streets walking down Battersea Rise towards the crossroads with St John's Hill and Northcote Road. As I stand out at the foot of the hill, the derelict church some 300 yards ahead of me is bathed in glorious light – its spire aglow, I kid you not.

A song courses through my head – 'Solsbury Hill' by Peter Gabriel, his first solo effort on leaving Genesis (and still my favourite piece of music ever). Ahead is this spire atop

the hill – St Mark's, Battersea Rise, derelict at the time, but destined down the line to become Holy Trinity Brompton's southern sister when renovated in the early nineties.

To my left is the market street of Northcote Road, home to Dove's the butchers, only recently departed. To my right St John's Road heads toward Clapham Junction station, behind me stalks a white cat. To me this is a powerful moment – my diary at the time captures it thus:

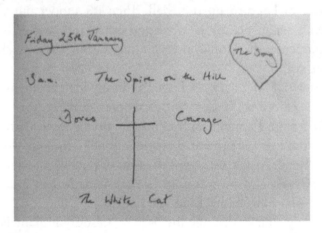

Back home I go – to have a bath where I laugh about this game of life …

The Great Game.

***

It is the day of Mary Rose's funeral – we are due at Castle Rising Church north of King's Lynn in Norfolk at 2 p.m. This is Greville's family area, a ruined castle, home to the Howard family over centuries past. Many Howards had been buried here and now it was Mary Rose's turn, although her roots and life were really in the New Forest, London and latterly the cottage in Wiltshire. I buy *The Times* and *The Telegraph* and am convinced pictures inside relate to my week but subsequent investigation pours doubt on my manic theory.

At 8.30 a.m. Cha and her friends arrive at my house – we pick up her car and head to East Anglia. First stop is The Lodge at Elsenham, home to my eldest sister Anne. Why we bought marmalade at Mr Buttle's shop I remember not. Then on past Stansted Airport, Saffron Walden and San-dringham, arriving at the pub in Castle Rising where I recall spouting my thoughts and feelings in frenzied fashion to anyone who might listen. Most there were friends I knew, who knew of my love for this girl.

I was part of the ushering squad before taking a seat next to Cha near the front left of the little church. There are well over a hundred fellow mourners. Jamie Chichester, her elder brother, and cousin Robin read the lessons well. Behind Cha and I are four ladies in red coats emblazoned with lion motifs. The service is moving with splendid hymns – it seems to me that my singing improves.

Outside, the burial happens – short of a bouquet of flowers, I grasp some grass and cast that on her wooden coffin. Earth to earth. We then all assemble at a nearby friend's house, Valentine's. I remember the tears of Julian, her younger brother, the busy kitchen ladies providing the wake, the tea and sandwiches round the kitchen Aga. A life cut short, so sad.

Eventually our car heads back to town. There appears to be good news on the radio and it seems to me that we all sense the magic – but then there is news of a murder on Clapham Common. We pass a small factory named Just Jamie Co. in Whitechapel. It feels as if there are signs all around – on reaching Altenburg Gardens I turn my attention to the basement and stuff stored there and elsewhere.

My mind is racing. News comes in of the release of Paul McCartney in Japan – yo. Somehow I want to greet his return ... planes landing at Heathrow pass over Fulham so passengers on the left-hand side might see my house. I start a bonfire in the garden (we are not yet in a smoke-free zone) – some marketing material from Aeroflot is turned to ash – that'll learn them for invading Afghanistan. Papers relating to my father get similar treatment, my mind has turned against him too. On the windowsills at the front of the house I assemble a montage – the massive family Bible, leather-bound, dating from 1850. Brian Redhead uncovered

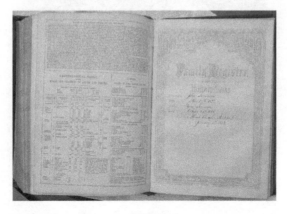

a second one in existence when he wrote his book on the Summers family. A rustic pair of garden shears joins the display.

This behaviour leads to a confrontation with some of my house-mates and others present. My GP Michael, who I trust, administers a double-dose syringe of calming medication but there is no change in my disposition.

Below are word for word Michael's medical notes of these days:

25/1/80 Has become even more hypomanic since Mary Rose's funeral today and is now talking as though he were God. Telephone call from Cha Weychan who says that he has become madder than ever before and needs hospitalization. Talking about visions, about the Good News that can be seen on television or in any newspaper. Considers the world to have an overall plan which he and God are running. Refuses to see that anything is wrong with him or his viewpoints. Given Serenase 15mgs iv. Admitted to the Priory Hospital under Dr. Desmond Kelly.

27/1/80 Narcosis unit at the Priory. Has slept most of the time since last seen. Taking Serenase 10mgs t.d.s., Largactil 200mgs q.d.s. Lithium Carbonate 250mgs q.d.s., Mandrax 1 tab q.d.s.

Serenase is Droperidol, which featured in Chapter 1.

And so he gets into his car, a red Mercedes roadster. "I know the place for you," he says, and he drives me the four miles or so to the Roehampton Priory Hospital. It is late on Friday night and the next four or five days pass in a blur of amnesia. One of the doctors' initial drugs of choice for me is Mandrax. This is a super-powerful sedative derived from the mandragora root which gave me daydreams of flying, night dreams of playing golf at 3 a.m., but caused me to lose touch with the world. Mandragora officinarum, used as an aphrodisiac by Jacob with Leah as told in Genesis 30, verses

14–16. Betcha bottom dollar that Mandrax is no longer used in acute psychiatry – they have tried so many 'cures' have they not … immersion in cold running water, insulin coma 'therapy' – all to no avail.

Some time in this amnesic four days they also added Largactil to my medication mix because my writing style begins to become tight – a tortuous script that is hard to decipher. I was keen for others to learn of my experiences and chose dear Bernard Levin, *The Times* journalist and author, as the recipient of my outpourings. My friend Minnow had furnished me with Tintin books to read in hospital and on the blank backs of some of the opening pages I scratched out a long letter to Bernard Levin. This was kindly typed up for me by a fellow patient and dispatched on 30th January. Graciously on the 6th February he sent me a short reply thanking me for my letter and "this account. I offer you my sympathy."

What is extraordinary, weird, spooky or whatever adjective you choose to use is that his reply would have been typed up by Honor, his secretary. When I got married some four years later I discover that Honor is the best friend of my wife's sister. Coincidence or what?

This month of January 1980 closes with notes in my diary of appointments with the Priory's top consultants – taciturn Dr Desmond Kelly and his senior at the time, Dr Thomson. The latter tells me that he has treated both my mother and my grandmother in times past. This was news to me – shall we leave 'madness' for a while and take a look at some hard times a decade later.

# 9

# FINANCIAL MELTDOWN / LLOYD'S / DIVORCE

I don't expect too much sympathy here – 'rich kid loses most of his money' isn't a headline that engenders empathy nor should it. However, a little compassion wouldn't go amiss as I explain the circumstances. The chapter heading indicates a triple whammy of money woes which happened concurrently at a time when I was weak. But when you are in the gutter the only way to look is up. The 'financial meltdown' was caused by one Graham Millar – I have two bulging lever-arch files called 'The Graham Millar Saga'. Lloyd's bumph merited two thick files' worth – divorce took up two thinner files' worth. They were all upsetting; revisiting the divorce ones has been particularly painful.

A bit of background then on our family trust funds. All my sisters and I benefited from these chunks of inherited wealth passed down over generations of Summers and Patrick relations. There were the 1946 and 1953 Marriage Settlements, the 1956 J.D. Summers Marriage Settlement, the C.B. Patrick Trust and others. The first three Dad had set up to safeguard the steel money that had come his way, administered by top London lawyers Allen & Overy, accounted by more City financiers Touche Ross. Old Army friends of his gave recommendations – Peter Rodier, Sir Godfrey

Morley and Desmond Reid who later became Chairman of Prudential Assurance. The idea was that his children would be entitled to the income from investments in stocks and shares from age eighteen to the age of twenty-five when they would become entitled to spend the capital.

We all had our education, our first motor vehicles and flats paid for by our Trustees. Fantastic. But when Desmond Reid died in 1983 things began to go awry. Dad had been impressed by the jolliness of a younger lawyer at Allen & Overy, a protégé of Peter Rodier, who dressed smartly, wore a bowler hat and carried a rolled-up umbrella. This was Graham Millar. So he was appointed co-Trustee back in 1973 on many of our family trusts at quite a young age. Desmond's departure left 'Swiller Millar' (as colleagues knew him) in sole charge of a lot of our family money.

One should always have at least two Trustees on these things, but the braggadocio of Mr Millar bewitched my father. Dad's poor judgement became my undoing. Millar carried on as sole Trustee having left the confines of the Queen's solicitors to become a stockbroker with Dunkley Marshall in the late seventies. None of us noticed the conflict of interest nor were aware of his drinking and gambling proclivities. He moved stock portfolios over to his firm from the previous trust stockbrokers, Phillips & Drew. In 1987 Dunkley Marshall became Parrish Stockbrokers – Graham Millar then moved to Raphael Zorn at the end of 1988, becoming an associate on half commission when the firm became Raphael Zorn Hemsley in October 1989 – in other words brokerage fees on stock trading were shared equally between him and his employees. I think that soon after that the arrangement changed to a 60 / 40 split between the firm and its employee. Because he came with several wealthy clients' money aggregating to many millions he must have seemed a good catch to Raphael Zorn.

I had always treated my trust fund as something not to be

touched – to be left in the background. Okay, so in 1977 I had asked for a chunk to be released to buy a house near Clapham Junction as the Belgravia flat had horrendous service charges. As I said, each of us children were bought our initial flats – the Ebury Street one had originally been bought for Carole who sold it to Kitten who sold it to me. It fetched £24,000 when I sold it and I needed £33,000 for the purchase of the house. This was when Desmond Reid was still alive and he agreed to my request for funds. I had also asked in July 1975 for £3,000 to buy a silver BMW 2002 – sort of a 21$^{st}$ birthday present to myself. (If only I'd kept it – such a classic car.) When I turned twenty-five and became 'absolutely entitled' to all income and capital I chose not to exercise these rights. Instead I relied on a monthly allowance and would only touch the capital in emergencies. This arrangement continued over the years to 1992 – I just felt I was a custodian of this inherited wealth, guarding it for future generations, particularly as I now had P and C to provide for. I was no financial whizz-kid and relied on Graham Millar to do what was best on my behalf.

Mistake. The man had become increasingly difficult to contact from the mid-eighties – meetings with him were sporadic, light on detail. When in 1987 I transferred the deeds of my house into S's name to thwart any possible Lloyd's of London future claims, S's solicitor father who oversaw the transfer found him 'infuriating' to deal with. Fast forward to early 1992 when yours truly had just left Springfield for the last time and was setting off for a much needed holiday in the Holy Land – the very first entry in my diary dated 18$^{th}$ January says that I posted a letter to him about trust funds. Even at that very difficult phase of my life I was starting to have concerns as to what Millar was up to.

On my return from Israel the misgivings continued. Surprisingly, my brother-in-law Andrew Ingram and I successfully summoned him to a meeting in King Henry's Road,

Primrose Hill in early February. Here we aimed to establish my monetary wealth in precise terms – divorce proceedings were in the air and I guess I was anxious to secure my own position. Millar's answers to our questions were evasive and limited. He was handed letters from Lloyd's and from my Lloyd's agents (R. K. Harrison) which required his urgent action. This did not transpire despite his promises. And this turned out to be last time I encountered the man.

Once again I turned to family members to assist me. My initial focus was on the inexplicable and abrupt decline in the value of my Lloyd's deposit – to remain as a 'name' one had to deposit some £100,000 in solid shares with them as security. I enlisted Jamie Thomson-Glover (my brother-in-law Mickey's brother and occasional golfing partner) who was twiddling his thumbs, living in Kingston Bagpuize while his son Edward attended my old alma mater Cothill School. Jamie was a fully-qualified accountant and forensically approached the task of investigating Millar's share dealings. We soon were joined in the quest by a cousin of his, Anthony Thomlinson who was a partner in Bischoff's, the city solicitors who provided valuable legal advice as to how to achieve some restitution. Both did this entirely 'gratis' and I am forever grateful to them.

Our investigations during the spring of 1992 revealed the most extraordinary catalogue of 'churning' my portfolios and selection of unsuitable stocks. We discovered that in his 3½ years at RZH he had reduced the value of my shares by some £300,000 whilst earning himself and his company some £150,000 in commission. Further digging at Companies House showed that my few remaining holdings were with 'penny stock' companies such as GRI Group, Sempernova, Tower Group, Sea Search and Ocean Treasure all of which had personal connections with Millar – he had been Chairman of GRI Group from 1984 to 1988, termed 'incompetent' and 'a bully' by its next Chairman, Tony Twine. He too, it turned out, had been dumped into dodgy stock and suffered heavy losses (£60,000) from financial involvement with Mr Millar. It later became apparent that others had been "churned and burned" – notably the Jersey branch of the Royal Bank of Canada (£6 million lost) and architect John Bonnington (£30,000 gone) who had designed No. 1 London Bridge.

By July we were ready to start the formal process – Jamie T-G and Anthony Thomlinson helped with the wording of the letter I typed up on a friend's word processor asking RZH for an explanation of the performance and level of activity since January 1989 on six accounts managed by Millar. Also requested were copies of any signed client agreements that they held. I said reply please within seven days otherwise I would approach the Securities and Futures Authority. I soon discovered that this friend passed a copy to my wife with whom relations were deteriorating fast. A breach of trust in my opinion.

Raphael Zorn were adamant that they bore no responsibility for Millar's actions and correspondence ensued as to the nature of agreements signed, dealing with whether they were 'Advisory' or 'Discretionary'. Towards the end of August the files were passed to Fiona Bisset at the Complaints Department of the Securities and Futures Authority and Anthony Thomlinson's involvement ceased.

By now another Anthony was about to take up the cudgels on my behalf. Anthony Bonsor, then a senior partner at Denton, Hall, Burgin & Warrens (later simply Denton Hall) was Trustee of the C.G. Patrick Trust along with Mark Patrick, my mother's half-brother, and Nicholas D'Arby. Anthony's mother, Sheila, was Mark's half-sister so I guess this makes him a second or third cousin – I'm not very good at divining these things. I had met up with Mark Patrick in June at his London flat where family finances were discussed – if Lloyd's wanted to break up the Patrick Trust (or divorce for that matter) to release my share of its assets, it would cause all sorts of problems, he said. In early September I stay with Mark and his wife June up in Lincolnshire and it is then that Anthony Bonsor is persuaded to help his distant relation.

We make plans to set in motion the dismissal of G. Millar as Trustee of the 1956 Settlement and instate Mark and Anthony instead. This involved serving papers on him in person or at least his wife – this we managed to do on 5th October at 7 p.m. when she answered the door to their flat. All rather cloak and dagger stuff – we were sure he was inside too. Anthony had also been brilliant in effecting the transfer of my remaining funds from RZH to the care of his friend Willie van Straubenzee at J. O. Hambro Investment Management who was able to put realistic valuations on RZH's inflated ones – it now seemed my entire share portfolios were worth about £14,000, down from the dizzy heights of say £350,000 a decade back. Anthony now took over as my chief negotiator with RZH and their solicitors, Lovell White Durrant. He worked tirelessly for me; his advice would normally cost one £500 an hour and yet for me it was all free. Deo gratia.

In late November, Fiona Bisset of the SFA's Complaints Bureau passed my file to Oscar Worthington-Edridge in their Investigation Department. She stated that Raphael Zorn "is not prepared to answer my questions in any detail" (nor those of Anthony or myself either) but reassuringly said that "Raphael Zorn would be liable for the actions of Mr. Millar in his capacity as your investment adviser as he was an employee during the period in question." This was a fact that they had constantly tried to dispute over proceeding months.

So Oscar and his younger assistant, Andrew Sowter, set to work investigating my complaint. They did a very thorough job indeed – Oscar came round to the flat I had managed to rent after many months of temporary accommodation – it had been a difficult time financially. I had survived by paying for just about everything I could by Diners Club card. Not everyone took this card so it was a struggle, made very much worse when my bank bounced the cheque when I was trying to settle the monthly invoice. Until I got paid employment in November I was close to being destitute as the income due to me from the Patrick Trust didn't come my way until all concerned were happy that it should be paid to me direct and not to Graham Millar. Nicholas D'Arby, a Trustee who worked for the Trust's accountants, was a stickler for the rules and protocol which delayed my payments.

I continued to feed information to the SFA. In a letter sent to Oscar in February I updated him on my investigations, tracing an alleged loan between family trusts sanctioned by Touche Ross with a cheque for £11,179 made out to the Inland Revenue which was nothing of the sort. I discovered, courtesy of a partner at Parrish Stockbrokers, that 'Swiller Millar' used to provide his own valuations of unlisted stock on Parrish company notepaper – he left their employ under a cloud. Contacting the GRI people up in Scotland revealed he had bullied fellow directors, had been "invited not to be chairman anymore" in 1988 and swindled the current chairman out of some £60,000. My angst against Touche Ross was based on their apparent ignorance of any wrongdoing within the 1956 Settlement, the accounting of which was costing me some £4,000 per annum.

Wouldyabelieveit, the £11,179 referred to was actually filched from my funds to pay one of Millar's own income tax bills. Incredibly, despite there being a clear paper trail to this effect, and despite meeting me at my place of work, officers of the City of London Police Fraud Investigation Department eventually telephoned me in mid-July 1994 to say that the Crown Prosecution Service were satisfied that Millar was 'mentally ill' at the time of the offence, and therefore he would not be prosecuted. Oh, the irony. The CPS … "What a shower," I wrote at the time, "hoodwinked by a gambling drunk." I never got that money back.

At the end of July 1993, with Andrew Sowter's help, I prepared my statement for the SFA's Investigations Department. It was a comprehensive account of the history of my dealings with Millar and it led eventually to a settlement of some of my losses.

The more you have, the more you can be milked.

La di da. Scurrilously, his churning activities continued right up to the day when his firm 'de-registered' him as a stockbroker in July 1992. Equally scurrilously, the SFA determined that his most prolific buying and selling sprees took place when I was languishing in loony bins. Just how ghastly is that?

Although I wasn't party to the final deliberations of the Investigations Department (nor sent the closing report) it seems they told RZH to pay me £85,000 in compensation. This they tried to recoup, without success, from Millar. So it wasn't until early 1994 that I received partial restitution. Almost at once I invested the money, along with the paltry remains of my stock portfolios kindly guarded by Willie van Straubenzee, in a small house in Earlsfield. Anthony Bonsor felt that the result achieved from RZH was a fair one and naturally we expected to get that additional £11,179 that Millar had nicked back as well – but as stated before that didn't happen. Oh well.

William Lewis, a journalist on the *Mail on Sunday*, was fed the torrid details by the SFA and published a short article on 6th February 1994 outlining the case under the heading, 'Sacked broker faces police probe'. Justice can be elusive can it not, but God sees all – Millar apparently died just a couple of years later. No contrition had been evident.

Let's turn to another drain on my resources, Lloyd's of London, which I had joined as a 'name' in 1976 at the age of twenty-one when I was probably too naïve to know what I was doing. Actually, not probably ... undoubtedly.

Basically Lloyd's was like a large insurance company, one of the differences being that the financial backing, should there be losses (i.e. more claims than premiums) was provided by wealthy individuals and not the capital assets of companies. It had started back in the late 17th century as a small coffee house on Tower Street, EC3 where people underwrote marine insurance policies for their friends. It grew to the vast outfit in the late 20th century where thousands of 'brokers' sought insurance for their clients' needs with hundreds of 'underwriters' sitting at 'boxes' in the busy atmosphere of the 'room'. It was more of a large gentlemen's club really than a traditional business model.

I suppose the more intelligent public school leavers and university graduates at the time gravitated towards other City jobs, joining banks or becoming lawyers if they wanted a career in the financial world. If you were less bright then the Armed Forces or Lloyd's beckoned. Added to the 'Hooray Henrys' in the eighties was an influx of 'wide boys' from Essex keen to make money. Of course this is a possibly unfair allegation, but there were definitely dodgy dealings and fraudulent activity going on at this institution. Many insiders managed to avoid any losses when the meltdown occurred.

The whole edifice crumbled at the end of the eighties. There were huge losses from the Piper Alpha oil rig tragedy, 1988 claims from asbestos sufferers (mesothelioma) and those with black lung disease after long exposure to coal dust. Gullible investors, many recruited to dilute losses already known about, it was alleged, lost all they had. You see, when you became a 'name' you showed you had at least £100,000 of solid capital assets. Should the syndicates (groups of names together writing business at one of those boxes) to which you belonged call in cash to cover their losses you weren't just liable for that £100,000. Lloyd's could (and did) come after you for everything you owned – famously they were entitled to leave you with just an armchair and a sixpence (2½p). This was the concept of unlimited liability that distinguished Lloyd's from a standard insurance company.

In the fifties, sixties and seventies names at Lloyd's enjoyed healthy returns year on year. It was a way of using one's money twice – shares lodged as a deposit earned their usual dividends but also provided the backing for gaining income from Lloyd's. Premiums generally outweighed claims, commissions earned by brokers were not substantial and many people did very nicely thank you from this system, Dad included. His annual cheque from R.K. Harrison, his agents, paid for all his children's private education.

So with his encouragement, I joined up on 1st January 1976. Because at the time I was employed as a trainee reinsurance broker, my first cheque which arrived in early 1979 (there is a three-year accounting delay) could be treated as earned income, attracting less tax. And bingo, it was a large one … £7,003. Over the next ten years the income averaged £5,000 per annum. There were other tax advantages too that accountants understood.

This became my main source of income after I'd stopped working in the City, to travel the world, to do part-time jobs before the bakery started. The baking enterprise never yielded large profits as we shall see later. So when Lloyd's started demanding money to fund syndicate losses times became difficult. I tendered my resignation from Lloyd's at the end of 1990 and joined (at considerable expense) many of the Action Groups fighting for the rights of their syndicate members – that run by Michael Denny for the Gooda Walker names was particularly efficient and effective. Others I joined were for Hazell, Janson Green, Secretan and Cuthbert Heath syndicates.

Fortuitously in the later years of Lloyd's membership I had

taken out 'stop loss' insurance. For the 1987, 1988 and 1989 years I was covered each year for £200,000 losses over an excess of £30,000. For 1990, because premiums had soared, it was only for £50,000, excess of £60,000. Nevertheless this proved enough and my overall losses remained within the insured section. Cash calls flooded in from 1992 onwards and soon what was left in my Lloyd's deposit after Millar's decimation thereof, was all gone.

Meanwhile, Lloyd's itself was seeking a way out of this debacle and began working on a Settlement Offer to its beleaguered names. Eventually they changed their under-writing rules to eliminate the unlimited liability, reinsured their past losses into a new company called Equitas which was ultimately bought by Warren Buffett, the American financier.

I imagine many suicides resulted from the cataclysmic events that were unfolding. Remember this was hitting me at the same time as divorce proceedings (more about that coming soon) and the Graham Millar saga – but I was resilient. Suicide wasn't on the cards.

Pragmatically, it appeared that I would need to pay Lloyd's about £60,000 to achieve 'finality' – trouble was I no longer had any shares and I wasn't going to sell my little house in Earlsfield. So I started negotiations with the Hardship Committee, partly in a bid to buy some time. Reams and reams of paperwork ensued – goodness me, the amount of detail they sought. This coincided with similar requests coming from my wife's solicitors so the figures were at least to hand. Lloyd's wanted full disclosure of all trusts with which I had connections and in intricate detail. The C.G. Patrick Trust Trustees played ball up to a point but eventually said it was completely unrealistic to arrange a professional valuation of the properties as this would incur costs to be spread amongst the other beneficiaries as well as myself. By the end of 1994 I was getting fed up with this Hardship Committee – they had even been to Fulham to have a look at the Lillie Road parade. In March 1995 they came up with their offer to solve my, at the time, £40,000 debt to Lloyd's. I wrote to them soon after, declining their offer, which involved ceding the deeds of my property to them when I died and sending them an enormous cheque once I had somehow sold on my share of the Lillie Road properties. So I told them, "I therefore agree for my Lloyd's affairs to be passed to the allegedly more vulture-like Financial Recovery Department."

That turned out to be contrary to reality. The Debt Recovery Team seemed more humane. By early August 1996, my general 'pissedoffness' showed in a letter to them where I said that I wasn't in the 'can pay won't pay' brigade, more in the 'will have great difficulty in paying' but agreeing to abide by my original membership contract. I asked for a little more time to settle my debt and said, no chance were they going to get access to the Patrick Trust deeds.

The renewed 'Settlement Offer' showed I owed them £55,579 and in late September I sent them £35,000 which I now had in my savings account. By mid-November I was able to send them the balance of £20,579 – this was after I arranged a mortgage on the Earlsfield property with the Woolwich Building Society who had a friendly branch on Wandsworth High Street.

Finality, closed, end of – although it wasn't really until 2009, so some thirteen years later, that we were reassured by Hugh Stevenson, the Chairman of Equitas, that our potential liabilities were at an end. There remains the remote, remote possibility that Lloyd's could still lay claim to people's estates – I would prefer them to go after those names who refused to pay their dues or fled the country.

The third part of the 'triple whammy' on my finances was running contemporaneously with the other two. I suppose ultimately it cost me more financially than Millar or Lloyd's but that pales into insignificance in comparison with the emotional cost. Nobody can brush off divorce and its effect on children. Of life's great traumas, a family bereavement, losing one's job, ill health and even moving house it is reckoned that divorce ranks number two after the death of a spouse.

As we have seen my marriage was effectively doomed on the last admission to the loony bin. "If it happens again, I'm leaving you"; and it had. Nevertheless, I tried my utmost to rescue things – a battered family unit being better than one broken up I thought. However, from Christmas 1991 S's mind was made up – she was adamant she wanted out and this became abundantly clear when I later read my medical notes. Initially I tried to use mutual friends as mediators but to no avail. It appears that the stigma of mental illness truly runs deep. Then I turned to S's sister who I knew she trusted. I believe her sister simply binned later letters that I sent her, although she did read the first two.

Mentioning the wedding vows … in sickness and in health, for better for worse … was greeted by her storming out of a restaurant. Friends who had themselves recently been on the wards at Springfield kindly offered to let me stay on their sitting-room floor. I was grateful for their company. From their Tooting flat I used to return to the bakery, using the garden gate door, just finishing up the existing bags of flour and eventually closing it completely after some twelve years of production. After a few weeks there, I rented a room up in Southfields where fellow resident and Christian counsellor, Dorothy, encouraged me in my quest to remain married.

I had also invoked help from Tony Yeldham, the mental health chaplain at Springfield – here is an extract from a letter I sent to him:

… how can I assure my wife that yes, okay, I have my moments of madness (or spiritual torment more like) but basically there's a decent bloke underneath it all? ... I felt you had noticed *something* in me, a touch of His grace in me ...

Before I left for my much needed break in Prague and Israel I said to her, "Please, please ring Tony Yeldham," and that's all I said ... no extra words. When I returned I asked, "Did you ring Tony?" The reply I received was in an unpleasant smirking nigh laughing tone ... "Yes I did, and he told me a thing or two about you I can tell you!" and that was all she said.

Now I wasn't privy to your telephone conversation with my wife but I hope you understand now why I did feel let down. I continued for ages to try and save the marriage, attempting to use other advocates in addition to my own efforts but it wasn't to be.

It took well over two years before I got a reply to my letter. Tony left to do social work in Devon before becoming part of the team at Exeter Cathedral and now has a more exalted status as Chaplain at Westminster Abbey. After the Israel trip I donated a rather special communion cup to his church, St Peter and St Paul Springfield and a friend, Alex Murray, was later commissioned to make a cross – both items are now lost which is sad.

Accusations started flying around when we both spoke separately with a lady from Relate. It appeared to me that S kyboshed the idea of being counselled as a couple, asking if Relate could help us separate. Her recollection was, "she made it very clear to me that she felt she would not be able to help you". In my session I spoke at length about my 'manic depression' and what steps I was taking to understand things – namely attending local Manic Depression Fellowship meetings, volunteering twice a week at Springfield Patients Council, joining MIND, seeing Desmond Kelly back at the Priory. I was trying to save our marriage.

In Chapter 12, 'Work', I talk about my efforts with other

members of the Patients' Council to instigate talking therapies for people diagnosed with schizophrenia or manic depression. We failed because the psychology department considered such people to be impossible to help. It does now seem the Relate lady was of a similar mindset. To me this is arrant nonsense, an arrogance designed to keep the mentally ill in their place as the lowest of the low, beyond redemption, 'the least of my brothers and sisters', according to Christ.

Here are some plaintive extracts from a letter I sent S in late February...

I spoke to your sister on the emotional aspects of our marriage over the past couple of years for, as I hope you will agree, before that we seemed to manage pretty well, particularly in the years before children when we were both working full-time. Things changed dramatically twenty-two months ago, with my 'up' during C's pregnancy. You may have been unaware of it but in the months before this you had been giving me a particularly hard time, I could do nothing right. I felt that my lot was an unduly burdensome one. This phase culminated with your accusation, blurted out of the blue, that I was having an affair with [name deleted] – so obviously untrue as to be ludicrous. Everyone always looks for 'trigger factors' causing my 'flips' and it could be that your loss of love caused my brain to go into overtime [marijuana more like – Jamie].

I know that money is currently one of your biggest bugbears but I have consistently told you that all you have to do is ask me and it shall be given. Twenty-two months ago, when I am sufficiently drugged up in Springfield, you obtained £5,000 (without my knowledge or consent) from my Trustee, Graham.

Again, this time in early December 1991, with me coshed and safely out of sight and mind, you contact Graham and ask for not only a large cheque but a regular standing order. Ignoring the lump sums, this would have given you an annual tax-free income from me of £17,400 comprising £6,000 housekeeping from me, £6,000 being your personal PEP scheme coming from my funds and nothing to do with school fees, plus your intended £5,400 standing order bonus. No small wonder that I had to put an end to your standing order scheme.

Whilst you may choose to deny the fact, I have not been ungenerous to you over the years. Apart from buying theatre tickets and the running costs of the Fiesta, the entire financial cost of our marriage has fallen to me – all household bills, rates / poll tax, holidays home and abroad, meals out, cinemas, drinks / entertainment, house insurance, BUPA and much of the annual food bill. I even covered a significant portion of our wedding reception bill. On the present side, you can hardly have grounds for complaint – you have received many expensive items of jewellery. Galling to me was how you greeted your last anniversary present with a shrug of your shoulders and no thank you. There are no two ways about it, you have been cold and selfish but I forgive you, because the whole is always greater than the individual parts and our life as a family unit has to transcend our failures as parents.

You say that you can tell when I am about to go 'up' – well, then why have you never put such prescience into effect? For me there is no such knowledge – I have no forewarning and I am sorry but there is nothing I can do about it. Afterwards, I do as the doctors tell me, take all my pills and even accede to your request for me to seek psychological help which as it turned out didn't seem to help … perhaps with one or two sessions with the right counsellor our problems could well ease. For my part I have undertaken to see Desmond Kelly and to cease baking soon which I feel are two steps on the road to marital recovery … what are you going to try to mend the bridge? As much as you may think it is, the current mess is not entirely of my doing.

I know that you are enjoying your present privacy and solitude but put yourself in my shoes for a moment – just at the time when I needed your love and support most during my six weeks in Springfield you made me feel unwelcome at home. Did you really care when their evil doings came within a whisker of killing me? No, you wanted to have me subdued and tranquilised more – I recall you were furious that I had the sense to refuse the Largactil and Droperidol cocktails. One phone call from you and my nightmare would have been ended. Even now you are trying to make things difficult for me by wanting me to restrict myself to visiting home at times which suit you. I am afraid that under the law I have the right to be at home 100 per cent of the time; it's only because I happen to be a reasonable human being that I am not enforcing my rights and am just hoping that in the not too distant future you will eventually see the light and give us a chance to resurrect our union.

Despite everything, I still love you and the children's love for their Daddy goes without saying. Let us pray for conciliation, not arbitration at court which ultimately would help none of us.

I held out glimmers of hope over the months from February through to October – here in my diary for 25$^{th}$ May … "S very relaxed all day, laughing & joking – week in Cornwall seems to have done her good." Again, in September … "Felt good about S. She was warm & friendly & interested about [Patrick] family weekend." But behind the scenes a different scenario was playing out. Back in March she had already primed divorce solicitors, sussing out likely child maintenance payments, had taken copies of all my bank statements, tax returns etc. – she was even opening letters addressed to me.

The friendliness that was sometimes shown was just a chimera. We went to a couple of large parties over this period – the first, deep in the Wiltshire countryside, was a lavish event. She got very drunk and I looked after her – kindly, I thought. At the other party in Ealing we seemed to be getting on well again but it was all a front – I was being hoodwinked into a false sense of security.

Just when she was about to issue her writ for divorce for my 'unreasonable behaviour' (these legal terms are so unsuitable are they not?) her father dies in the early hours of 9th September 1992. This delays her writ, but *alea iacta est,* the die is cast. Interestingly, a few days before her father's death a friend had been for an interview with a local private tuition firm which S used for gaining mathematics clients. They asked him, "How do you know Mrs Summers?" "I know her husband," he replied. "Ex-husband you mean," said his interviewer. Charming eh.

By the end of September I had secured a half-time job with Hammersmith & Fulham MIND after narrowly failing to get a similar post at Kensington & Chelsea MIND. Things were looking up – I had slowly reduced my lithium carbonate dosage (my decision – that ghastly psychiatrist Gundy wanted me to take the stuff for at least five years) and was now down to half the original dose. It's always wise to reduce slowly one's prescribed medication. My mind was clearing.

Divorce proceedings started in February 1993 – initially I had used solicitors down in Canterbury because of a Sandwich golf connection, but now moved to my friend Bill Warburton who worked for Simon Wakefield & Co. up in London – Bill and I shared mutual friends, he'd just gone through a divorce himself and I thought would thus be sympathetic. I was asked to supply documents, reams and reams of them detailing every aspect of my finances over the preceding three years, valuations of personal effects, tax returns etcetera, etcetera. Much of this information I had been feeding to the Lloyd's Hardship Committee but I certainly kept the photocopier at my new place of work busy. Because my heirlooms were assessed as having a value of about £29,000 by the London Legal Aid area office, I was turned down in my request for help with divorce costs.

It was around this time that a very disturbing incident occurred. There I was in the little office of our drop-in centre in the basement of 703b Fulham Road near the Munster Road junction – this was my new place of work, and out of necessity I was storing much of my inherited furniture in the adjoining rooms we shared with Broadway Housing – more bits crammed cupboards under the stairs. These I had rescued from the marital home. It was early days for my career at Consumer Forum, H&F MIND's 'user' group, not many people were dropping in, and I was able to base my own office needs there – remember, I was still tussling with Millar's shenanigans (indeed the City of London Police Fraud Department visited) plus Lloyd's plus the divorce paper requirements.

Anyway, one morning the phone rings. It's my wife on the line berating me for not having visited the previous afternoon / evening – probably because of a verbal battering leading me to believe I would not be welcome at my old home. "You are never going to see the children again," she avers and puts the phone down. Wow. This wounds me to the core and for the only time in my life I contemplate how to end it. I envisage attaching some sort of hose to the exhaust of my Bedford Rascal ex-bakery van – I even have the venue sussed out … there's a tiny lane that emerges onto the A3 just north of Getty's Sutton Place leading from Send Grove – Potter's Lane it's called – how apt; for Judas Iscariot ended his days in the Potter's Field. I reckoned that parking up on this quiet lane, sorting out the carbon monoxide hosepipe, would attract no unwanted attention.

So I am left to stew, pondering her words. Was it one hour? Was it two hours later that she rings again to apologise for her outburst and retract her threat? A close call.

At the end of June her 'unreasonable behaviour' petition is filed – I had let it be known that I wasn't going to fight for five years and would go quietly after two years' separation. By now I was starting afresh in a new relationship. But the allegations are way OTT ... one in particular irks to this day. When she is asked to give details of the proposed arrangements for contact she writes, " ...the respondent [that's me] visits the children on a regular basis at the former matrimonial home but *as he is a manic depressive he does not having staying contact.*" I see, and what has that got to do with the price of fish?

By the end of August I am in the throes of changing my divorce solicitors once again – here are extracts from my letter to Bill ...

As I am sure you will agree the whole nature of a divorce case is emotionally disturbing and the parties involved want their questions answered instantly and satisfactorily. Perhaps you at Simon Wakefield & Co. are overloaded with other people's files but I have not felt that my personal case was getting enough attention.

It seemed that I was doing all the groundwork on your behalf, assembling reams of financial documents and chasing up Legal Aid departments all over the country. But what disturbed me most is that whenever I telephoned you leaving messages for you to return my call urgently, this never happened. Partner / secretary communication at your offices appears inadequate and there was that appalling time when important letters (including one relating to me) were dumped in a bin rather than the letter-box by one of the secretaries.

For £150 per hour + VAT I believe a client is entitled to a quality of service that gives value for money. Obviously I will settle the charges incurred up to now so please send me the total bill in due course...

... Thank you nevertheless for your endeavours – no personal hard feelings but I hope you understand my reasoning, having been through the mill yourself.

Yours ever,

Jamie Summers

In hindsight it might have been better to stay with Simon Wakefield & Co. throughout, because as we shall see I felt the final settlement greatly favoured S at my expense. My new divorce solicitor was a Mrs Crabtree at Ashby's on Barnes High Street – she had acted against a friend of Graham Millar's and he was impressed. In retrospect I regretted acting on a recommendation of that man, albeit given over a year before.

S and her solicitor were now making overt threats to turn me over to the Child Support Agency, already notorious for their high maintenance demands on fathers. I believe she instigated this referral in November 1993. At least Ashby's insisted on a bit more financial disclosure from her side which revealed income pretty much in line with my own. Initial enquiries by my solicitors indicated that the CSA would demand I pay some £112 per week towards P and C's maintenance i.e. more than a third of my net income at the time. When her solicitor's offer of £60 a week but with S keeping the house outright came through, it seemed this 'clean break' deal was "most advantageous" in Ashby's eyes and, "you will wish to accept," they said. So I did. Please note, however, that when I got full-time work at MIND I voluntarily upped my payments to £100 per week.

On reflection, I believe my solicitors and I could have secured a better deal – the London property market soared in subsequent years. S had the marital home valued at £165,000 at that time ... nowadays it is worth well over £1.5 million. A friend got divorced some years later and was able to get a deal whereby the mother stayed in situ with the children but when the youngest reached the age of eighteen the property would have to be sold with the parents getting half each – that seems to me to be eminently fair.

The decree nisi was granted in December 1993 but recrim-inations continued. In a fax sent to Ashby's on 9th March 1994 I stated, " ...two days ago I had an angrily abusive call from my wife saying she would 'fight to the end' any application for my having 'staying access' to the children." The decree absolute followed in June 1994.

Goodness gracious, as I've said before these divorce proceedings really pained me and cost me dear. Twenty-five years down the line the whole episode still rankles. On reorganising much of my filing system late in 2011 I came across her draft 'Behaviour Petition' which fortunately Bill Warburton had shielded from me, pruning back its pernicious acrimony to the final agreed version. But in it she virtually accused me of sexual deviancy. I was hard-pressed to recognise the truth of what she alleged on many matters. What plagued her and still does is that I have passed 'mental illness' to our children – but in my reflections noted down at that time I write:

Here we are some twenty years down the line with *no* further manic / hypomanic episodes. I feel the 'manic depressive' tag has been disproved – hands up to 'cannabis psychosis'. There may be some genetic disposition to vulnerability to mental problems although medical opinion is still uncertain over inheritance issues. There again, not to be overlooked is the mania / creativity link viz. Blake, Byron, Michelangelo, Mozart, Stephen Fry etc. I did not 'conceal' anything from S – indeed it probably wasn't until the early nineties that any mention of 'manic depression' was made by psychiatrists.

I was also aggrieved on rereading her comments, made through her solicitors, about the projected expenditure figures I had assembled as regards golf costs, holidays and gifts which she deemed to be "grossly excessive" and wanted all that expenditure to be used for the girls' education. This is what I wrote twenty years after the divorce…

The holidays & gifts figure totalled £1,300, most of which would have been spent on P and C. Golf etc. costs were estimated at £867 p.a. – how petty to seek to deny me my prime leisure activity (& one at which I was pretty competent at the time) – this sum would have only paid for a portion of one term's private education for one child.

If S was so keen on their private education then why did she offer me no support when I was trying to persuade P to accept the place she had gained at Alleyn's? – I said would pay her basic fees if she covered the additional expenses. S remembers this differently, saying the discussion centred around splitting Alleyn's fees between us and felt I was applying undue pressure on P. To me any public school education would have been superior to the state system – indeed for both children I had secured, before their births, places at houses at Eton. As girls this could never have happened and I very much doubt the funds needed would have been available had they been boys. Because S was teaching in the state system her loyalties were to comprehensives, although she had been partially educated at a public school herself. To be fair, as education was her field I delegated didactic decisions to her.

Overall, she did very well out of the divorce. Having brought virtually nothing into the marriage she now has a house worth well over £1 million – the appropriate course in my view would have been to downsize and buy the girls & herself a flat each but apparently she sees Altenburg Gardens as her 'pension'.

Bitter? Moi? Yes, guilty m'lud.

What is sad, however, is that she still sees me as a sick manic depressive. As do plenty of other members of my family. Once you are labelled it sticks. Divorce is always bad news, particularly if there are young children involved. Regaining the full trust and love of our two daughters when I was persona non grata for part of their early development is an ongoing process. How powerful is that stigma of mental illness when allied with divorce.

I suppose slowly over the years her position did soften somewhat. She required chaperones to be present for our first three or four ski trips in the February half-terms. I was keen to instil a love of skiing into them but have only been half successful – so thanks to Stuart Hall and Mark Jones for their help. "What will happen if you go mad again?" was the reason for her insistence. Later, this constraint wasn't enforced and the girls and I were able to enjoy boating holidays in England and Ireland, a trip to Disney World in Florida and other ventures just the three of us. For many years I spent time over Christmas with S and the girls either at the old marital home or at her sister's place in Kingston.

Many of you who have been divorced will recognise the traits of behaviour that I have described – my own diffused anger and frustration and the antics of a woman derided. It has been cathartic to set the record straight.

So my triple whammy of woes was now pretty much over. As that adage goes…

'Pick yourself up, dust yourself down, start all over again'. Strength comes from weakness does it not? Let's move to sunnier climes, let's go travelling.

# 10

# Travels when younger

Having kept all my passports over the years – they get returned with the top right corner clipped off – verifying my movements over the years is a doddle. The first passport, one of three old-style blue and gold ones, was issued on 20th March 1964 and renewed five years later at a cost of £1. Costs a bit more these days does it not!

There's a stamp dated 6th April 1964 by the Sûreté Nationale of France which must have been that exchange visit to the St Lagers down at St Germain les Vergnes when aged 9¾, mentioned in the Early Years chapter.

Next big trip as a solo traveller was in the summer of '68 – not to Woodstock, New York with flowers in my hair, but kindly invited by school friend Philip Remnant to join his family at their villa outside Dénia near Benidorm on the Costa Blanca. There was younger brother Rob and even younger sister Melissa – we spent our days splashing in the swimming pool, learning to water-ski behind Philip's father's boat in the bay at Calpe, attending a bullfight in Alicante and visiting Benidorm. Wouldyabelieveit, there was just one high-rise hotel there – nowadays there must be three hundred plus.

I remember well the return journey – Spanish sword in my luggage, fortunately no stuffed donkey or sombrero – I was so tired that I slept through Moreton-in-Marsh station and awoke at Evesham. So, I caught a return train and on exiting at the correct stop, albeit one hour late, I see Dad's grey Land Rover (AD1760 was its number plate) disappearing back towards the Fosse Way – rats, we have just missed each other. Undaunted, I manage to get a lift all the way to our home with a kind motorist. Dad is aghast that I have done this, offers to pay the man thinking he must be a taxi and on reflection it was an unwise move on my part – but perhaps they were more innocent times and anyway, at just turned fourteen, I was naïve about paedophilic possibilities.

Of course, the marvellous yearly ski-trips continued – one was to Verbier, just me this time, where I was able to stay with sister Carole who was working as a chalet girl. Relations between us were good in those days and it was fun skiing with some of the British ladies ski squad … Sue MacInnes, Divina Galica and others. One year, with Dad now ensconced in his Vale do Lobo villa, we organised a half-term trip for the Eton golf team. Peter Breeden's parents, David and June, had a cliff-top villa nearby so we were able to put everyone up – Richard Hurst, Nick Myles, Peter and I and a couple of others played against local expats and locals at Penina, Vilamoura and Vale do Lobo.

The famous Henry Cotton, British Open victor in 1934, 1937 and 1948, was the professional at Penina. He gave us all a clinic, whacking his hanging car tyre with an assortment of clubs, encouraging us to keep a firm grip with one's right hand. Peter Breeden, cheeky monkey, thought he knew better and questioned Mr Cotton's techniques!

1973 was a good year travel-wise. Between leaving school and going up to Oxford there were big trips to America and Europe. The latter I covered at the end of Chapter 7, the former followed on from a stint of work in New York (more about that later). Philip Remnant and I set out at the end of June on a road tour, criss-crossing some 35 states with our Greyhound bus passes. Down the East Coast through

Williamsburg, Virginia; Charleston, North Carolina; Savannah, Georgia to Orlando, Florida. Disney World was such fun – a pleasure for anyone from eight to eighty and beyond, so clean, tidy and well organised. On through Alabama to New Orleans where we stayed 'on the bayou' with friends of friends. There was such generosity from our hosts to these two young English gentlemen. Over to San Antonio, Texas and then up to Denver, Colorado. We were hosted again in a lovely house in Vale – unbelievably, I was lugging an old-fashioned suitcase and a full set of golf clubs on the buses. The golf sticks at last got an outing in Vale … funny to play golf there and not ski really. Along with Aspen, Vale is the premier USA ski destination.

We continued over to the west coast after a visit to the Grand Canyon and the Hoover Dam. Los Angeles and adjoining Hollywood were a bit grim – Greyhound bus depots were usually in the 'worst' bits of town – but we had a special time up on 17-Mile Drive outside Monterey. A beautiful part of the world – our hosts here, the Hills, were exceptionally generous, lending us one of their cars and arranging for us to play at Cypress Point. Deer on the fairways, seals clapping their flippers under the coastal cliffs – one of the great golf courses of the world with its neighbour Pebble Beach regularly hosting the US Open.

We had dipped our toes into Mexico down at El Paso / Cuidad Juárez and now popped over the border into Canada at Douglas just south of Vancouver. Then it was a few days in the spectacular Yellowstone National Park, across to Detroit, Michigan via Minneapolis and St Paul and eventually back to New York and home to the UK. To save money we had often travelled through the night from city to city but I found it nigh impossible to sleep either on the seats, the floor or even in the luggage rack.

Even before the bus trip, we had been treated royally by friends of our families around New York. Weekend ventures out to Long Island, around Connecticut, down to Union-ville, Pennsylvania. There was even an invitation to attend a splendid and sumptuous 'coming out' ball – Philip being particularly welcome ... we were often introduced as, "This is the Honourable Philip Remnant and his friend Jamie Summers". Philip's dad happened to be a Lord, hence the elevation of his son.

The first summer 'vac' at Oxford I was back on the East Coast, this time with geography and old school pal, Sam M-I. We bought an old VW Beetle, stayed with his sister Josie in Boston before tootling down to Miami, whereupon I decided to leave Sam to his own devices and bussed non-stop through the night right up to Maine. There I struggled out in the pouring rain to the dockside of Medomak, a little lobster fishing port, and out through island channels to Cow Island. My Lymington friend, Timmy Beddow, was there, helping out owners Donald and Patsy Ryan with building and gardening work at their idyllic home. Timmy and I stayed in a white clapboard cottage near the main house and I joined the payroll, helping to tile a barn down by the quay. Patsy and Donald were such kind people, playing host to several of us itinerant English travellers. Dear Donald was a true alcoholic, come 6 p.m. he would take his first drink of the day and almost immediately be sozzled. They paid us handsomely for our toil, enjoyed our company as we did theirs – supper was in the big house, sometimes boiling live lobsters in big saucepans whose lids would rattle up and down until the grey crustaceans died and turned pink. Most kind way to kill them apparently but no one ever asked lobsters. There was no television reception so conversation reigned after supper – fellow guest David Ogilvy played the piano beautifully and sang too.

Toward the end of August 1974 it was time to return to England, which I accomplished in some style. Dru Mon-tagu, one of the finest old Etonian golfers playing in the

Halford Hewitt tournament over many years, was a keen amateur pilot with his own twin-engined Cessna. He flew regularly from the UK to Houston, Texas where he was boss of a small oil exploration company, Pemex.

We had kept in touch since the previous summer when Dru had most kindly lent to Philip and me his Upper East Side New York apartment on East 83rd. This time he arranged to pick me up at Rockland Airport which wasn't far from Cow Island – goodness knows how we coordinated this pick-up in the days well before mobile phones. Fantastic, off we flew on a semi-circular route staying the first night at Goose Bay in the province of Newfoundland, Canada, having cleared customs further south at Sept-Îles. From there it was over the Labrador Sea, enjoying games of backgammon at 20,000 feet, our cruising altitude, and winding our way over the majestic icebergs into Narsarsuaq Airport, Greenland. I shall always remember flying over those icebergs up the fjord – pure white bergs with $7/8^{ths}$ of their mass under the water, which appeared a metallic blue fringed by the dark blue sea. As we refuelled, a Boeing 727 landed up the short airstrip – it left before us, accelerating down the runway and back out over the fjord.

Dru piloted us out in the opposite direction, up the airstrip, climbing rapidly to clear the Greenland ice cap which loomed menacingly close to Narsarsuaq. Exhilarating stuff – then over the high ice plateau and the Denmark Strait to land a few hours later at Keflavik, Iceland's airport. The colourful wooden houses of Reykjavik almost toytown-like over to our left. We stayed the night in the capital at great expense (most fortunately at Dru's kind expense), window-shopped for thick jerseys (£50 apiece as I recall) admired the beauty of the local females and then left Keflavik, heading for Prestwick Airport outside Glasgow. Here we parted company, me down to Heathrow on a British Airways shuttle, Dru probably to score a few birdies at nearby

Troon or the enigmatic Prestwick Golf Club itself. Thank you Dru, what a trip that was.

As I continued my time at Oxford, Dad was all settled in his villa to the right of the 5ᵗʰ hole at Vale do Lobo, often peppered by golf balls sliced off the tee so he rigged up a cordon of netting and no one got hit. The villa, 379 Vale do Lobo, Almancil was fine – much of his old brown furniture, sofas and armchairs had been installed so it wasn't a usual holiday home. Sadly there was no pool, so one had to borrow other people's or head the half-mile to the beautiful sandstone cliff-fringed beach (once dropping a whole roasted chicken in the sand, oh dear!), tennis, romantic flirtations and typical youthful exuberances. One night I overdid the cheap Portuguese brandy but survived – more about that in Chapter 14.

Once a group of us drove out from London – a fine ferry from Portsmouth to Santander, then crossing from Spain into Portugal at Badajoz. This was in my swank new silver BMW 2002, more comfortable than the old white one but perhaps a bit slower – it had one of those 8-track players. I

had persuaded my Trustees that as I was now twenty-one this was the car for me – it soon got sold as finances dwindled but Mary Rose had used it, earning money chauffeuring round town Henry Wynberg, Elizabeth Taylor's lover at the time. She was friends with Liza Todd (Elizabeth Taylor's daughter) when at Heathfield School, hence the connection.

Let's fast forward – something you couldn't do on those 8-track players – to the autumn of 1977. By now I had done two years working in the City (more on that in the 'work' chapter). Timmy Beddow had recently returned from a long trip around South America full of tales of wonders to behold and experience. His photographs then were particularly inspirational and he continues to be an acclaimed landscape photographer. Anyway, wanderlust set in and I devised a plan whereby I would take a year's sabbatical from the reinsurance world in London. The idea was to travel overland as much as feasible to Buenos Aires where I could perhaps work for a while for the Argentinian agent used by my London firm, before returning to the United Kingdom to continue in their employ.

So, the journey starts once again in New York. There are many young Brits strutting their stuff in Greenwich Village at various bars (the 'Bells of Hell' was our favourite), others enjoying the music scene – I made friends with Maggie Lapiner who worked for Island Records as Director of Publicity for the North-Eastern United States and became a bit of a ligger, getting a free Grace Jones T-shirt and enjoying Graham Parker and the Rumour playing live downtown. Music journalist mate Robin Eggar, who had been at Bristol University with some of my friends, got me a ride in a limo out to Daryl Hall and John Oates' gig in the suburbs – silly boy had been playing silly buggers in his hotel room and perversely had stabbed a lighted cigarette into my face while we eyed each other through the door peep-hole. I still have that scar.

Others in New York at the time were Sophie Whately and her girlfriend Nicky L-T. Adam Edwards, another journalist, and I larked about in the apartment where Sophie was staying, belonging to a girl called Aurora, creating surreal sculptures out of the rented fixtures and fittings. Must have been the marijuana talking in my case, and our efforts were not appreciated by the girls. Sophie, Nicky and I formulated plans to travel together, certainly as far as Central America, possibly further.

Before we left I had flown down to spend time with Eton / Oxford friend Kim who was learning American insurance practices with a small firm in Atlanta, Georgia. He was destined to remain in insurance, like his father before him, for most of his career.

Anyway, we had fun for a few days in Atlanta. We busied ourselves on Peachtree, one of the main arterial roads of the city where Kim had an apartment. One day I sat all day with the caddies at the Peachtree Golf Club hoping to be hired and wasn't. $6.98 I spent at Peaches Records & Tapes buying a copy of J. J. Cale's *Troubadour* album because we were privileged to have tickets for a concert he was giving at the Great South East Music Hall & Emporium in a local shopping mall. There were perhaps just 300 people there to hear him play – his band that day included vocalist Chris Lakeland, while he spent most of the concert perched on a stool. Not that I've been to many music gigs but this one was super special – I love his work; 'Cocaine', 'Ride Me High'. It was he who wrote 'After Midnight', made famous by Eric Clapton who also covered the 'Cocaine' track. At the end, I got all the band's autographs on my copy of the *Troubadour* LP, which I still have.

Kim and I hatched a plan to launch a new career as advertising copywriting geniuses. Plan A was to do voice-overs for Atlanta FM radio commercials. Oh the hopes and dreams of youth … we composed what we thought were inventive jingles and ditties. One for Otis Elevators – "Wanna get high? Wanna come down smooth an' slow? Step into an Otis elevator." This we backtracked with J. J. Cale's 'Ride Me High' guitar chords. "Add a third dimension to your record collection," we enthused as an aid to selling Jean-Michel Jarre's *Oxygène* album. "Take away a piece of England and grace your home" – that was Wedgwood china. "Lipton's Iced Tea – even the British approve." Our spoof advert for a perfume, Jean Patou 1000 ... "for the woman who has everything, and yet wants more," which sounded a bit like, "and yet once more," encouraging one to repeat the refrain. We then spent three hours with Bruce Baxter at Stone Mountain Music Studios getting our ideas professionally recorded at a most reasonable cost of $28. Needless to say our zany efforts came to naught – no advertising agency took us on as aspiring account executives. No talent agencies took an interest. 'Twas fun trying though.

Delta Air Lines flew me back to New York a few days later. Sophie, Nicky and I set off 'travellin' light' (another J. J. Cale track). We had bought a car, a Mercury Monarch, for $100 up in Harlem I seem to remember, which broke down in Cincinnati, Ohio. However, another $100 in repairs later we were on our way to Louisville, Kentucky and Knoxville and then down to San Antonio, Texas. Here we were generously hosted by the Westons at their Santa Clara Ranch outside Marion, Texas. Sophie and I both knew Carolyn Weston who was Georgie and Mary Rose's aunt. From there we flew to Cancún on the Yucatán peninsula close to Merida, on a Southwest Airlines flight from Houston at $67 apiece. The car was sold in San Antonio for $75 – not bad going really.

Most Americans are scared witless by Mexico, Donald Trump included, but us Brits have no such qualms. Mind you, Cancún, where we landed, was and is a luxury holiday resort full of swanky apartments, five star hotels and golf courses. We had sat next to a kind lady, Lissa Kelley, on the aeroplane who invited us all to spend night one at her place. From there we headed out to hippy hotspot Isla Mujeres for a few days chilling. We rented bicycles to circle this small island, the highlight being snorkelling over the little coral reef close to the shore. It was a crowded little beach that gave access to this underwater wonder world – iridescent blue ones, angelfish, rainbow-coloured larger ones, lumps of white coral resembling human brains, wavy brown fronds of vertical coral. But it's a magical world, one of life's must do's, gazing down through goggles above a coral reef.

We visited Chichen Itza with its manicured Mayan ruins and were together for Christmas 1977, moored off the Yucatán coast by Isla Contoy, staying on a fancy yacht. Sophie had fallen for its owner and we enjoyed mini-cruises, more snorkelling offshore where we came face to face with barracuda and even sharks. No harm done luckily. We barbecued lobsters on the beaches, caught by new friend Dave, a long-blond-haired Canadian, and his spear gun. But by now, the threesome of Sophie, Nicky and me as a travelling unit was approaching its end. It's never easy travelling as a team and we tended to be interested in different things. I had found Nicky hard to fathom, hardly ever laughing, and reserved.

I'd already spent days lolling about at a beach idyll just south of the Tulum Mayan ruins with Swiss friend Benoit Vulliet and his Argentinian girlfriend, Ana. Tulum is some 100 km south of Cancún and stupidly I had lost my wallet (holding $350 cash), leaving it on a bus station counter at Cancún. On returning it was nowhere to be found – Lissa put me up for one night again and then it was back to Tulum. For a couple of weeks we all enjoyed the beach bum life, walks on the beach and on the starry nights sometimes seeing the Moon, Mars and Venus all casting their light beams in a row on the gentle sea.

The girls and I parted company in little Belize, then still

a British colony swarming with British troops ostensibly engaged in preventing an incursion from hostile neighbours Guatemala but also active in attempting to stop marijuana and cocaine from South America being run up the coast towards the USA. I found Belize an unhappy place – in a letter to my friend Piers back in London I termed it "the anus of our Empire". I remember spending a couple of days and nights on Caye Caulker close to Belize City – this island was heralded as the best of Belize but I found it oppressive, overcrowded and full of American bullshitters there for the dope.

I hitched a lift, now solo, to the Guatemalan border – given a ride at 70mph in the back of an Army Land Rover which dropped me half a mile short of the border – some war zone eh? Close by were the fantastic ruins of Tikal which feature in the early scenes of the film *Star Wars* – the temple tops peeking above the dense jungle canopy. Less pristine than the ruins at Chichen Itza, steep climbs up the pyramids, monkeys and other mystery mammals lurking in the undergrowth. From Flores, I flew to Guatemala City for $20 for the 20-minute flight – I had read in my *South American Handbook* that the bus, although just $8, sometimes took up to twenty hours to make the journey over some of the worst roads in Central America. So a flight it was.

Next sojourn was Panajachel (or 'Gringojachel' as it was known), a small town on Lake Atitlán full of health food freaks – the lake is surrounded by dormant volcanoes and has twelve villages like a clock face around its circular shore. For three days I hitched, rowed and bussed round them – it is a beautiful place, meriting its popularity with the gringos. By now I had met up with a charming Frenchman, thirty-year-old Didier Rousseau, who was teaching me all sorts of useful French idiom and slang. In company, he used to pass me off as Swiss ... my French was improving daily, Spanish as yet very patchy. We gelled did Didier and I, and were destined to meet by chance again months later in Rio de Janeiro and many times over subsequent years in France and England. I tried to track him down recently in his home town of Royau, north of Bordeaux and learnt from neighbours that he was married and living in America, they knew not where.

From Panajachel I bussed to Antigua, the elegant colonial-style (Spanish) old capital of Guatemala, sitting underneath another volcano, up which I climbed to two-thirds of its height. Here I met up with Sophie and Nicky briefly – they had decided to stay with families in Antigua to attend the language school the Escola Popol-Vuh for a month – I decided to learn the lingo en passant as it were, while travelling. Quite soon I was on my way down the Pan-American Highway on local and long-distance buses through El Salvador, bypassing Tegucigalpa the capital of Honduras and Managua the capital of Nicaragua. Progress slowed a bit through Costa Rica – I must have stayed a couple of days in San José. Costa Rica is the richest and least communist of these Central American states; one had to prove substantial funds and an exit-strategy in order to enter. But soon I was crossing the Panama Canal and holed up in a poor hotel in Panama City.

Rather than trek slowly for days by track and canoe through the Darien Gap, the swampy mosquito-ridden isthmus that defeated early Scottish colonial endeavours, I opted for a short flight on 30th January, from Panama City to Bogotá, the capital city of Colombia. Here in Chapinero, a district in the north of the city, I had an address of a friend of friends, Chris Sanford, and he was expecting me. It was great to have a place to stay, close to a splendid shopping mall (I like shopping malls) probably financed with cocaine money, Colombia's principal export. I made forays around the fun capital, the Museo del Oro, the gold museum with its Inca treasures, enjoying the excellent coffee … un perico was an espresso. Wonderful too to be back in a country with good dairy products so café con leche became my staple.

I began to like the refreshingly upbeat Colombian people, their music and their culture. Chris busied himself teaching English and proselytising, for he was an ardent evangelical Christian – I found some dope to smoke, not that hard a proposition in Colombia, and wrote loads of letters while watching hummingbirds out of his kitchen window. Letters to and from home were a lifeline – my best correspondent was Georgie Chichester, and Piers Fox-Andrews was great as well – to him I had entrusted my affairs back in Blighty poor man, so he was often negotiating with my bank manager to mail out money to various places in South America plus dealing with errant tenants back at my house in Battersea. Thank you, Piers. Chris Sanford became a regular correspondent too.

On I went south – first stop San Agustín in Huila province. Just a delightful place of which much more later, across to Popoyan, sadly devastated a few years later by an earthquake, and down to the Ecuador border after less than two weeks in Colombia, crossing the Equator just north of Quito. I didn't tarry in Ecuador – there were many tales of Hepatitis B and worse, best avoided I thought, so it was a twenty-eight-hour bus ride to Lima, Peru. Once recovered from the bus journey, I flew up to Cuzco and its rarified air to avoid a two-day bus trip – here it took a while to acclimatise to the lack of oxygen. There are impressive Inca ruins in and around Cuzco but obviously the pick of the crop is Machu Picchu, only 'discovered' by archaeologist Hiram Bingham in 1911, the superbly situated Inca citadel, 8,000 feet up in the Andes above the Urubamba river. I stayed in the valley at Aguas Calientes before hitching up to the site and hiking around the ruins. It was too expensive to stay close to Machu Picchu so it was back to Cuzco after a good look round. From Cuzco it was down the Andean cordillera to Puno on the shores of Lake Titicaca, 12,500 feet above sea level. It's arid up here, a bit desolate and I gave the reed islands a miss. Next it was on to dry and dusty Bolivia, entering at Copacabana. Here I remember witnessing the slaughter of a calf in my hotel's inner courtyard. Somewhat gruesome with throat slitting, blood and rigor mortis etc., but if you are a carnivore to be endured and expected. The following day I was in La Paz, walking very slowly because of the altitude, on a level with Lake Titicaca. Chewing the local coca leaves gave respite from the assault on the lungs as did the gram of cocaine I scored for $6. I was no cocaine addict ever in my life but up here it definitely helped one to breathe.

My day-trip to ski on the Chacaltaya glacier on Mount Illimani I have already mentioned (this was on the very day that Mary Rose married Greville Howard in Beaulieu Church. I had sent a telegram saying, "Wishing you an amazing peachy day. Regrettably absent on Bolivian leaves. Jamie." Apparently there were no speeches nor telegrams read out so that was a shame!) – another site of interest visited in Bolivia was the city of Potosi, even higher than La Paz, where silver mining over the centuries has practically demolished the rich mountain, el Cerro Rico, initially exploited by the Spanish conquistadors in the 16th century but still being mined today. Somewhere south of Potosi, when I am travelling with other gringos in their minibus, we encounter a guy coming in the opposite direction pulling a golf trolley holding his backpack, tent and sleep roll. This turns out to be George Meegan, from Rainham in Kent ("Best fish'n chips in the world!"), who is walking from Tierra de Fuego to Alaska, i.e. the entire length of the Americas. He had left Ushuaia in January 1977 and hoped to reach the Panama Canal by January 1979 averaging about 20 km per day. He eventually hit Prudhoe Bay, Alaska in 1983 having taken 41 million steps on his 19,019 mile journey. Hats off to you, George. He had been hassled by the police in Argentina who had stolen $10 from him – worse was to come in the Darien Gap apparently where he was shot at and survived a knife attack.

Then it was into Argentina at Villazón, past Salta to Tucumán deep in the pampas country. Non-stop to Buenos Aires I recall on the much improved roads.

Here I holed up in the Hotel Victoria at 55p a night, enjoying occasional red wine and steak suppers. I remember that one could buy a kilo of fillet steak for 40p in those days. Buenos Aires was a bit dull so I spent much time watching movies. My insurance job never materialised, my Spanish not being good enough, but contacts made through Greig Fester in London, the Blanchard family, were very kind to me, inviting me out to parties in the posh suburbs of San Isidro where vast 'parrillas' of barbecued bits of beef would be the central attraction. I bussed and hitched around the vast expanses of southern Argentina – getting as far down as Trelew, Gaiman and Puerto Madryn with their Welsh connections and even down to Comodoro Rivadavia. Then inland to Esquel and Bariloche, beautiful alpine-type countryside where one can ski in summer. Amazingly I got a lift back all the way from Bariloche to Buenos Aires in a large lorry. My lift spoke not a word of English so communication was limited.

After a few weeks in Argentina I crossed into Brazil at the enormous Igauzu waterfall where Paraguay meets Argentina and Brazil. More bussing through the night brought me to Rio de Janeiro. Here too I had an address to head to – on Avenida Delfim Moreira in Leblon, one bay beyond Copacabana beach lived Mike Cobb, who kindly put me up for a few days. We enjoyed a weekend at a cottage in the hills with Pippa Jenkins and her friend Julia. Extraordinarily, I ran into my French friend Didier at an English pub in Rio – great to see him again. We taxied up to the summit of Corcovado, one of the volcanic plugs that gives the city its special character. There stands that huge concrete statue of Christ with his arms stretched out. The barrios, the slums of Rio, tumble down the ravines spilling close to the expensive streets of downtown – a city of huge contrasts, rich and poor cheek by jowl, exuding an unhappy, slightly menacing air.

I was never entirely comfortable in Brazil – there was no marijuana to be had, it was too dangerous to obtain, let alone cocaine. But that wasn't the reason for my reticence. From my times in Portugal I had a smattering of the words and phrases of the Portuguese language, but wherever I used them I was met with blank looks. Okay, Brazilian Portuguese is earthier than the original and was hard to emulate – also whenever I spoke in Spanish people chose not to understand. This made life quite difficult. So methinks, time to head back to Colombia aiming to get back to the UK mid-summer.

Through Brasilia, the strange capital of the country … vast eight-lane highways dissecting blocks of apartments and government buildings. To Cuiaba, and then hitching up one of the worst roads in the world towards Manaus. My ride came courtesy of Pedro Caldas in his red camionetta (SUV-type vehicle) packed with meat products that he was taking north from his home in Cuiaba, Mato Grosso province. Earth and rain equals mud so one encountered huge queues of traffic stuck behind trucks stuck in ruts in the mud. We stood still for eleven hours at one stage. At Porto Velho I caught a bus for the final leg to Manaus – here one is deep in Amazonas, where some of the cowboy types of the Brazilian wild north-west were perpetrating evil deeds against the indigenous tribes of Indians in this huge region. We heard stories of multiple murders, poisoning of flour with cyanide and a complete disregard for human life so that forests could be denuded of teak and mahogany, slashed and burned for a brief spell of cattle ranching. This area provides $\frac{2}{3}$rds of the world's oxygen and its protection is essential – the rainforest too is a source of flora and fauna vital for developing new drugs. Was not quinine, the anti-malarial wonder drug, isolated from the bark of the cinchona tree, found here in the Amazonian forests? There will be others awaiting our discovery. Short-term destruction by these Brazilian bandits of both the forest and its inhabitants helps no one long-term.

At that Porto Velho bus station I had an unpleasant experience with the custodian of the men's toilet. Not having the correct 20 centavo coin to enter his establishment I was denied entry in no uncertain terms, eventually finding relief in a quiet side street. On the 4 p.m. bus to Manaus I was subjected to taunts from fellow passengers throughout the night … "eh gringo!" they would laugh. Manaus is a weird place, thousands of miles up the Amazon from the coast, famous for its faded Opera House. Hot and sweaty, me as well as the city, I stocked up on essentials for the two-week boat trip up the river to Leticia in Colombia. Sellotaped into my diary is the receipt from a shop on Avenida Joaquim Nabuco ... 54 cruzeiros, 60 centavos (when a US dollar fetched 17.5 cruzeiros) for plasters (5.30), loo paper (3.40), mosquito repellent (8), candles (11.50), yoghurt (5.80), large matches (2.60) and two packs of batteries at 9 cruzeiros apiece – vital to keep my little cassette player pumping out my music.

My money is running low – I need 800 cruzeiros to pay for my passage upriver and manage to sell a pair of jeans and a sleeping bag for 500 which helps. We eventually leave Manaus at 6.15 p.m. on 19th May 1978 – our cargo is gas canisters and we are latched to a smaller craft belonging to Rolf Scherrer and Barbro from Sweden who are hitching a ride upriver. Hammocks slung on deck are the sleeping arrangements, the diesel engine chugs away twenty-four hours, food is rice, frijoles (beans) and 'bones' I write, occasionally nourished with a caught river fish. This is no Danube cruise boat but it's okay – we make periodic stops to deliver gas at Cajonas, Tefe and other villages. We spot snakes slithering on the water, the odd dolphin and exotic birds.

Rolf and Barbro are fine companions – he has played guitar for John Mayall and Boz Scaggs and has an excellent Uber tape player, so we listen to the Allman Brothers, Lynyrd Skynyrd and the Marshall Tucker Band. On arrival at laid-back Leticia – lovely to be in Colombia once more – we stay for a few days. My billing is at the Hotel Manigua, pesos 315 for three nights ... that's $9. My Swedish friends adopt two leoncita monkeys, mother the size of a small hand, the baby not much bigger than a fingernail, who spends most of its time in Barbro's hair. Rather than spending days on a bus I spend 1,200 pesos ($34) on the Aeropesca flight to Bogotá and am back in Chris Sanford's flat at 6.30 p.m. on the evening of 31st May. Rolf and Barbro are heading further up the Amazon to Iquitos and Pucallpa in Peru.

We spend a very pleasant few days in Bogotá, up near the Unicentro shopping mall with excursions to Chris' friends in the outlying hills. More of his friends from England arrive – Nick Murray-Wells, Miranda Cumming-Bruce and Robin Parrish, another Eton / Christ Church alumnus. On the 8ᵗʰ June my last tranche of money from England arrives and the following day I am on a bus to Neiva (six hours) and the following morning on the 7.30 a.m. bus back to San Agustín (six hours). There follows a week or so exploring this wonderful area by foot and on horseback. I'll let the tourist office bumph tell you about the place:

San Agustín is perhaps one of the most beautiful sites of all Colombia, but in addition it is an archaeological zone filled with all the enigma and mystery of a distant past. A sacred place, San Agustín was the destination of neighbouring tribes who pilgrimaged to the area to perform religious ceremonies and render homage to the dead.

The area is surrounded by formidable mountains, protected by the canyons through which flow tributaries of the Magdalena, Naranjo and Sombrerillos Rivers.

The town is famed for its indigenous sculptures, dating back to AD 6 to just a few years before the arrival of the Spanish conquistadors. In the midst of its incomparable landscape, the small town of San Agustín and its surrounding area house statues, some of gigantic size, ceremonial fountains, tombs covered over with the plant from which straw is obtained, and artificial mounds which cover coffins and statues.

Just a few years ago I was attending a 'How to Get Yourself Published' course outside Bournemouth. Ali Hull, course leader, asked us participants to write a short piece entitled 'A Significant Moment'. Here is what I wrote …

It is June 1978 – having 'pushed paper' for close on two years in a City reinsurance broking firm I have chosen to take some time off for travel. Wanderlust rather than work.

Two hundred kilometres south of Bogotá, Colombia and 50 kms east of Popoyan lies the charming village of San Agustín in the Andean foothills – one could be in the Cotswolds ... rolling hills, friendly people, excellent coffee and dairy products. This village became my favourite archaeological site in the whole of South America – eat your heart out Machu Picchu! In San Agustín itself is the exquisite Lavapatas ... volcanic river rocks scoured out to make animal patterns for the water to flow over and around – monkeys' tails, lizards, snakes – all beautifully done some 2,000 years ago.

A couple of English girls, Gail Bishop and Tessa Cormack, are also 'gap yearing' before gap years have been invented, and with a couple of other travellers we take up an offer of rooms at a local farm with horses from where we explore the outlying ancient stones and sites.

One glorious morning we have ridden for an hour or so to reach 'Alto de los Idolos' where there is a menhir and other standing stones – as we approach the site, me on a young chestnut bay of about 15 hands, there are a few houses. Out of one of them comes a middle-aged lady in a flowing skirt who walks straight up to me, takes my right hand off the reins and thrusts into it an object –

It's an oval amulet, made of grey stone, carved on one side with an eagle and snake motif and the reverse carved with a fly agaric mushroom set against the mountains and the sun. An unexpected gift that I have kept safe over the years.

From San Agustín I journey back towards Bogotá spending a night at San Andrés de Pisimbalá and a day exploring the Tierradentro underground tombs. Dave Sykes, a crazy Yorkshireman and his friends are my companions here – we procure avena con leche (oats and milk) and cook up a nourishing porridge for our supper. The following morning Dave and I set up an impromptu gringo stall in the village selling items we no longer need – this generates much local interest but little revenue. In fact I recall one or two trinkets got nicked. Touring the tombs, unique in South America with their elaborate paintings and carvings, is fascinating but not quite so enchanting as San Agustín. Then it's north of this beautiful country with Tessa and Gail who I had arranged to meet again in Bogotá. We go by bus through Bucaramanga and Ciénaga to the tranquil town of Santa Marta on the north coast. We stay at the more than adequate Hotel Titimar, along with 30 American Peace Corps missionaries, close to the beach.

Excursions are made to the Tayrona National Park and its empty Caribbean beaches and to bustling Benidorm-style Rodadero where I do a spot of water-skiing costing just 200 pesos for half an hour. From excitable local Pablo, I score a gram of cocaine for $14 – it was of such quality that I was inspired to give away at least half! For a similar price I buy a wonderful sisal shoulder bag made by Arhuaco Indians up in the hills above Santa Marta which served me well for many years thereafter. I am now planning my return home and entrust Pablo with a stash of 6,800 Colombian pesos to convert into low denomination US dollar bills – he is Mr Fixit, the local wheeler-dealer. Oh dear, he returns with two $100 notes, clearly counterfeit – what a sucker I can be.

Many months later, Mark and Rich, two of the American missionaries, write to me in England to say Pablo was shot dead on Sunday 9th July at the Manuel Restaurant between our hotel and the beach. Colombian drug cartels were notorious then and now. The civil war between the FARC guerrillas and the government was yet to start but would continue for decades. Such a shame that a beautiful country blessed with good people should degenerate thus – perhaps with my purchase of coke ('blancita' in the local lingo), I was partly responsible, not forgetting the Colombian weed, also of the highest quality. Progress is slowly being made by subsidising the campesinos (local farmers) to grow cocoa beans not coca bushes, to plant coffee and bananas instead of cannabis. But boy do I wish this country well – all this is fuelled by the decadent habits of Westerners, Americans and Europeans. Cocaine has its uses as a decongestant and anaesthetic (indeed it helped keep my nasal passages clear from clotting after breaking my nose in a cricket match). Now marijuana is on sale in the UK with its THC content virtually eliminated, leaving just the apparently beneficial CBD components. Tea bags and oil are very expensive but this marijuana is touted as a painkiller, a sleeping draught and overall panacea. This is overstated in my opinion, or should I re-evaluate my thinking in light of its alleged efficacy as an anti-epileptic medicine? But the misuse of both drugs is epidemic and widespread. It has to be said that hemp hand cream is an effective hand cream salve, however.

Early on 29th June I take the bus to the fine Spanish colonial city Cartagena along the coast west from Santa Marta, via Barranquilla. Beautiful buildings and marimba music. I secure a flight a couple of days later from Cartagena via San Andrés island to Tegucigalpa and on to Guatemala City with Honduran carrier SAHSA. San Andrés was meant to be a Colombian Caribbean idyll but wasn't. From Guatemala I flew to Miami, back in the 'First' World – the overweight people and the extravagant waste pained me. I'd been six months amongst poor folk contented with their lot – Georgie had written to me from the Lötschental valley in Switzerland extolling the virtues of the people there. In reply I wrote, "Your mountain people sound like the mountain people of Colombia – full of humour, very little need for money and an undying respect for the people and nature around them. Revelling in their simple, unmuddled, day to day existence, just delighted to still be alive.

"And when you become part of their system, you are astounded at their open generosity – so different from the people one is used to meeting. Mountains breed honest, hard-working people, unpretentious people don't you think?" Poor Georgie got a diatribe of Jamie philosophy in that long letter.

Anyway I then bussed up the East Coast back to New York – to my friends Jerry and Georgia Rose on the Upper East Side, 155 East 70th, who had been so kind to Philip and me back in 1973. Name-dropping briefly … Georgia was born a Rockefeller, thus with a silver spoon in her mouth. Kind Jerry Harden Rose was jovial and on the board of the American film classifiers determining whether movies are U, A, X or whatever. What I'm saying here is that many richer scions of industry play their philanthropic part in this life. From Andrew Carnegie to Bill Gates, Americans have performed well. Oh that modern entrepreneurs would do likewise – Vladimir Putin, probably the richest man in the world … what has he done to help those who are weakest and most rejected? Not a jot I fancy.

This trip around North, Central and South America was reaching its end – not quite $10 a day but not much more, for travel, accommodation and food. I was back in London on July 6th anticipating a party at my house on my birthday, the 13th, my mind full of plans. It's funny isn't it but friends had hardly noticed my absence. The summer continued with trips to Devon, Cornwall and Sardinia – Johnny Barclay's wedding on 16th September to Mary-Lou and a dance down in the New Forest accompanying Sue Gernaey to the Drummond daughters' bash. A big highlight was on Saturday 19th August when Steve Winwood headlined a little festival in a dry valley a few miles north-east of Cirencester. We threw frisbees across the valley on a glorious afternoon – Steve is now a Cotswold resident living close to Northleach.

That winter I drove out to Switzerland, Kitty Barrell lending me her Mini, skiing first at Klosters and then joining Kitty and others to stay in Georgie's cherished Lötschental valley. Spotting a route directly through the middle of the country I was thwarted by ice and snow and had to detour in a big circle on bigger roads at lower altitudes. Advance planning is easier these days with satellite navigating and the internet helping us out.

But my mind was elsewhere really – planning my next big overland adventure, this time the better-trod 'hippy trail' eastwards. No job as a goal this time, but a very well-organised trek in Nepal instead. My fellow trekkers would fly out to Kathmandu for the April walk in the Jugal Himal foothills and I decided to get there by road and rail. So in early January I am at Calais hitch-hiking my way towards Geneva where I am due to stay with my Yucatan friend, Benoit Vulliet. Lift number one is a bloke in a small Renault who soon pulls off the main road, gets out of the car and proceeds to 'pull himself off' trying to engage my interest. No thanks mate, but fortunately no harm done. Lift number two is a lorry driver who takes me further but starts putting his hand on my knee – quickly removed. Not a great start is it to a 4,000-mile journey?

Trains now take me to Benoit's farmstead outside Geneva where I stay one night. Then it was on to freezing Venice for a two-day quick look-see before train once more through Slovenia, Serbia and the rest of Yugoslavia. Five days followed in Florence at sister Kitten's flat, central, but up many narrow stairs and a bit of a trial for her with daughter Sarah's pushchair. Husband Mickey had the flu which cannot have helped – I spent my time sightseeing and noticing the countless spent syringes in alleyways courtesy of the city's heroin addicts. Greece and on to Istanbul. Culture shock ensues – I stay up near the Blue Mosque and the Hagia Sofia close to the 'souk', the covered market selling all sorts of stuff at inflated prices to Westerners. The film *Midnight Express* had recently come out – a powerful piece showing the dangers of smoking dope in Turkey and the ghastly, ghastly conditions of Turkish jails. Billy Hayes, the subject of the movie, was dealt with very harshly by the legal system ... initially sentenced to four years and two months. With just weeks to go before his release the sentence was increased to life imprisonment. In 1975 he finally managed to escape.

Anyway, *Midnight Express* put me off attempting to score while in Turkey. After several days traipsing around Istanbul up and down to Taksim Square over the huge Bosphorus bridge I felt the urge to move eastwards to Ankara. Many years later I learnt that my mother had done stints for MI6 here – a chance encounter in a car park in lower Ankara proved fortuitous. Several second-hand German Mercedes buses were parked up, their new owners mooching around, charming Afghans trying to get paperwork in order, so that they could continue the export of these vehicles to their native land. Turkish bureaucracy was thwarting their progress but they welcomed me and a fellow German traveller to sleep on the back seats of the buses. While we waited, the lads made frequent forays to the red light district – eye-opening stuff, rather less sophisticated than the Amsterdam equivalent. Depressing actually, but as they say, the world's oldest profession. I am pleased to report that I have never paid for sex.

Occasionally we made progress with the buses in an easterly direction but a frequent refrain was, "Benzin yok yok" – just about the only Turkish I remember, which meant there was no diesel fuel available to fill up the bus tanks, stalling our progress once again. But in due course we passed through Erzurum into the bleak east of Turkey and reached Doğubayazit close to the Bazargan border with Iran. For some reason we chose to abandon the bus sleeping arrangements that night, possibly due to sub-zero temperatures. We checked into the worst hotel in the world, dirty, smelly, grotty – all of us trying to sleep on one tiny shelf-like aperture. Room service and reception were equally poor!

The next day we parted company at the Iranian border – home to the worst loo in the world on the Turkish side, an excavated pit on a hill shielded by corrugated iron sheets and certainly no sheets of loo paper and no soap, just use your left hand. Your right hand is to use for eating – if you are convicted of theft it is the right hand that gets chopped off under sharia law, adding to your humiliation by leaving just the 'unclean' one to eat with. Praise the Lord that we in the West live under a civilised legal regime, not 8th-century Arabic rules. This was an interesting time in the Iran story – the Shah has fled the country in the face of the 'theological revolution' against his dreaded SAVAK secret police and his Western leanings. Autocrat-in-waiting was Ayatollah Khomeini, at this time enjoying his exile in Paris but destined to return in triumph on 1st February 1979. Reza Pahlavi had left on 17th January. Me, I arrived in Iran during this brief interregnum – the streets of Tehran were full of anti-USA and anti-UK posters, it wasn't a great time to be British in this troubled country. One night in the capital was enough and next day I took a decent train up to Mashhad in the far north-east, making friends with a zany Kurd.

Memories make one smile sometimes. I remember buying a small bucket of delicious yoghurt in Mashhad and sweetening it with local honey. Yum after the standard 'chelo' dish of rice topped with meat or veg. So after just two days in Iran I was at the Taybad border and reaching sanctuary in Herat, Afghanistan. Here I holed up in the Faez Hotel for a while, starting to learn a bit of the Dari language from the kind owner. Here was peace, away from the traumas of Turkey and the dangers of Iran. Marijuana grew wild on the side of roads. Herat was a sleepy city, nestling under hills where I walked with French friend, Optijesh. The Faez was up near the World Heritage ruins of an ancient capital – at the other end of town was an elegant mosque, renowned for its architecture.

Tempting as it was to traverse the country on minor roads through the central spine of Afghanistan – a route walked I believe by our ex-prisons minister Rory Stewart – I opted for the faster southern circular route to Kabul on a bus via Kandahar. This was dry, dusty almost desert terrain.

In Kabul I rested up for ten days or so – playing hours of frisbee in a local park with Juma who was on the staff of the simple hotel where I stayed on Chicken Street. I collected my mail from the British Embassy – thanks go to my correspondents, Georgie Chichester and Mary Clare Wilson in the main. I wandered around the city window-shopping at beautiful embroidered shirts and cloths, carpets in the markets and enjoying the genial atmosphere of Kabul with its vistas of snow-capped peaks and orchards beneath. It is such a shame that this country was destined to be invaded by the Russians, used by bin Laden to recruit his al-Qaeda rogues and then swamped by the dreadful Taliban from neighbouring Wazaristan.

I was fortunate to be there before freedom atrophied and was then abandoned. Strong dope was freely available around the hippy enclave of Chicken Street and, truth be told, much of my time was spent in a daze, drinking pots of black tea, munching on the local flat-bread and listening to Genesis tapes ('Wind & Wuthering' a favourite then) on my little cassette player. Then onwards east again past Jalalabad to the epic Khyber Pass frontier with Pakistan – scene of fierce battles between the British in India failing to conquer Afghani tribesmen back in Victorian times.

My own personal mental battle came there too. Idiot that I am, I had secreted a lump of excellent Afghan hash in my left sock. The Pakistani customs man asked me if I was carrying any drugs from Afghanistan. "No," I lied. "We're going to search you," he said and left me alone in this bleak room. Okay Jamie, option one is to reach into your sock and try and dispose of the dope somehow. Option two is to do nothing, adopt an air of insouciance, a casual lack of concern, whilst contemplating many years in a Pakistan jail. Option two prevailed and fortunately was the more successful. The man returned after an anxious minute and said, "Okay, you can go now." There must have been a peep-hole that I hadn't noticed or a two-way mirror.

Hypocrisy really, because within yards of the frontier, scores of locals were trying to sell me coils of oily black hash. From travellers' tales and advice I had decided not to spend much time in Pakistan, so from Peshawar I sped to Lahore and crossed into India close to Amritsar. Train up to Jammu where I check into a cheap hotel and roll up a joint to celebrate a successful passage to India. Oops, there follows one of the few times in my life when an intense feeling of paranoia takes over – I explore a bit of Jammu, take a few bites of a street-bought onion bhaji … the combination of the insufferably hotly spiced bhaji and the powerful Afghan hashish sends me into paroxysms of paranoia. Everyone's looking at me, everyone's following me it seems. Gordon Bennett this is not good and I struggle to find the way back to my hotel. Usually my spatial awareness is pretty good but it deserted me here.

The next morning I am fully recovered and catch a bus up to Srinagar, the capital of Kashmir state and a source of tension since 1948 between India and Pakistan. Exacerbated these days as both are now nuclear powers. Trouble is there are more Muslims than Hindus up here but on partition the territory was awarded to the Hindu-dominated India – resented by their Pakistani neighbours. The road up from Jammu was twisty and treacherous in parts but scattered with amusing signage – here are some examples that I noted down…

This is not a race or a rally / Drive slow / And enjoy
   Kashmir Valley
Valley's charms are a pleasure / Only driving when
   at leisure
Drive with your nerves calm / And see the valley's charm
Less fast, move sure / A safe journey ensure
Make safety a habit. Safety saves
No hurry, no worry
Do not show your strength on accelerator
Sleeping with steering in hand prohibited
We would be better off without you than without trees
Divorce speed if married
You are on a hill road
Better be late than the late

On arrival in Srinagar one is bombarded by houseboat owners seeking custom – these are the oddly ornate boats sitting cheek by jowl on Dal Lake. Overrated as idylls in my view, so after one night afloat I was on my way to little Gulmarg close by, site of India's only ski 'resort', well ski station anyway. This was the day that Margaret Thatcher became the UK's first woman Prime Minister. Up at Gulmarg I rented some adequate skis, sticks and boots and after a bit of practice on the one slope with a lift, at 4 the following morning I climbed up with a friend way above the village. The temperature was minus 40°C as we left, slowly rising as the dawn and the day broke. Fun and good exercise at least – there seemed to be scope to enlarge the skiing area should India decide to do so. The caste system was in evidence here – overweight Brahmins and their children being pulled on sledges by 'lesser' mortals.

From Srinagar it was down to Jammu then overnight train down to Delhi where I checked into the Ringo Guest House just off Connaught Circus as recommended by my long-time friend and like-minded traveller, Rupert Johnson. From minus 40°C it was now plus 40°C so I paid a little extra for a single room with a fan, after a night in the airless dormitory room. Finding my feet in Delhi took a little while – the contrasts in this country are so enormous. Basically it was hard work being a gringo – there was little respect for Christians and an oft-repeated mantra of, "From which country are you coming?" I liked the no-nonsense attitude of the Sikhs who unlike others would cross streets diagonally to save a few seconds – and if I ever needed directions I would seek out a Sikh haha! Other Indians would deliberately send you off in completely the wrong direction – I sensed not because they wanted to please you by being 'helpful' but with a mischievous air of assumed superiority and a deliberate desire to confuse.

So many people, so much traffic, tuk-tuks, bicycles, cycle- and hand-pulled rickshaws, Ambassador cars, mangy dogs, monkeys – mayhem. Cows wandering around, beggars in poor shape and health, people scratching a precarious living everywhere. I loved sweet lassis: yoghurt, water and sugar twizzle-sticked for you at the roadside … good for counteracting the curries. Railway station tea, surprisingly refreshing, hot, milky and sugary – all boiled together with tea leaves in large pans on the platforms.

From Delhi I trained down towards Bombay, stopping for one day at the Mount Abu carvings (a thousand feet above the plains, a blessed relief) and then took a ferryboat down to Panaji in Goa. Colva beach offered a bit of Portuguese colonial-influenced change from the India of the north. A quick look at Varanasi on the Ganges after a brief visit to Udaipur and Jaipur. I was learning that reasonable places to stay were the Dak Bungalows, government-run guest-houses usually in pleasant garden environments.

It was now time to join the trekkers up in Nepal. From Gorakhpur, I headed up to Kathmandu and its Guest House, meeting the rest of the troupe in their fancier 5* Annapurna Hotel or was it the Hyatt Regency. Anyway, we were now at the fulcrum of my journey – it was for this trek that I had covered 4,000 miles overland from Europe. My fellow trekkers were led by Edward Montagu, joined by two of his nieces Georgie and Caroline, their friends David, Jenny and Nick, and Gerald and Janet from South Africa. Gerald took thousands of photographs. I shared a tent with Nick Vesey (who later became a vicar) – he was great fun and had scored a baseball-sized lump of Nepalese Temple Ball in town before we set off.

This was trekking in style. Our bags and supplies were carried by some fifteen Sherpas and porters over the ensuing two weeks. They were able to carry enormous weights, their foreheads taking the strain as they clambered nimbly up the narrow paths. Single-file we followed – beautiful views of Himalayan peaks, terraced agriculture mostly rice paddies, a few native rhododendrons. We were in the Jugal Himal region before crossing the 14,000-foot ridge and returning via the Indravati valley. Up at that altitude it was cold and miserable – poor Georgie succumbed to 'soroche', the mountain sickness that puffed up her face, and she had to be taken to a lower altitude fast.

The whole thing ran smoothly – Jagatman, our Sherpa leader, was an experienced guide. Whenever we approached our camping destination in the evening, tents would have been erected and tea would be brewing while others prepared our evening meal. Luxury.

On return to Kathmandu most of our group travelled back to the UK but I took Georgie under my wing for a bit more basic travel – down we went to Patna back in India, over to Delhi squatting on the roof of the overcrowded train and then up again to Srinagar and Gulmarg where we met up with David and Jenny once more. Romance had blossomed between these two on the trek. We all stayed at the Tourists' Hotel & Guest House, 'fitted with modern sanitation' apparently. But this was the only time on my long-distance travels when temporary illness struck – I recall eating a bag of apricots which I think caused (and apologies offered if this offends you) my poo to come out in hard round nuggets for a day or two. Georgie departed, with some difficulty from unpleasant airport staff at Delhi Airport, back to the UK. I then waited for the arrival of Mary Clare Wilson and her mother who treated me to an excellent supper at the posh Akbar Hotel – several notches above the old Ringo Guest House.

Mary Clare, as I have said, had become a regular letter writer to me on these travels – much appreciated, the flavours of home … she was renting a room in my house in Battersea, and kept me informed of all comings and goings. With Mum in tow we were driven in one of those Ambassador cars to the Taj Mahal at Agra – a great day out. By now I was a bit blasé about travel in this place but I think Mrs and Miss Wilson were astonished at the number of Zebus and Zebu-cross cows we had to avoid along with the potholes, pedestrians, buses and assorted rickshaw-wallahs. Such is life in India. To be endured rather than enjoyed. There was always a contrast between rich and poor, Brahmins versus Harijans (untouchables), backstreet squalor versus the Taj hotel chain, the air-conditioned tourist trains versus the usual crammed carriages. India prides itself on being the world's largest democracy and it sort of works – but underemployment abounded and life was cheap when I was there.

So now I start my long journey home, taking pretty much the outbound route in reverse. I won't bore you with too many details this time, just some highlights. Two weeks again in Afghanistan – more frisbee in the park with Juma. I recently was given a copy of Jamie George's book, *Poets & Saints*, in which the American describes his family and friends' bus tour around Europe. On reaching Assisi, he and his children had befriended a friendly Franciscan friar called Andrew. Son Jordan converses with his father thus:

"He was one of the highlights of this trip, Dad, Andrew has such a love for God. I want that kind of passion. Oh, and you're not going to believe this. The man plays frisbee!"

"What?"

"He plays frisbee for the Turkish national team."

"Andrew, the Franciscan friar who studied in Indiana and lives in Italy plays frisbee for the Turkish national team?"

"Yeah, totally," Jordan responded, his eyes wide with excitement. "And he taught Pope Francis how to play! Well, not the entire sport, but he was carrying his frisbee when he met the Pope, and the Pope asked him what it was for."

"What did Friar Andrew say?"

"You toss it back and forth to share joy," Jordan said with a smile.

"Best definition of frisbee I've ever heard."

I concur.

I travelled up to Mazār-e Sharīf through the Salang Tunnel close to the border with Turkmenistan. Just one night there, witnessing a communist-inspired demonstration, red banners and placards in the evening – remember, this was just a few months before the Russians invaded on the pretext of supporting their recently-elected puppet leader and his government. A fellow guest at the hotel was an intelligent intelligence Englishman, unimpressed by the marijuana I was toking.

I had hoped to break my journey back to Kabul by getting off the bus at Charikar to visit the extraordinary massive images of Buddha carved into cliff faces at Bamiyan. Somehow I missed the opportunity – such a shame as in March 2001 on the order of Mullah Omar (friend of Osama bin Laden) they were destroyed by those extreme religiously intolerant idiots, the Taliban. Perhaps one day, assuming Afghanistan can reassert its independence, they can be re-carved further along the cliff face. Sadly, it looks like we have years to wait.

On the trek the males had not shaved, and it was time for my straggly beard effort to come off, although the moustache remained. At a barbers on or close to Chicken Street a guy started to tackle the mop on top but I was so horrified by his scissor-work that I fled halfway through! At the Intercontinental Hotel the job was finished but at more expense. The Taliban have launched two devastating attacks on this edifice, killing twenty-one people there in June 2011 and forty-two people in January 2018 with many more maimed. Evil personified.

So my route home continued … Kandahar, Herat, back into Iran at the Qala border crossing, to Mashhad to Tehran, through Turkey to Thessaloniki this time across Greece to catch the ferry to Corfu. My stepsister Helen (Hutchy) was working as a travel rep at the Messonghi Beach Hotel and we had a couple of fun days with her friends before I took another ferry across to Bari in Italy. Hutchy was the best thing to emerge from my father's second marriage, a great correspondent and introducer of me to her female friends at Benenden School. Neither of us got on with our new step-parents but that didn't interfere with our own friendship.

Another brief stay followed in Florence – Kitten's family swelled by the arrival of second daughter Rebecca. Then on about 10th July I am back in Battersea with preparations well underway for a welcome home party; pink invitations sent out by Mary Clare – one last photo of self with moustache taken in front of paternal grandfather's rather better effort immortalised in his posthumous portrait. Funny isn't it, one goes away for six months and nothing seems to have changed back home. Indeed many of the party guests appeared to be unaware that I'd been away at all.

Thus ends my two odysseys overland on the 'hippy trail'. Wanderlust now led to wondering what to do next work-wise, but before we examine my curriculum vitae let's do some more travelling – broaden that mind further, pick up a smattering of some more languages, meet people.

# 11

# TRAVELS WHEN OLDER

The last chapter descended into a bit of a travelogue … then I went to etcetera etcetera. I shall endeavour to do better with these post-1980 journeys. Before we head to Israel and other places let's quickly chart where I went in the eighties and nineties. Quite a few golf holidays in Portugal, Spain, Scotland, Ireland and many skiing trips already itemised. Before S and I were married we had spent three weeks in Jamaica, on honeymoon we were in Mexico, Belize and Guatemala and some years later took another three-week trip to Thailand. Over the years I've been all over Europe, strangely never to Scandinavia nor Russia. Australia has never appealed. New Zealand one day perhaps.

A great joy has been long-distance walks across southern England. With my wife I walked one summer from Winchester to Canterbury along the Pilgrims' Way staying in hotels, B&Bs, and friends' houses. The following year, choosing once again the second week of Wimbledon when rain seems rare, it was from Blockley near Chipping Campden to Bath along the Cotswold Way. Later, with my next paramour it was from Winchester to Glastonbury. On my own another year, I did Glastonbury to Brecon – each time one learned more about the flora and fauna of our beautiful country.

On release / escape from those horrendous times in Springfield Hospital I felt I deserved / needed spiritual respite. Thus in January 1992, I made my first trip to Israel, going via Prague in a somewhat elementary Tupolev Tu-144 aircraft of Czechoslovak Airlines. Lithium plus the remnants of neuroleptics were still coursing through my veins so my diary recordings of this time are a bit frenetic but get this…

On Sunday 26ᵗʰ January I am driving in my yellow number plates (Israeli) rent-a-car, a little bit lost on the outskirts of Hebron south of Bethlehem in the West Bank occupied territories. I write "… suburbs to the right then suburbs to the left before explosion rocks car! Assume direct hit from intifada stone-throwing youth & curse Arabs but soon discover interior light (inches from my head) has its plastic cover blown off, although mysteriously the light still works!? Made one heck of a noise I can tell you." It is many years before I fully evaluate this incident and its only explanation is that a bullet caused this – someone shot at me, assuming I was a Jewish citizen because of the Israeli number plates. Enmities run deep out here with fault on both sides.

Next day I am at the wonderful Garden Tomb near to the American Colony Hotel in whose annexe I am staying. Diary entry again … "This is the site of the cross and site of the resurrection – lovely garden run by society based in London. Plants thriving – you name it they got it. Anti-clockwise to

wooden platform overlooking bus station, past well / wine press to tomb entrance, one bay dry, one damp in the corner – out to take photos. Listen to guide with group, sitting to their right when kerblam SONIC BOOM shatters our peace. Ta very much, Israeli Air Force."

Next day after visiting Megiddo, I am atop Nazareth in a Force 9 wind – a 'ley line' connects through me from the University on Mount Carmel to the summit of Mount Tabor. "Feel inner strength," I write. There follows time within that amazing Antonio Barluzzi church on Mount Tabor,

the Church of the Transfiguration. The Spirit is moving, no doubt about it. Next morning, after a night in Tiberias, I am at probably my two favourite churches in the world – first the Church of the Multiplication of the Loaves and Fishes with that special mosaic under the altar. Close by is the Church of the Primacy of St Peter which this time I found more impressive than the first church. "You are Peter, and on this rock I found my church." Jesus' only recorded joke as 'Peter' means 'rock' in Latin. Amazingly one is able to sit on this very rock, the Mensa Christi, the Table of Christ. More diary: "I sit on the edge of the Table. Outside is fine bronze statue overlooking lapping Lake Galilee. Walk on foreshore (where Jesus walked post-resurrection), take

photo & return to entrance of church where lady tourist is sitting. Suddenly it starts to hail – 'Hail Mary,' I say & walk through rocky gardens & underneath two arches of ancient well-type structure."

A couple of days later I am back in Jerusalem wandering around the area between the Nablus and Az Zahra roads – "an incredibly strong wind in my face as I stand at eastern edge of wasteland and parking square, on east side of Salah El Din.

What happened here? Into small park further east with olive trees, very strong winds again. Jewish Synagogue at corner ... round garden and back to wasteland square where stands a tired-looking donkey." Later that same day I have motored out via Solomon's Pools at Atlit, these are three largish reservoirs built thousands of years ago, and arrive at a possible site of Herod's tomb, Herodium. It's those winds again, this time the fiercest ever ... here goes the diary – "Army checkpoint, drive up to near summit & park. Fierce wind shakes the car. Pay to enter & struggle against wind to walk round. Roman temple inside top of hill. Do not linger as wind in danger of pushing me over cliff – brief glance at Roman city below hill. This is where Herod, good man turned evil, dispatched his troops to murder the children and babies of Bethlehem, 5 km away." I cared not to seek his tomb.

That evening the prayer service at St George's Cathedral, centre of Anglicanism in Israel, is given by Ian, the vicar of Shotton, home to John Summers & Sons Steelworks. Such little coincidences are a frequent occurrence in my existence. Perhaps they could be called 'God-incidences', a term I first

heard coined by Gerald March, composer / vicar living in Witney, preaching at nearby Swinbrook. Once they seemed only periodic but in recent years have become mainstream. I shall share many of these moments with you in this book – I told you in the opening chapter about the time that I happened upon a funeral taking place at Springfield, where I witnessed ethereal light radiating from someone's coffin. There was no one else attending the funeral apart from the coffin-bearers and the vicar.

Some people would dismiss these as mere coincidences, nothing more, but to me they are examples of mystical and visionary synchronicity. Jean Vanier, in my opinion for most of his life the holiest man living (he sadly died in May 2019), is quoted in the 1990 biography written by Kathryn Spink as saying, "It is one of the advantages of getting older, that you can see how everything had meaning. You think everything is your choice but it's not. Gradually there is the discovery of being chosen, of being shaped in order to be an instrument." This is how it is for me too. I once said to Jean that, "we are in the same boat, nous sommes logés à la même enseigne, but it's a good boat to be in."

I was back in Israel in December 1995 after a couple of interesting side trips to Northern Ireland and Croatia. Both places slowly healing from decades of violent conflict – Corrymeela near Ballycastle was an inspiring Catholic / Protestant union centre. In Croatia I was a bit underwhelmed by the tales of the Medjugorje Virgin Mary viewers, some of whom I encountered, but was fascinated by the bullet-splattered buildings and broken bridge in Mostar. Both countries are melting pots of religious rivalries – so hard to overcome … Arabs and Jews have battled since Ishmael and Isaac.

So back to Israel it is – more illuminating memories. Down in Eilat, Israel's port on the Red Sea mirrored by Aqaba on the Jordanian side, there is a commotion of sparrows in a palm tree outside the airport terminal. Eilat's airport is right in the middle of town although plans are finally afoot to build a larger one up at Timna in the Negev desert. The flutter of birds I feel too, as a small frail nun from St Catherine's Monastery in Sinai walked up the wide steps towards check-in.

Having checked out the marble halls of the Royal Beach Hotel ($212 a night) – I am at the Marina Club Hotel which is fine – and enjoyed a reasonably-priced lemon pressée in one of its elegant bars, I converse with the concierge about earthquake damage to pillars that I have spotted. "Only superficial," he says. "You only cemented over the cracks," I say. "You need wider (stretch out arms) pillars. Another quake?" (Frown). I am getting entranced by Enya music here, birds and trees outside my hotel window have been singing and swaying in harmony. Even the swanky Royal Beach Hotel evokes her lyrics – one of her songs dreams of

dwelling in marble halls. Having chatted with the man at
the nice hotel about earthquakes what follows next was a bit
spooky – here goes the diary entry then…

Monday 11<sup>th</sup> December 1995
Well, I thought it was Monday when I woke refreshed, but
guess what, I had read my watch upside down & instead of
it being 4.50 a.m. it turned out it had in fact been 11.20
p.m. By the time I realised, I'd washed down a couple of
coffees using the hot bath water and smoked a couple of
white Silk Cut so it was too late to sleep again.

Might as well set off earlier than planned methinks. So,
after some diary scribbling it was pack the ruck-sack, more
carefully this time as a longer trudge is likely – quietly exit
the hotel, leaving room key at night reception at 2 a.m.
Some late stragglers are returning to rooms after discothequ-
ing; for some the day is ending, for me it's just beginning.

Walk some distance to the edge of town to the last neon
street-light where I park up. Thumb out a few times, car
& timber transporters pass in pairs but the few vehicles
are mostly the busy bee concrete mixers heading up to the
cement works. Get bored after ¾ hour & decide to walk to
army post near only Jordan crossing 2 km or so up the road.

Nice night, nice to be on the road again. Reach the post
at 3.30 or so. The two men there are kind – one divorced
with two kids, one has seen 30 years' service. Give me tea &
biscuit & we chat about army matters. A few vans, a car &
some lorries pass but thumb fails.

Then at 3.50 Bingo – lady in Subaru stops for me. She's
going to Jerusalem too, hallelujah. Radio crackles, tense
driving, cold air rushes through the car. Her reason for trip
is sad – her young & only sister, 22, has been knocked from
motorbike and died in Jerusalem hospital.

We are speaking in French because she's Tunisian, though
30 years in Eilat – at 3.30 a.m. *that morning* she tells me
there had been another quake shake, she on 2<sup>nd</sup> floor &

frightened, 5 on the Richter scale. The second in a month in Eilat, but perhaps another 'small earthquake in x, not many dead' news story. During the first quake in November one man had died from a heart attack.

So, strangely avoided was this earthquake and most fortunately I have never felt the earth move in my life. Back in Jerusalem a couple of days later there came another extraordinary revelation … moseying around the Christ Church enclave close to David's Tomb at Jaffa Gate, I enter its little museum dedicated to the memory of Michael Solomon Alexander, the first Jew to become Bishop of Jerusalem, installed in 1842. As I briefly described in Chapter 2 there are little handwritten cards explaining the exhibits and these have been done in my mother's neat and recognisable handwriting. One of her roles in World War II had been as secretary to the Chief of Police of Jerusalem, Colonel Bryant, I later learned. His office was just here – extraordinary; perhaps Mum was involved in setting up this museum and was asked to do these cards.

Recent refurbishment of the museum rooms meant that Mum's cards have migrated elsewhere – to be honest the team at Christ Church over the years have been less than helpful in my quests to see these cards again. Mum's roles in the Middle East, which I learn in dribs and drabs from my sisters' archives, we shall revisit soon on my next Israel trip.

But first of all in summer 2012 there is a long-haul holiday to Sri Lanka which turned out to be the first of a few as it is a genial country to visit, where on the whole Buddhists, Muslims and Christians rub alongside each other fairly well. Daughter P and I flew out via Mumbai on 29th July and taxied down Sri Lanka's only motorway to a nice little hotel, the Flower Garden, tucked into a side street in busy Unawatuna Bay, near Galle. After a week, she flew home but I carried on in backpacking style for a further fortnight.

Rather fun it was to be on the road again, bussing and training around this awkward-to-negotiate sub-tropical island. The bus journey back to the airport from my final beach idyll near Tangalle was long and tiring – much walking, which stupidly I did in a pair of flip flops – my feet took several days to recover.

As paid work began to dwindle and a period of property development started (more on this in the next chapter) I was once again able to travel at will. In May 2013 I fancied some more time in the Holy Land.

More spiritual moments were in store on this week-long holiday. A quick word about the journey out – undertaken from Luton Airport with EasyJet, the flight had cost £442 return. Airport facilities were poor, the flight itself notable for the abominable behaviour of some of my fellow passengers. Look, these people are very much the exception to ordinary Israelis who are generally charming. However, this sect in my opinion do themselves no favours. My diary records, "many Hasidic Orthodox Jews with British passports – their hats overcrowding the on-board lockers thus forcing others to check in their hand baggage. The one next to me spent the whole 4½ hours tweaking the unusual hair arrangement around his ears and constantly leaning over part of my seat – space invasion! They seem oblivious to the presence of others and seem to plough their own furrow. Rather rudely I thought. Chosen race? Je le doute."

I have subsequently learned that the reason my space was being invaded by this bloke was because in the aisle seat on his right was a woman. Heaven forbid, a woman. These Hasidic Jews have an aversion to the other gender and treat them like schmuck. On the return flight I am on their case once again…

… throughout the flight those Orthodox Hasidic Jews have behaved abominably. Luckily this time there were only about 20 of them but honestly, it's the men who are tiresome. They stand in the aisles chatting away (about God knows what) leaning on other people's seats, blocking the poor steward's trolley and particularly blocking stewardesses' trolleys. What a nightmare they are – so selfish. I berate one of them who impedes my passage to the loo at the back – a weak sorry and I say "Are you really sorry?" with one of my sterner stares. They get my goat this particular sect.

Aha, those stewardesses were women.

On day one of this week I am back at the American Colony Hotel shop, although staying this time in the guest rooms at St George's Cathedral. With the shop owner we are discussing the Middle East Peace Envoy, one T. Blair whom he berates … "Greedy man. Gets $1.5 million salary for doing f*** all." At least he no longer gets a free flat at the American Colony where as I've told you my parents had a flat during the British Mandate. Blair was at St John's College in Oxford when I was at Christ Church but I don't think our paths crossed.

On day two I encounter the security fence, the barrier put

up by Israel from the year 2000 – this blocks my way from Bethany to Jericho but a kind man gave me directions up and down steep side streets in Palestinian territory. I give him a brief lift in my little underpowered Toyota Aygo and … "then, perhaps the strongest surge of the day greets me as I descend towards the big new road avoiding dissident youth … (those yellow number plates again?)

"A young crippled boy struggles up the pavement on the left hand side – looks at me, his legs not working very well but our eyes meet for some seconds and it feels very strong and good. Thank you Lord."

Day three brings experiences aplenty at Vered Hagalil, close to Corazim above Lake Galilee, in a lovely hotel room overlooking the Upper Jordan Valley. Pottering around the area in the evening with Peter Gabriel's 'Solsbury Hill' running through my head, seeing the lights of Tiberias way down on the right, " … I could see the city light. Wind was blowing, time stood still …" I am approaching the end of a lane where stands the largest spina-christi tree in all Galilee. The ziziphus tree is its other name. I shivered spine-chillingly as a bird chattered out of the upper left branches of this tree in the moonlight … "eagle flew out of the night". Perhaps it was one of those snake-eating eagles that inhabit these parts. Spooky it was – this tree has soft leaves but spiny spiky twigs.

The following evening I am again wandering around the Hagalil properties. Underneath House No. 16 the fence below the car park is quivering for no reason. It is that plastic security tape. I quieten it down with some judicious handiwork – not sure what was happening there. There was no wind.

I made a few visits to Tabgha with those special shoreline churches. The Primacy of Peter Church was now festooned with bits of paper from pilgrims' prayers, the Tabula Christi partially roped off and it was all a bit tatty and tainted. My allegiance transferred to its sister church, the Church of the Multiplication of the Loaves and Fishes. Its excellent shop, its cool pillared interior and all the animal and bird mosaics now elevated it to my favourite church. Goodness me, I was soon to learn that at the adjacent convent buildings my mother (aged twenty / twenty-one) had run the Rest and Rehabilitation Centre for all Allied officers fighting in the Middle Eastern theatre. What a star. No wonder the church had a special resonance with me.

Back in Jerusalem I am shopping once more – finding, on the Via Dolorosa, a fabulous piece of Uzbeki embroidery which costs me just 150 shekels. Another great purchase on this trip was a little silver cup of Shevach filigree work that will also become a family heirloom. Up at Christ Church I meet a remarkable German giant of a man, Elijah, some 2 metres plus tall. He has walked from Potsdam to Jerusalem via twenty-four concentration camps because he wants to enunciate his personal grief on behalf of his nation in a gesture of atonement. At the same service I had become aware of a girl, standing in pole position on the aisle seat front left. She is quite skinny and appears to be having trouble with her legs – why, I don't know but the back of my own calves stiffen up and I have to do a bit of self-massage. The piano-playing and accompanying singing are truly outstanding – I tell the lady afterwards that she reminded me of Enya of whom she had not heard. The sun shines bright on her as she plays.

I discover more about the little teenage girl who is called Vora and from the Ukraine. No one knew where she had appeared from – she had announced herself as a Sister of Jesus. I shake her hand and say, "Hello, I'm Jamie." I tell the lady who had been sitting next to her that I think she's in a better space than when she arrived. "She is so happy – she is indeed in a good place," says her neighbour, also from Eastern Europe.

More walking and bussing brings me to a rendezvous with Tineke T'lam and her husband Peter who I had met in the shop at the Garden Tomb. They help run Jemima House on the outskirts of Bethlehem at Beit Jala. This is a home for children sadly not wanted by their parents – I dish out peppermints and as much loving care as I can muster to floors of twisted little bodies, bent limbs, hands and feet. Most of the time I spent with a prostrate pony-tailed girl who could not move, poor angel. I'm not sure if I had made any contact or impression upon her. Peter then drove me in his rickety van up to his charity 'House of Hope', where he and the more able of the handicapped youngsters carve out masses of olive wood crosses and other souvenirs.

I contemplate taking the 21 bus back to Jerusalem, but decide on a different course of action. I'll let the diary tell you of what transpired next, one of the weirdest moments of my life.

… so, I thought, why not? Let's walk back to Jerusalem … it's not far on the map. Enjoy a caramel-type ice cream tub and then something extraordinary happens close to David's Caves.

A guy and two girls are walking on my side of the pavement – she catches my eye, this first girl because she is very attractive, long dark hair and fine décolletage encased in a white top. Has this happened to anyone before? But anyway, she walks *straight* into me, chest to chest, *bang* –

and moves on without saying a word. I say to her compan-
ion, as though I'd done something wrong... "it was her,
she walked straight into me." It was my T-shirt wot done it
apparently – it reads in Hebrew, 'The Golden Dove'. Her
friend had a large gold watch. I've had that T-shirt over
twenty years & it's had some of Jamie's remedial sewing
work done on it but I like it.


Getting through the security force proved an ordeal. Arabs
working in town often take two hours each way because of
queues morning and evening.

My last day on this trip started with a couple of church
services, first up at Christ Church and then the 11 a.m.
communion in the Cathedral. Then it was back towards the
airport – one last 'coincidence' for you ... the Aygo gets its
tank refilled at a petrol station as I am inside buying iced
tea and biscuits. "153 shekels, please" – the number of fish
caught on the north shore of Lake Galilee where Jesus asked
his disciples to cast their nets as recounted in John 21 v. 11.

There were the usual shenanigans / rigmarole to leave Israel
– paranoid as they are about being targeted by Arab / Islamic
fundamentalists. Okay, perhaps with some justification, but
the security questions at Tel Aviv airport for predominantly
Christian European travellers once more went way 'over the
top'. Rude Israeli women soldiers asking unnecessary questions – one mention of Arabs and you are referred to Mossad
agents who repeat the original interrogation. At least this
time I wasn't asked whether I had made any friends on the
trip – how ghastly is that question, how pernicious of Israeli
security to demean human contact and friendship?

Luton Airport continued to disappoint – on arrival in the
early hours no aircraft steps were available for about half an
hour. Later I dispatched one of my shirty letters to EasyJet
in complaint – not easy is it, complaining these days. Try
haranguing Ryanair; no chance. EasyJet passed the buck,

until I got hold of their chairman's home address when suddenly action happened. Customer service among airlines is woeful, Lufthansa being a notable exception.

Just a few months later in August 2013 a new country is added to my repertoire – well, three new ones actually. The inspiration to visit Georgia emanated from seeing a documentary on RT television showing Doukhobors gambolling in the hills around Gorelovka looking radiantly happy – it turns out they believe God resides within us and at death the soul passes into another body by metempsychosis (yeah, me neither). The Gospel of Matthew is their chosen New Testament book to the exclusion of others. Mind you, when you see a photo like the one in Lonely Planet of the awe-inspiring Georgeti Trinity Church nestling under Mount Kazbek you realise that this is somewhere you just have to go.

And wow, what an amazing country this is. Subjugated under the Russian yoke for so long, losing the state of Abkhazia in the early nineties when it became a Soviet republic before independence beckoned with the Rose Revolution in 2003. Sadly the Russian bullies annexed the South Ossetia enclave in 2008 and the democratic status of Georgia remains in peril. Scene in medieval times of appalling atrocities ... in 1227 Sultan Jalal ad-Din and his Turkmen Army attacked Tbilisi, Georgia's capital. Rather than convert to Islam, 100,000 people were beheaded, babies too, on the Metekhi Bridge, their severed heads cast into the Mtkvari River.

I stayed just above this bridge at the GTM Hotel and explored Tbilisi for a day or two. Highlights included the Jvaris Mama Church (dating from the 5th century) with its carved figure on a rock reminiscent of those carved on the font at Toller Fratrum, Dorset and high up in Burford Church in the Cotswolds. Peaches on sale were the size of Ogen melons – local wines and brandies are renowned worldwide. Fortune favoured me when a German / Canadian couple returned their Hertz rent-a-car early and I thus secured the last vehicle available for hire in Georgia! It was a Toyota Yaris, and together we set off – first to Gori, Stalin's birthplace. This little town houses a museum to the dictator's memory and remains a pocket of pro-communist voting in modern pro-democracy Georgia. I left a copy of the photograph of my grandfather Mark Patrick shaking hands with the ogre when Mark was 1st Secretary at the British Embassy in Moscow. The lady curator appeared delighted and I followed it up with more information that I sent in October. Stalin was responsible for the murder of up to 60 million people, including millions of his fellow Georgians – yet this strange museum rather ignores his evil legacy.

At Kazbegi, local man Georgi drove me up to that astonishing church in his remarkable Lada Niva. The rutted super-steep track was beyond Yaris' capabilities. Next day I am in the eastern Kakheti Province seeking the burial place of Saint Nino, the Armenian nun who brought Christianity to Georgia, fleeing a massacre of her fellow sisters in about AD 320. Her grave is in a chapel at Bodbe Monastery; in the valley beneath is a little shrine built over St Nino's Spring, which burst forth after she prayed on this spot. I made a scrapbook of my Georgia travels – here is what I wrote about the approach to this special shrine…

Yaris and I approach Nino's shrine down a bumpy gravelled track. Some 500 yards short of the car park we are serenaded by a sweep of swifts and / or swallows soaring around us – marvellous.

This is where she prayed and a spring appeared – now wait for this: when Stalin invaded his own country in 1922 the source completely dried up only to reappear when the Russians left in 1988.

Pretty good eh?!

From the sublime to the decidedly dark at David Gareja, monastic cave dwellings close to the Azerbaijan border…

After the delights of Bodbe I drove to Ninotsminda and turned off towards David Gareja looking for a place to stay. Excellent new paved road led through epic desert land-scape, arriving at the lonely monastery at dusk. Nobody around initially apart from some stray horses and the pair of monastery dogs (good cop bad cop). Later one of the monks deigns to talk to me. "Catolicos?" he demands. "No, Christian," I reply in the vain hope of a bed for the night – access denied. So sleep, most uncomfortably, in the little Toyota Yaris, even retreating back down the road a bit towards Ninotsminda to avoid the prowling dogs' atten-tions. At 8 a.m. I head back for a hoped-for stroll round the site but am brusquely treated once more … "Closed." Apparently, this sect of Eastern Orthodoxy is in conflict with other calmer sections. Anyway, I was made to feel des-perately unwelcome in this place, in Georgia where a guest is a gift from God. Never mind – left to a very threatening angry car-chasing barking accompaniment from the resi-dent mongrels.

The leaving proved equally torturous:

Spotted a signpost to Rustavi near David Gareja and set off into the unknown – mistake … the road soon became a track, really only suitable for a 4x4 vehicle. It was touch and go many times through scrub, over streams and rutted ravines. After several slow hours we appear on the edge of an odd Soviet-style dormitory town but are soon in beautifully hilly country around Marneuli heading for the Armenian border.

Once I'd found the necessary car documents lurking in the glove box, I crossed into Armenia for one night, driving through the Debed Canyon to Ijevan after stops at Sanahin and Haghpat churches. Then it was back in my preferred Georgia, not without a little local difficulty...

Day seven starts early at 6.30 a.m. with a visit to the rather sterile town of Gyumri, levelled in 1988 by an earthquake. On up towards the Georgian border where I am pursued, overtaken and stopped by an Armenian traffic cop presumably because my car sports Georgian number plates. Much document production is required before he decides my paperwork is not in order and he writes 15,000 dram (i.e. £34) in his notebook implying I should pay this pronto. I am having none of this and try to telephone Hertz in Tbilisi on my mobile whereupon he now concedes defeat by saying, 'normal, normal' and gestures me towards the border. Pretty outrageous really.

Once back in Georgia, now in Doukhobor high plains country, I head towards Gorelovka, the initial inspiration for this trip. But one village short of my goal I encounter three local elderly hitch-hikers who I transport through Gorelovka (pausing for one photo of a stork's nest atop a telegraph pole) and into Ninotsminda. No English spoken but charming people with an admiration / fixation for St Matthew's Gospel.

Then it's on to Vardzia Monastery, the most visited cave monastery in Georgia, which swarms with tourists from Israel, Poland, Belorussia and elsewhere. Good that Israelis are welcome here as visitors, even if they are pariahs in most of the world. Last port of call before a comfortable night in Kutaisi is Zarzma Monastery, off the beaten track, but a welcoming gem where a monk showed me round accompanied by friendly dogs and some cheeky children. A nice contrast to my treatment at David Gareja.

From Kutaisi I head to the 'monastery complex' of Martvili –

such a special place, dating from the 7$^{th}$ century. I was given a marvellous welcome from clergy and congregation alike. So friendly – there was an excellent shop within the main church (as there usually is in all Georgian churches), people wandering about during the service touching and kissing various icons and pictures, wonderful plainsong chanting from a small female choir and an open confession area on plastic chairs at the back. I'm a big fan of the Eastern Orthodox Church and its ways – only occasionally let down by diffident priests – but not here at Martvili where I was conversing about Rooney, Drogba and Petr Čech (the latter two Chelsea footballers) before buying crosses and a key ring. The road up here was a little hard to locate initially and of course populated by goats, cows, sheep, chickens, pigs, ducks, geese, horses and naturally pedestrians, who prefer to walk not on pavements but the middle of the road.

Thwarted in my attempts to reach Batumi on the Black Sea coast by a massive traffic jam, I turn back on the back roads to Tbilisi where my favoured GTM Hotel has a room available. Next day I return the rent-a-car and spend frustrating hours securing my visa for Azerbaijan. I have chosen to return to the UK from Baku on a British Airways flight on a splendid Airbus A321. Odd to go east for 40 minutes to Baku before the six hours west to Heathrow but it gave me nine hours in the totalitarian state of Azerbaijan administered by the Aliyev dynasty. The Yanar Dag was interesting – a 10-metre-long wall of fire accidentally ignited by a shepherd's cigarette back in the 1950s. The whole of Baku smelt of crude oil and there were those nodding donkeys pumping up oil everywhere and oil rigs out in the Baku bay.

Depressingly, the oil wealth was being squandered on vanity architectural projects all over town – the old city buildings were bulldozed to make way for yet more Heydar Aliyev (that's the current Ilham dictator's dad) Centres, Heydar Aliyev flagpoles etcetera, etcetera. Out at the Heydar

Aliyev Airport at least the duty-free chocolates were reasonably priced but the wretched security people had nicked three packets of Georgian cigarettes intended for my daughters out of my bag – bastards. A weird country, not on my list of favourites and such a contrast to Georgia where I shall return. There is so much left to explore, particularly the mountain regions of the north-west, Mestia and Svaneti.

Let us leave Georgia with the anecdote as to how they got their gorgeous country. God had been handing out the rest of the world to other nations but the Georgians were too busy eating and drinking and turned up late. Sorry, said God, I've no lands left. Never mind, said the Georgians, who invited Him to join them in food, wine and singing. He enjoyed himself so much that He decided to give the Georgians the last spot on Earth, which He'd been saving for Himself.

At the end of October, I am on the move again at Pisa Airport, being fleeced for extra payments by Goldcar Rentals on a prepaid pre-booked Fiat 500 – sometimes it is better to pay a little extra for a car from one of the bigger players like Hertz or Avis. My autumn journey will take in some of the main towns of Tuscany and Umbria. I enjoy Assisi, particularly the Eremo and San Damiano churches but develop a soft spot for nearby Gubbio. Staying at the Hotel Bosone Palace, not as grand as it might sound, I have the most excellent meal (second best of my life I reckon – top was the Hotel Millon in Argentière, France) in the Bosone Garden Restaurant just below my hotel. 20 euros for the 'menu di oggi' with a glass of white Grechetto – four varieties of bruschetta, penne pasta with broad beans and bacon, calves' liver with grapes and lemoned spinach, chocolate cake with Kirsch. Prima.

I love the fact that Gubbio (Igurium) was where Rome exported its lunatics, 'which has left a lingering influence on the populace' says *Cadogan Guides*. It should be noted, however,

that Rome considered Gubbio to be one of its better-run city states – a case of the lunatics being perfectly capable of running the asylum. It was in Gubbio that St Francis tamed the wolf at La Vittorina that had been eating local residents. Another famous local saint was Saint Ubaldo, who a century before Francis had personally stopped Barbarossa from attacking the city, with divinely inspired intervention.

The Italian tour continued with visits to Perugia, Spello, Urbino and lovely Siena before a night with Dave and Sasha Hart and children at their house close to the beach at Orbetello. Then one last foray up to Lucca, before returning to Pisa and England. Okay, having promised you only spiritual sensitivities this trip was more prosaic but being in the orbit of 'little Jesus', the exceptional St Francis of Assisi, had some moving moments especially up in the hills of Eremo delle Carceri, the sanctuary, where he preached sermons to the birds and animals – mercy, joy, humility, fraternity and love were his abiding qualities.

In May 2015, I went on a 'humanitarian' holiday out to Nepal. A chance encounter the previous month with John T. Bach on a golf course playing in the intercollegiate Oxford event encouraged me – he was a Trustee of the Gurkha Welfare Trust and kindly rang round other Trustees in advance of my visit. Notes taken at the time again tell the tale...

At the suggestion of a friend whose father commanded the Gurkhas in World War II, and after talking to the UK head of the Gurkha Welfare Trust who kindly put me in touch with several people on the ground, I decided to visit this lovely country where I hadn't been for thirty-six years. "What can an individual do to help?" many said, "you'll just get in the way," said my brother-in-law Mickey, with several disparaging comments from others who enjoy trying to wound me. Nevertheless, I ignored my gainsayers and went anyway.

Armed with the latest Lonely Planet publication, Sainsbury's instant coffee and tonic, a mini kettle, a litre of Jersey milk cosseted by freezer packs, plenty of music but sadly the wrong-sized bath-plug, my Oman Air flight circled above

Kathmandu airport on the afternoon of Tuesday 12th May while they checked the runway after the second big 7.4 quake.

A short taxi ride later through streets thronged with people (too scared to stay indoors) and I am ensconced in the relatively luxurious Hotel Annapurna on Durbar Marg, albeit with no hot water, lifts or working pool. There appeared to be only limited damage to these newer sections of town but all shops and restaurants were closed because of the tremors. Luckily I had brought some home-made flapjacks and duty-free Gilbey's gin so my survival was not in doubt. Dropping names here … my initial contact was the super-efficient (and teetotal at least while on duty) Defence Attaché Kathmandu, Colonel Sean Harris, who filled me in on the UK's efforts to firstly deal with our citizens in distress and then the more needful Nepali people. He and his hundred men were only able to do limited rescue work with their Land Rovers because as it turned out, our wimp of a Prime Minister did not insist that the Nepalese Government accept the use of three Chinook helicopters which were poised to help in Delhi and wouldyabelieveit he withdrew them back to the UK on my last day.

The following four days saw me touring the city and out-lying towns Bhaktapur, Patan, Bungamati, Dhulikel and Panauti by bus and on foot. Of these Bungamati was the worst affected; it reduced to rubble, me reduced to tears.

I had spent a few quid in Poundland and Flying Tiger before leaving and brought out DIY / gardening gloves, face-masks, antiseptic hand-wash and soap along with balloons, pens, booklets, crayons, candles, napkins and all sorts. About half my stash I gave away amid great jollity at a Nepalese Army camp in central Kathmandu. I was able to leave many gifts for Anjana to distribute from her little church in the back streets. Surprisingly in a predominantly Buddhist country there are well over 500,000 Christians.

Of course I raided the hotel's soaps, combs, toothbrushes and paste to dish out to people. I think the gloves were my most successful import because people were removing bricks and beams with their bare hands. Balloons (starry ones from Sainsbury's) went down best with the children. Working on the Starfish Principle (Google it) to bring a smile to maybe 350 people can't be a waste of time.

Different countries were bringing different approaches to

'helping' Nepal. It was galling to see a 15-acre 'field hospi-tal' with thirty immaculate khaki tents set up by the Paki-stan Army outside Bhaktapur that was completely empty. Disturbing too were the ubiquitous smart blue tents with windows provided by China, but sparsely populated – they could pick and choose who they wanted to admit. These arrived without being requested by Nepal. India too is play-ing political games – their media swamped the hills after the 25th April initial quake bringing not food and tents but just cameras and inane "how are you feeling?" questions. I guess they have provided much canvas but it seemed to me the little Nepalese Army were doing more and with better grace.

The Yanks, bless 'em, sent 120+ fire-fighters from Fairfax County, Virginia and Los Angeles with sniffer dogs (all stay-ing at the Annapurna) who were on 24-hour alert.

So much brilliant work was being undertaken by the NGOs and small organisations ... the Salvation Army, Christian Aid, Tearfund, CAFOD, the Gurkhas and richer local individuals. I was somewhat appalled to read an article by Sarah Sands, then the editor of the *Evening Standard* on Friday 22nd May making what I considered to be a snidy remark about Israeli help, coming in without consultation, she said. Easier to pass judgement on them than the Chinese I suppose. She had cadged a ride in a tiny helicopter char-tered by Justine Greening's lot in the Department for Inter-national Development up to Chautara, when quite honestly two bags of rice would have been more worthwhile cargo.

Amazingly the earth stayed still for all the time I was in Nepal.

A word on some of the elite mentioned above – David Cameron, self-styled 'heir to Blair' (how preposterous is that) was a weak Prime Minister but apparently a good constituency MP. Sarah Sands now presides over the decline / demise of the BBC's flagship *Today* Radio 4 programme – her old position at the *Evening Standard* now taken by

that buffoon George '11 jobs' Osborne. Justine Greening has resigned from parliamentary responsibilities and I have sought her help concerning one of her previous Putney constituents which I hope will bear fruit one day.

Sandwiched between the Nepal trip in May and a French odyssey towards the end of July was a five-day jaunt exploring Cyprus, where I hadn't been before. Staying in Paphos in a package-tour-type hotel – Roman mosaics nearby and disturbing to see St Paul's Pillar outside the main church to which he was bound and lashed, poor man.

Renting a small car again proved wise, taking me up into the hills, through forests, past the Mount Olympus ski resort and over towards Nicosia. Depressing to see how the Turkish north side of the island had announced their continued occupation with banners and flags pinned to the hillsides,

but wonderful to discover the painted frescoes of Our Lady of Asinou, a little church not far from Nicosia which somehow escaped destruction from Islamic invasion. These were absolute gems, painted in 1105 apparently and the undoubted highlight of the trip.

Later that summer, on Monday 20th July 2015 in fact, I met Jean Vanier face to face for the first time. In the chapel at L'Arche, Trosly-Breuil we greet each other warmly at the end of the evening mass – wonderfully he knows who I am because of my previous visits to La Ferme de Trosly and letters I have sent. I give him a framed photo of Akiane Kramarik's painting of Jesus and a copy of Todd Burpo's book, *Heaven is for Real*. Both these children have had extraordinary revelations through meeting Jesus.

This journey I am undertaking in my cherished Mercedes roadster – hard top, soft top, no top as one wishes. The following morning I am back in the L'Arche car park … sitting in the car, stabbing at the sat-nav with Elbow on the Sony CD player when soudainement the 6 foot 4 inch frame of Jean leans into the Merc on the passenger side: "Jamie, I read the book. Very good."

He reaches over and clasps my hand with both of his … I say, "You know that letter that I sent you when I returned from Nepal? Well, this is one of those songs I told you about

– the birds are the keepers of our secrets."

He listens – I am wracking my brain for the sentence in French that I want to say, but it doesn't come – of course the man speaks perfect English anyway, so I say, "You and I are in the same boat, but it's a good boat to be in." What a broad genial smile he has.

Superb to be in his presence – uplifting.

A long journey south goes via Souillac, Sarlat, the fascinating Cabanes du Breuil at St -André-d'Allas, Les Eyzies and I experience one of those surging senses whilst walking steeply up the stations of the cross at Rocamadour. As I approach No. 11 (Christ being nailed to his scaffold) a two-year-old girl with dark hair in a pushchair is coming downhill. Our eyes meet and lock. She looks a bit startled but the mutual moment is intense. On via nice Cahors, Rennes-le-Château (Holy Blood and Holy Grail mysteries), a superb road through Cathar country from Estagel over the Col de la Dona toward Perpignan and Ceret.

Here I stay with Geoff and Ula who are already hosting my Oxford mate Simon Williams and his wife Amutha. Great hospitality at their beautiful home overlooking the town. Then it's on to Saint-Girons, via Foix over the high passes of the Pyrénées. I am due to meet my friend Louise Good–all who is staying with fellow walkers at the fancy Château Beauregard, Nazi headquarters during World War II. Fortunately, there was one spare room available albeit costing some 198 euros for the night where Louise, her friend Janie

and I slugged back some gin after a disappointing supper in town. Coincidences abound again that evening – at the restaurant I am seated on the right of a nice man, Dennis, who it turns out is CEO of Tala Kitchenware employing ninety-two Suffolk folk. I tell him about my vicar friend Greg Cushing, now of Loxwood, to whom I have recently sent an old box of Talaware sourced at a car boot sale because his Labrador puppy is named Tala. Opposite me is Anglican Mandy married to Catholic John who has just spent a week at Lourdes with Ampleforth people – I am due at Lourdes the following day. I am wearing a Celtic T-shirt sourced near Santiago de Compostela where their daughter had arrived yesterday after a long Camino. My own trip to Santiago had been earlier in the year, four days in April, renting a car from Corunna Airport – interesting to see James the Great's tomb and hear how his friends transported his coffin from Jerusalem, across the Mediterranean, round the Rock of Gibraltar up the coast of Portugal, turning right into the Mino Estuary at the A Guarda Celtic castros, ancient round stone and thatch settlements. It was here, outside the Museo da Citania de Santa Tegra, that I bought my Galicia Celta T-shirts, black and green ones.

Then another of Louise's walking squad turns out to be Ed Creasy, a KS (King's Scholar) at Eton and member of Pop one year my junior. Small world innit? – poor man fell and broke his leg on the ensuing walk.

So at Lourdes I walk round the allegedly miraculous sites of interest, even the Bergérie out at Bartrès where stands the shepherd's hut where Bernadette Soubirous looked after her father's sheep back in 1858. I am astonished to discover that this hut now houses a few plastic sheep and a statue of the Virgin Mary. My take on Lourdes – for what it's worth, is recorded thus:

5 million visitors a year – so it's a congregation of Christians

with those massive churches (one can hold 5,000+ people). But sacred sites they are not. I think this bored little fourteen-year-old school girl invented her visions perhaps to please her parents and the local Catholic priests and boy, did it work! Many shrines and associated relics have brought wealth to many towns and villages. Lourdes is just the largest. Who really cares if 'Sainte Bernadette' (not in my book) invented the whole thing? Does it really matter? It's a convocation of Christianity / Catholicism and it's not going to change.

Lizzie Peasley and her hound, Peggy, I had dropped at the Gare Montparnasse in Paris on the way out. On the return journey I dropped in at her sister's house near Juignac. Sister Jane had met Mother Theresa when she was in Holland – she had always sent money to the 'Little Sisters of Charity' despite being on a teacher's salary and Mother Theresa insisted on thanking her personally. Nice. I then tried to locate the whereabouts of Didier Rousseau by tracking down his old house in Royau just north of Bordeaux, and leaving messages with its new owner. Sadly, all to no avail.

Up north again, picking up Lizzie and Peggy where I had dropped them, and up to Compiègne to introduce Lizzie to the happenings at L'Arche, before we motor north again after a bit of cheese & wine shopping at the Trosly-Breuil Intermarché supermarket, one of my favourites. Of late, however, the Moroccan black olives at Leader Price have become a must-buy when in France, Sainsbury's version sometimes hard to find.

One little coincidence soon after my return occurred on renewing my travel insurance with InsureandGo on 26th August. The call centre is on Southend High Street (near the home of my ex-wife) – £46 per annum is tendered to one Tobias Smith. I give my date of birth ... "Wow, that's my dad's birthday!" Literally, 1954 too – how extraordinary. Thank you Lord.

Goodness me, I'm doing a lot of globe-trotting in 2015. Mid-November finds me heading off to Kuala Lumpur – a few days with Scruff (that's Simon) and Amutha who we met in Ceret, plenty of Bombay Sapphire on their terrace plus nibbles – hot and sweaty climate but I manage a bit of sightseeing and a visit to the Islamic Art Museum. Then quick hops with local carrier AirAsia, first to Siem Reap and its Angkor Wat temple complex in Cambodia and then to Yoghakarta Airport, Indonesia to see Borobudur and other temples at Ratu Boko. Three more countries thus added in less than a week. One felt most at ease in Malaysia.

2016 dawns and I'm back in Aqaba, and once reunited with my luggage lost by Royal Jordanian Airlines, am starting to write up my first book (*Pastoral Care in Mental Health*) on the Red Sea beachfront at the Mövenpick. Then continuing the process at Abbey House in Glastonbury and the Mill House retreat near Tiverton. But at the end of February it's pilgrimage time with friends from Southwark Cathedral and its diocese, guided round sites in Jerusalem, Bethlehem, Ramallah, Nablus, Nazareth and Lake Galilee – this wasn't cheap but McCabe Pilgrimages were pretty efficient and their tour guides knowledgeable. This is my fourth trip to Israel and although not as spiritually momentous as the previous three, memorable for friendships made – Alma, Martin and Christine, Peter and Irene. Bishop Christopher Chessun it

turned out had been at University College, Oxford around my time there – he let me read one of the lessons when we had a service outside the Primacy of Peter Church and then surprised me by speaking warmly about my mother's role in the area in his homily.

One last trip I shall mention was a month later, and one of the hardest undertaken. Going via Istanbul with Turkish Airlines to Addis Ababa, Ethiopia. I found the open poverty pretty galling – never have I handed out so much cash to people begging in the streets. I was befriended by Baruke, a university student, who walked me round most of the capital – I was generous in supporting him, buying him medical dictionaries for his course but felt used.

Getting from A to B in Ethiopia on the roads is hard, hard work – it was a whole day's bus travel from Meskel Square in downtown Addis, via Bahir Dar to Gondar. The bus broke down just outside Bahir Dar and we waited hours for a replacement vehicle. There was abuse from some locals who taunted me as a 'farang', a Thai word for Westerner, but in use here too. My hotel on the outskirts did have a pool but like my hotel in Addis seemed to have very little to eat. My health was beginning to suffer as I was surviving on tubs of Pringles and bottles of Sprite lemonade bought at considerable expense in local shops.

Breakfast in hotels comprised scrambled eggs and perhaps a piece or two of unappetising white sliced bread. I then bit the bullet and bought an air ticket to Aksum, ancient capital and allegedly home of the fiercely protected Ark of the Covenant. My dollars ran out and I spent hours trying to secure more funds at various banks, even resorting to ringing Scottish call centres to discover why my cards were being rejected. Eventually I succeeded with a cash withdrawal on Mastercard and was able to book a flight on to Lalibela, home of those mysterious churches dug out of the local sandstone.

Aksum was a nice enough little town and I had enjoyed walking in the hills above – some of the church frescoes were charming and in Aksum I bought basic silver but nicely wrought crosses that are a feature of the towns, Gondar, Aksum and Lalibela each having their own designs. In Lalibela I toured those interesting churches and walked the streets. Then there was unwanted attention from a local boy insisting on escorting me on what appeared to be the wrong path to a landmark hotel / restaurant. Sure enough, up a side path he grabbed the silver cross and chain from my neck and ran off. Easter Sunday on the Gregorian calendar.

"Thief, thief," I screamed. Other local lads hearing the commotion ran after my assailant. Fortunately the cross fell onto the rocky ground and he only got away with the chain.

But soon he was apprehended apparently, and punished by being put in the police cells for one night. I was thrilled to be reunited with my chain by one of my rescuers, Bashan was his name, and bought him a beer or two at this cliff-top restaurant. No harm done really – it is sad that the Ethiopians have so little and life is very tough for all. There were very few Western tourists, facilities were meagre, supermarket shelves even in Addis Ababa devoid of fresh produce. A desperately poor country – probably the poorest I have ever been to.

# 12

# WORK

People have said that my career path is an inverted one. Somewhat unusual to start off as a Wall Street banker, spend years as a baker before ending up as a minicab driver and most recently as a gardener's assistant. Would it have been any better in reverse order? Too late now anyway, and in the words of Edith Piaf, "Je ne regrette rien."

Leaving Oxford early might have given me a head start over my peers in employment had I been taken on by either Barclays or Schroder Wagg, merchant banks with whom I had interviews courtesy of friends of my father's. While I waited for interviews for proper jobs, I earned 50p an hour washing dishes at the Anglo-Belgian Club in Belgrave Square and a little more serving the rich locals at Justin de Blank delicatessen on Elizabeth Street. Both these places were easy strolls from the flat on Ebury Street where dear reader, I confess I was cultivating marijuana in the spare loo under 'gro-lux' bulbs.

The washing-up job I inherited from an acquaintance, Sloan Hickman – it involved dealing with the glasses and plates of large lunch parties upstairs with up to 400 guests. Hot soapy water and a good rinse in cooler water for the glasses before drying them on clean tea towels. A useful skill to learn. Us skivvies earned our free lunch of leftovers and were well-treated by a jovial big fat Greek manager.

The upstairs / downstairs role was reversed a year or so later when I hired the elegant main room to host my 21st birthday drinks party. Didn't the Romans have one day a year when the slaves became the masters?

The menial tasks came to an end when at last an interview was successful. A parental connection came to fruition when a friend of my father, who had a villa near his on the Vale do Lobo golf course in the Algarve, turned out to be John Greig, boss of the newly amalgamated reinsurance broking firms W. T. Greig and Fester, Fothergill and Hartung, now called Greig Fester. I started with them as a trainee reinsurance broker on £2,000 per annum salary at No. 52 Lime Street, adjacent to the Lloyd's building.

It was June 1975 – initially I often drove in to work, having to move the car to a fresh parking space every two hours or so. This chore echoed efforts around Oriel Square in Oxford, often poorly timed, which led to a plethora of parking tickets. It might have been more sensible to keep one's car somewhere down the Cowley Road where parking might have been free, but I was an irresponsible youth. They plagued me those Oxford parking tickets … every so often that lady would appear at my flat door in Ebury Street demanding their resolution. There is no escaping the claws of the parking police.

Whilst I am on the subject of Oxford's traffic management, let me have a brief rant. Even back then the situation was nightmarish. One was funnelled around the back streets when trying to drive around town. At least in those days one could use the High Street and St Aldate's – now they are closed off most of the day and clogged with buses. Oxfordshire Country Council seem to have little idea of how to keep traffic flowing – they recently built a massive new roundabout where the Woodstock Road meets the A40 which might have eased pressure there, but instead of letting the traffic flow naturally they installed a traffic light system which does not reflect the flows on the feeder roads that change throughout the day. Exactly the same problem besets the lights to the east where the Banbury Road / Kidlington / A40 junction regularly delays the A40 travellers – it is frustrating to look left and right and see precious few vehicles queuing when one has been waiting half an hour to reach this little roundabout. Further west there are interminable delays as people on the A40 crawl past the Cassington and Eynsham turn-offs. There appears to be no rhyme or reason – is it badly-phased traffic lights once again? The big Barton / Headington roundabout works well enough out to the east of Oxford, so why can't someone sort out the other areas? It can't be beyond the wit of man. To park in Oxford nowadays costs £7 for up to 2 hours … surely the highest charge in the country. And our country lanes are plagued with potholes. End of rant.

Greig Fester soon moved from Lime Street to larger premises at Regis House, close to London Bridge. I moved too, renting out the Ebury Street flat to Jamie and Veronica (it was he who helped investigate Graham Millar many years later) and moving to 36 Montpelier Street in Knightsbridge which I filled with friends. My salary of £2,000 wasn't really enough and this move augmented my income – the service charges alone at Ebury Street were more than £1,000 per annum. From here I began to commute into the city on a Suzuki 100cc bike, rather more sensible than driving in, and sometimes taking the tube.

As a trainee reinsurance broker, I learned the basics of how insurance companies minimise their exposure by 'laying off' percentages of their 'maximum probable loss' with other insurance companies. Brokers facilitated this, taking standard commissions and commissions on profits made. I was in the treaty reinsurance part of the firm dealing with the reciprocal and non-reciprocal quota share, first, second and third Fire Surplus treaties of insurance companies all over the world. There were some very bright middle-ranking executives: Charles Penruddock, fluent in German, Bob Fairman in French and both were fluent in Spanish I seem to recall. The directors were a jovial bunch, particularly those who had been with Fothergill and Hartung. One in particular took me under his wing, kind D. A. N. (Duncan) Allen, and I often prepared his notes for trips to South Africa, Europe and America.

Most of the time us juniors in the Treaty department did as little as we could get away with, composing letters, tying up changes in percentages and commissions, filing away copies and answers. Occasionally we would be trusted to head into Lloyd's itself and around the companies nearby to get someone's fire and accident treaty business covered by underwriters. If no one was keen to sign, you headed to the IRB, the Instituto de Resseguros do Brasil who were renowned at the time as willing to underwrite anything. It can't have done them much harm, as their website now boasts that they are the most profitable reinsurance company in the world.

I sat next to Charles Holman and David Long. Charles didn't last long and went off to become a Royal Engineer in the Army, but we were firm friends. David was an Essex boy from Upminster where we once enjoyed a round of golf. Di Davies was a bit older, worked diligently but always felt the glass ceiling was holding back her progress up the corporate ladder. I spent much time doing *The Times* crossword, a habit developed at school, or reading the newspaper. Lunch almost always comprised an egg and anchovy sandwich plus a cream cheese and tomato one from the same shop. We were given 40p luncheon vouchers each day, but I would usually cash them all in at a little supermarket in the Leadenhall Market where I bought groceries. Occasionally, I would whizz back home at lunchtime, smoke a joint and return sheepishly to work often well over the allotted hour.

Although my salary rose to £3,000 after a year, I think it

is obvious that the City life was not for me. Pushing bits of paper around I found tedious, friends were doing more exciting things and Timmy Beddow returned from South America feeding my wanderlust with his exotic tales. Also, the life I saw ahead of me as an insurance executive – perhaps a house in suburbia and a rail commute into town – just didn't appeal. Sylvan Surrey, somewhere in the 'gin and Jag' belt, 2.3 children – it suits many, but it wasn't my style.

After nearly two years I handed in my notice – kindly, Greig Fester agreed to keep me on their books so that any income from membership of Lloyd's in 1976 and 1977 would be treated as 'earned income' for tax purposes. It became a sort of 'sabbatical' when connections were made with their agent from Argentina, Senór Raoul Margottini, with whom it was agreed that I would work when reaching Buenos Aires on my travels. As it happened this carrot dangled in front of donkey me never materialised as my conversational Spanish wasn't considered good enough. The crumpled suit lurking at the bottom of my backpack therefore wasn't needed.

This time, spring and summer of 1977, was a time of change in my life. Looking back, I see much of the change was brought about by my developing dependence on marijuana, which moved from being a jolly social habit to be enjoyed with friends to being something that was done secretively. My relationship with Mary Rose stuttered then stalled – I remember, and deeply regret, one incident when she was tearful, wanting to talk and all I was interested in was getting back to Montpelier Street, where I could roll another joint and retreat into myself. Marijuana had become more important than Mary Rose to selfish me.

A year's rental at Montpelier Street came to an end – we had enlivened the living room with vertical blinds, a white perspex coffee table that I had rudimentarily constructed, new sofas from Enriqueta, a firm run by friend Sally's mum, and exposed rather fine Chinese-style wallpaper. Supertramp's

'Dreamer' blasted out from a music machine as I blasted out brain cells. Almost literally at times, as strong 'Red Leb' hash would create an extraordinary sensation of a rising crescendo in one's head followed by a sort of closing explosion – whoaargh, this cannot have been doing me any good. I turned twenty-one with this sybaritic lifestyle – throwing a large party back at the Anglo-Belgian Club, buying a brand new car (always a mistake innit?), another BMW 2002, this time a silver metallic paint one (KUV475P) with an 8-track player (more mistakes) – new it might have been but it never had the oomph of the old white one, plusher seats maybe and chrome strips along the sides.

Eton / Oxford chum John L-P had done a spell with couriers Pony Express on his bike and recommended I give it a try with a car. So, the silver BMW was sold back to the Park Lane dealership (at a much reduced price) and I bought a slightly weird Citroën GS Club from people in St Peter's Square, Hammersmith. Weird because one started its engine and waited awhile until its rear and front suspension raised the light blue UJD890M off the ground. Pony Express' offices were up the Preston Road north of Wembley, which wasn't ideal as most jobs emanated from thereabouts, the best ones were transporting computer parts from IBM all over the country from their base near Hangar Lane. This job lasted about six months while I planned the Americas odyssey and coincided with my move from Ebury Street to a house near Clapham Junction in the summer of 1977. The clutches of cannabis were very much in evidence, I would often stop in a lay-by to roll a joint in this first spell as a minicab driver. On exchange of contracts with the sellers of the Battersea house we celebrated with a joint, as it turned out we shared the same South London dealer.

Returning from America in the summer of 1978 vague plans to make some sort of documentary on the long-distance walker George Meegan came to nothing, as did a hope of employment with Intermediate Technology – I had been inspired by the 'Small is Beautiful' philosophy of E. F. Schumacher which this firm espoused in helping developing countries, but they felt I had no particular skills to offer them – true enough. Thus, I took a job on the King's Road as a store worker for Habitat over the winter months of 1978 / 1979. I was downstairs in the kitchenware department, really just filling in time before setting off on the next big overland trip out to Nepal. It was a pleasant environment in which to work, good products attractively displayed – friends would drop by and the journey to and from Battersea was easy by bus. Strangely, as my memory is usually pretty good, I can't remember what we did for lunch – there was a back room where we took the occasional fifteen-minute break, coffee and a cigarette I'm sure – I seem to recall a reasonable café / restaurant on site and salad-type subsidised meals, but the precise details escape me. Maybe the marijuana befuddled my brain. I do recall once snorting a bit of cocaine in the loos but this was not my drug of choice. Looking back, I wonder if perhaps coke might have been a wiser choice – these were the days before the more pernicious 'crack' variety. One could have lost one's septum to over-use of cocaine rather than one's marbles to marijuana. Better still would have been to stick to cigarettes and alcohol, those legal stimulants. Best would have been none of the above but hindsight was not available at the time.

Once back from the second big overland adventure in the summer of 1979 it should have been time to settle into something sensible work-wise. My fellow house-mates were pursuing honourable careers: Minnow Powell as an accountant at Touche Ross, Mary Clare Wilson at the Historic Houses Association, even Paddy Sumner was gainfully employed. I thought a little catering company might be the answer – frozen meals for couples: soups, mains and puddings.

Peter Breeden (of golf fame) and I started experimenting with recipes for the 'Mange 2' label that we had registered at solicitors Allen & Overy. Chicken goujons, Vichyssoise and carrot and orange soups, rhubarb and orange crumble, heart-shaped salmon fishcakes filled our freezers. It wasn't to be, however, despite our enterprising endeavours.

Without my realising it, seven or so years of cannabis consumption was starting to cloud my persona. Florid ideas, half-finished tasks, shortened sleep times, a generosity of spirit – my brain was all over the place. These are classic symptoms of the hypomanic side of 'manic depression' or 'bi-polar disorder' as it is known these days ... whether this behaviour was in my genes or aggravated by the industrial quantities of dope I was smoking I shall let others decide. Certainly, I now consider my own antics were caused by the catalyst of cannabis. Whatever, I was a bundle of energy, at times no doubt disturbing to others, but to me I was just 'going with the flow'. The flow came to an abrupt end at the beginning of 1980 when, following Mary Rose's death, I landed up in the Priory as I described in Chapter 8.

Part of the occupational therapy on offer at the Priory was a small kitchen where I made a few loaves – not the first bread-making I had done by a long chalk, but it was good to feel the therapeutic effect of hand-kneading dough. Previous efforts in the Ebury Street flat had included stretching out pizza dough, following the recipes of Peter Boizot's PizzaExpress cookbook and using special cast-iron pizza plates, probably bought from David Mellor by Sloane Square (the culinary emporium not the Putney politician). This Priory work may have sowed the seed for my next big working venture, the bakery years, which were to last from 1980 until 1992.

It all started in the week beginning 3rd November 1980, initially in the kitchen at Altenburg Gardens, the house in Battersea. That week I made and sold sixty-nine loaves, mostly organic wholemeal small tin loaves, some date and walnut ones and perhaps a few white plaits. The Tangled Web on Webb's Road, run by friends Lucy and Juliet was the outlet – a fun gift shop and café. Cakes were soon added to the repertoire, but it was the loaves that sold best. At the time I was using large tins of dried yeast that I sourced down at Lymington Market down in Hampshire, bags of flour, dried fruit and nuts from a health food shop's storage unit on Acre Lane in Brixton and the mixing and kneading was all done by hand.

Production in the kitchen continued for some two and a half years. It's hard to believe that I pummelled all that dough by hand for so long, but I must have done. New outlets were gradually added … Puddleducks Delicatessen on Battersea Rise in the summer of 1981, and Café Noir up by the fire station on West Hill in the autumn of 1982 who filled my large croissants for lunchtime punters. By now things had outgrown the capacity of the kitchen to cope.

So, in June 1983, architect and golfing friend Johnny Dunn drew up and submitted plans to convert a one-room cottage / coach house at the end of the garden into a bakery. Permission was granted so Steve Morris and I set to, tiling the interior and bringing gas and water pipes from the house. This involved digging a trench the twenty or so yards between house and bakehouse. Steve was the car mechanic for my Morris Minor convertibles but adept at anything mechanical as well as plumbing and general building work. We installed a large double sink, a small hand-washing basin, an Ascot water heater, work surfaces and two large gas ovens. My pride and joy was a Hobart 30-quart mixer with its huge steel mixing bowls and assorted dough hooks and whisks – this came from my baking mentor, venerable Mr Sporik, an elderly Hungarian who was ceasing trading down on Battersea Park Road. It weighed a ton but somehow PAC 632, my grey Morris, lugged it up to Lavender Hill.

As soon as we were ready to commence bakery activities, I organised a small opening ceremony. The vicar of St Mary's, Battersea, where I was to be married that winter, came to 'bless' the building, reading an apposite poem. Susannah York, a keen customer at The Tangled Web, had been asked to cut the ribbon but sadly couldn't make it. Angela Down did the honours instead, not as famous as Susannah but nevertheless another English rose. Funny that all these actresses were enjoying my bread – Angharad Rees (*Poldark*) was another, with talented RSC player Geraldine James becoming a regular later on ... every morning we would place a small wholemeal loaf on her back wall.

Production steadily increased – it was so much easier with the mixer and the large ovens. One could cook over thirty-five large loaves at a time or several large metal sheets each holding twenty-four croissants. One developed a routine whereby the next batch was proving while the first batch was cooking. My operation and output was similar to Karl's at the Old Post Office Bakery in Clapham but dwarfed by the much more professional business run by Marcus Hampton on the Shaftesbury Estate. Nonetheless, the area was well served by us artisan bakers.

My best customer became Dandelion, the health food shop by the Latchmere on Battersea Park Road. Gilda, its owner, enthused over my wares and her spread of breads was legendary. Small granary rolls I started to produce for

Pollyanna's, a fine restaurant at the end of Lavender Walk. Other shops, restaurants and catering companies began to take my breads, croissants and rolls ... Tea-Time on the Pavement in Clapham Old Town, Scotties, Organic Farm Foods, Yorkies, Holland and Barrett on St John's Road, Albert Wharf Market by Battersea Bridge, No Name Place near Wandsworth Common and others. By early 1987 Dandelion were taking close to £200-worth each week and that tax year my overall takings were over £22,000. Profits, however, were minimal – selling a small loaf for 32p, a croissant for 20p and a small roll for 10p means you have to produce a huge number to reach that sort of turnover.

By now the bakery's footprint had expanded a bit. I cobbled together a flour store with breeze blocks, timbers and roofing felt fixed to the garden's back wall. Being the quirky idiot that I am, this I then covered with a straw thatch that complimented the adjacent pillared portico construction, also with a thatched roof, which housed bread crates both plastic and wooden. This was in fact the old wooden gazebo front from North Rye House's swimming pool, re-invented as a porch to the cottage bakery building. It had sat for a few years in a shed outside Stow-on-the-Wold close to groom Mr Moreton's bungalow.

I engaged Danny Levitas as a part-time assistant and Steve Morris' girlfriend Margaret as occasional driver – before getting a brand new Bedford Rascal van (again a mistake buying a new vehicle) we had transported the crates of bread around in a clapped-out Honda and at one time in a delightful Austin A40 brown van. Laconic Danny lived in the 'hippy commune' flats near Clapham South with Steve and others – he surprised me once by spotting a portrait of me done in 1957 and saying, "That's my aunt." "No, it isn't," I said, "It's me." "No, it was painted by Eileen Chandler, my aunt," he says. Small world indeed. Eileen lived at Hampnett, near Northleach, and did fine pictures of each of the Summers children.

1987 proved to be the apex of production and turnover steadily declined over ensuing years. Daughter P's arrival in 1988, C's in 1990 and my mental blips allied to a general disinclination to continue this career were contributory factors. I delegated the Saturday shift to Danny, albeit setting up mixes on the Friday evening which allowed me fewer hours on the job. As I have said before, over these years I often managed to play a round of golf on Tuesday, Thursday and Saturday afternoons, mostly at Wimbledon Common.

The whole business came to an end in early 1992 after some twelve years – I slowly used up my last supplies of flour and dried fruit and sold or donated the ovens and mixer to a catering junkyard in Mitcham. An era ended. One suspects there are not many Eton / Oxford bakers – this one, prone as he is to a tendency to exaggerate notwithstanding, reckons he made about 1,000,000 croissants and rolls in his time and some 500,000 loaves. If ever I lamented that my choice of career was perhaps beneath my educational capabilities, friends such as Rupert Johnson would say, "Well, you gave pleasure to 400 people a day."

So, here we are again at a massive turning point in my life. No job, no home, not much idea what to do next. I made enquiries via Tony Yeldham, the vicar at Springfield, and via my second divorce solicitor in Barnes about training to become a vicar. But sadly, at that time, in the Anglican Communion anyone who had spent time in a lunatic asylum was not considered suitable vicar material. That avenue closed, I continued my voluntary work for the patients and ex-patients of Springfield as an advocate at the Patients' Council. Our primary focus was trying to persuade psychologists and psychiatrists that those termed 'acute' patients should be offered talking treatments but it all fell on deaf ears. I continued to search for more permanent work in the field of mental health, scouring Thursday's *Guardian* newspaper for suitable posts.

Having come second applying for a position with Kensington & Chelsea MIND in September 1992, I was taken on as part-time Development Worker for the user group of Hammersmith & Fulham MIND, namely the Consumer Forum. Slightly odd name; people often thought we were linked to Which? and their Consumers' Association. It was just that the group didn't want the stigma of being labelled 'users' or 'service users', the terms with which psychiatry demeans its denizens. Label jars, not people please.

Initially we shared basement offices and meeting space with Broadway Housing on the Fulham Road at the junction with Munster Road. These were hard times for me personally with divorce proceedings in full swing and the Graham Millar saga sapping my energy. Fortunately, I received much support from Anton Neumann, who had been on the panel to appoint me and from Nick Benefield, the charismatic boss of the local MIND. My 'steering group' or committee comprised these two, along with Silvie Stoddart (my chair) and Andrew Gidlow-Jackson. The Fulham basement rooms became temporary home to some of my bits of furniture, but soon larger, more salubrious rooms became available at 153 Hammersmith Road, underneath MIND itself. Following the move, Heather de Leon became the person I saw for supervision, another kind and wise employee of MIND. When Nick Benefield left to run Cheshire's mental health services there was an awkward interregnum period before Mark Logan was appointed as director. He was an ex-mental health nurse who greeted me you will recall with the words, "Your not another of those bloody Christians are you?" when seeing I sported a silver cross around my neck. We didn't 'gel', but plenty of other staff were supportive of our move to rooms close to our parent body. Geraldine Mason in particular was sympathetic to our cause and a strong ally to me personally.

It was here that the group blossomed, in Highmaster's House, a Victorian Gothic edifice which was the old St Paul's School Headmaster's domain. We had two large rooms overlooking the adjacent park gardens where we welcomed those deemed mentally ill for many hours, six days a week. These were Monty's London headquarters when he lived over the road at Colet Court – both buildings escaping the Blitz.

To try and give you a flavour of these times here are the introduction and conclusion to three reports that I penned for our funders between January 1996 and March 1997:

January to March 1996
It might be wise at the outset to emphasise that the comments herein are my personal reflections of life at Consumer Forum, expressing views not necessarily shared by anyone else involved.

The closing three months of the last financial year saw an additional 142 new people through our doors, bringing the year's total to 637. Without doubt it is a heavy workload coping with the demands of up to fifty souls each weekday and the logistics of feeding four score on a Sunday. In a sense we are victims of our popularity, hoist by our own petard. Being an open-door centre with no separate office, limited kitchen facilities and just two members of staff often creates an atmosphere of organised chaos which cannot be conducive to people's mental health.

Over the winter months my earlier attempts at promoting more responsibility amongst our membership proved counter-productive. Treading the tightrope between genial disregard and didacticism led respectively to accusations of indifference and of overly 'head-masterly' behaviour. Striving to achieve the right balance for each visitor remains as elusive as ever. Even humour can so easily be misconstrued. Nevertheless, each emotional setback must be viewed as part of my personal learning curve, however hurtful. If only the converse appeared true more often.

The financial year closes with the environment at Consumer Forum improving courtesy of the Art Group's pictures, elegant and sturdy chairs from IKEA and the new Windows 95 computer system.

Our place within the provision of local services feels more recognised, if not overtly valued. Staff commitment to a successful future for this project remains undimmed.

April to September 1996
This report covers the period from 1$^{st}$ April to 30$^{th}$ September inclusive and again contains the author's own comments. During this time 237 new faces have appeared here, meaning our 'client base' over the last eighteen months is 874 people. Of these some 800 will have been labelled schizophrenic, manic depressive, schizo-affective, clinically depressed, or worse, deemed to have a 'personality disorder' – to us they are just people.

One message given to the visionaries of Medugorje is that in order to combat the evil, injustice and wickedness that abounds, one must set a good example. Jean Vanier, founder of the L'Arche communities for the mentally handicapped sees personal growth emanating from a descent into the lives of the dispossessed. The process of helping others requires a willingness to acknowledge one's own weaknesses. I trust these values have influenced my four-year tenure as Development Worker.

Being a user led, user run project, albeit under the management wings of the local MIND, we have aimed to demonstrate that users are equally capable of providing quality mental health services as anyone else. With a different flavour, yes, whether better, who knows? Quantity served is no parameter of quality provided.

These last six months have been tumultuous at times but somehow it feels that Consumer Forum is at last emerging as a significant contributor in the field of community care. We seem to be gaining respect regionally and nationally.

The six-month period closes with the exciting news that our M.I.S.G. (Mental Illness Specific Grant) Target Fund bid for £55,000 over the next 2½ years to run a 'Cleaning Hit Squad' became the Borough's top priority and received Department of Health approval. Our scheme aims to help people sort out their accommodation using Consumer Forum volunteers armed with scrubbing brushes, hoovers and bin-liners, taking referrals from statutory and voluntary agencies but we hope mostly from the people themselves.

Our Management Committee recently voted that Consumer Forum should become an independent charity in its own right and we have begun to take steps in that direction, initially by consulting our general membership.

October 1996 to March 1997

The past 6 months have seen 163 new people pass through the portals of Consumer Forum. Statisticians might like to note that over the last two years we have welcomed 1,037 different individuals to the project. This report is my Parthian shot at reflecting life here for I tendered my resignation in February to leave in early May.

After more than four and a half years ensconced at its

helm, having washed over 100,000 mugs, taken no days off sick nor time off in lieu, the time felt ripe to relinquish the reins. Coal-face work at the sharp end of community care takes its toll and I wish my successor, Janine Woods, every strength. There is undoubtedly something magical about our rooms where Hitler's defeat was planned by Monty, Churchill and Eisenhower – may God continue to bestow his blessing on Highmasters House.

About a year ago, inspired by some words of Dorothy Kerin, founder of the Church of Christ the Healer at Burrswood, I penned and posted up a verse which talked of the dangers of selfishness, of people who cling to their illnesses blocking the path to their emotional healing. Its precise words are lost because it was torn down; too near the knuckle for one of our members. I stand by that message, adding a more recent observation that those who seek to criticise destructively merely fuel their own torment.

As this six-month period closes we await news of whether a £20,000 funding application to Smiths Charity has been successful. This is an attempt to broaden Consumer Forum's traditional sources of income. Diversity should encourage future strength.

Within three years this project has grown from a £14,500 outfit with one half-time worker to its present status of four full time members of staff and a likely income next year approaching £140,000.

There are dangers that even our unstructured approach to community care can develop into somewhat of an institution and this must be guarded against. There is a world out there and people must be prepared to re-join it.

This was a half-decade, a quinquennium or perhaps a pentad for us word pedants, of which I was proud. I had given back to society some of the benefits that I had received from my birth. Perhaps my best co-worker at Consumer Forum was my rescued brindle greyhound, Tikka (registered name

Halcyon Lady), who loved the attention bestowed upon her and appreciated being walked around the streets and parks of Hammersmith by willing friends. If nobody loves you, which regrettably is the plight of most of those diagnosed mentally ill, then the unconditional love of a kind hound works wonders.

In addition to endless cups of tea and coffee with biscuits, chat, music, books to borrow, sometimes free cigarettes to smoke, to our Sunday lunches we invited guest speakers from across the health spectrum or showed relevant videos. Summer outings were organised to Blenheim Palace and Bladon, with evensong at Christ Church Cathedral, Oxford, a canal cruise from Uxbridge to Camden Lock, a longer one up from Stoke Newington towards St Albans, down the Thames to Greenwich, up the Thames to Hampton Court. There were theatre and museum trips, art groups, a women's group, relaxation sessions and a Hearing Voices group guided by Alan Leader, a well-respected 'user' who became an advocate on our local mental health wards at Charing Cross Hospital where many of our people had spent time.

There were a few niggles in our efforts at Care in the Community. Of the 1,000 people who attended we were obliged to give temporary bans to three or four and a lifelong ban to just one damaged individual who later tried to strangle me outside. A safe space for all was our credo, but some individuals abused our efforts – illicit alcohol consumption being their catalyst. We once shared first prize as Best User Group in a National MIND competition and Lord Longford said kind things about me and Gabriel Mackintosh, my first co-worker, at a debate in the House of Lords on 15th May 1996, part of which I reproduce below:

I refer to a leading member of a small organisation called Consumer Forum. He was at Eton. That counts in his favour in my mind; but I hope that it does not count against him in anyone else's mind. That old Etonian found things difficult for a time but, like Peter Thompson he rose above it all. Currently, he and a colleague see fifty ex-mental patients per day. That is just one example of the work of these smaller organisations. Already 160 of them are interested in the Federation. I am told there are at least as many who are waiting to be asked to join. I put it to the noble Baroness the simple question: are the Government ready to back the Federation of smaller mental health organisations not only by word but by deed?

This came about because towards the end of my years at Consumer Forum I became involved with the UK Federation of Smaller Mental Health Agencies set up by Matthew Trust founder Peter Thompson and raised some funding for them. Frank Longford was a friend of Peter's and kindly invited me to listen to this debate behind the red benches.

At this time too I was serving on the committee of the important national charity APCMH – The Association for Pastoral Care in Mental Health. Jeremy Boutwood its chair was inspirational and a great motivator – he introduced me to the life of Jean Vanier and he, Pam Freeman and I went to the Quakers' Hall off the Marylebone Road to hear the great man speak. It was there that I bought my first copy of *The Broken Body*, which Jean signed for me. Treasured memories.

In May 1997 I left Consumer Forum. I tried and failed to get another job in mental health, coming second twice for quieter roles in the system. But I did carry on as vice-chair of APCMH, volunteering at an evening drop-in down in South Norwood run by Mary Hillier. Redoubtable and reliable Pam Freeman, the charity's co-ordinator over all of its thirty-five years, volunteered there too. My role on the national committee continued for a few years until I felt that my usefulness was compromised by not working in the field any more. It would be many years before I became involved again – I had made a large fruit cake for its 10th anniversary and would do so again for its 30th. Both events we held in Southwark Cathedral.

What next on this curved career path? Five years on the front-line in mental health was in retrospect enough for the time being – perhaps the two jobs lost were a sign. Maybe minicabbing would bring in enough income – it had been lucrative enough in those Pony Express days back in 1977. By now Tikka and I were well settled into our terraced house in Earlsfield, my daughters enjoyed coming over to stay Friday nights and much of Saturday. With brother-in-law Andrew's encouragement I bought a Renault 19 (G891TYL), trading in my reliable blue Polo (E382BGO). A friend suggested that Greyhound Cars in Fulham were a decent enough outfit. So, I head round to their offices in

Sands End near Wandsworth Bridge, and sign up with the directors there as a self-employed driver.

Here begins fifteen or so years in the taxi trade. Greyhound Cars had recently merged with Prestige Cars & Couriers so there was plenty of work for the liveried vans, motorbikes and us in our owner-driver cars, estate cars and MPVs. Once one had sorted out the ridiculously expensive hire and reward insurance (always in the £1,000 per annum region) a two-way radio system was installed. My 'call sign' was 72. A weekly rent was paid to Prestige to belong to their circuit, and jobs were issued on a rota basis (pretty much), partly depending on where you were parked up – the choice being Battersea, Fulham or Hammersmith. The job wasn't ideal for Tikka who had to put up with an early morning romp on Wimbledon Common, and then fleeting encounters when things were quiet on the job front and I could slip home for a while awaiting the next call. Soon I enlisted the help of a friend who came over from his flat in Streatham Vale at lunchtime to give Tikka a stroll around the local park. And later, in early 2000 after I spotted an advertisement in a local shop, the services of the 'K9 Carers' from the nearby Atheldene Centre took over the walkies role. Wonderful, a mutual bond developed between Tikka and a group from this learning disabilities centre. This arrangement continued for a couple of years until she died on 27th April 2002 – oh sad, sad, day for all of us, the K9 carers, my children and me in tears. She had given eight years of joy and touched the hearts of many.

The radio system was soon superseded by the advent of mobile phones and texts – shame in a way because one missed the banter from our controllers 'on the box' at base. Friendships grew amongst us drivers as we often parked up together – there was Brian, an old hand at this business who had once been Fulham's National Front candidate, John, call-sign 19, bent over with his bad back but a slow and careful driver, Steve Hodder who became a golf and skiing mate, Jen in her MPV whose daughter worked in the office and a host of other characters – generally we bemoaned the paucity of jobs but in fact earnings were pretty good in the early years. Airport jobs were always appreciated, sometimes one got a parcel to deliver way out of town ... twice I even had to deliver a company's tender documents up to Manchester which paid about £100.

Over the years I changed my vehicle several times – the Renault morphed into a VW Passat Estate (J350FWV), then a slightly weird Toyota Lucida Estima whose seats one could swivel, a Hyundai Trajet MPV (X468NNO) which served me well before I became enamoured with the clever versatility of the first Vauxhall Zafiras. YN02BHE I bought in 2008 for a hefty £8,000 and then my last minicab vehicle was another Zafira, AX03KXM. Payment rates for estate car jobs were 50 per cent more than a standard car and for an MPV job, taking up to six passengers, double the standard rate – hence in trying to maximise income most of us were driving these multi-seaters.

Before the days of satellite navigation, one relied on one's own knowledge of London, aided by those A-Z publications. Obviously, a minicab driver's familiarity with the complex warren of London streets was way below that achieved by the black cab trade but I've always been a proficient map reader and rarely made errors. Whilst on the subject of black cabs, whose rates were twice ours and who could be hailed anywhere unlike our pre-booked restriction, I have to pass comment on their trade body, in reality a 'closed shop' union, the LTDA (Licensed Taxi Drivers Association). This outfit constantly harangued the not very threatening challenge to their hegemony, us minicabbers. Posters abounded implicating us as potential rapists and yet it turned out that one of their own, John Worboys, probably drugged and raped some hundred women – witness the hypocrisy of the

LTDA who vilified us, when much of the poison was within their own ranks.

Regulations came in that required us to fully register with the authorities, yellow stickers and bi-annual checks with new monitoring centres like additional MOTs which necessitated visits down to South Croydon. This all added to our costs and each year my income declined in the new millennium. Prestige bought and operated vehicles of their own which meant those drivers were given the better jobs – private and cash bookings were discouraged as these generated no fees for Prestige. I had always logged on to the circuit for sixty hours plus per week, Monday to Friday 8 a.m. to 6 p.m. and all day Sunday too, often the best-paid day. At one stage I left Prestige and joined a local Earlsfield firm for several months but was persuaded back by the promises of one of the directors, more of whom later.

Nevertheless, earnings continued to plummet, and by 2012 I calculated that this driving lark was in fact earning me just 87p an hour! Naomi Campbell allegedly wouldn't get out of bed for less than £5,000 per day and here was little me on call for many hours for scant reward. It was time to seek ventures new, but before I recount the parting from Prestige let's consider some of the psychology at work between driver and passenger. A wise adage is: "Never assume, for to assume makes an ass of u and me" – I would add that how you treat others in life, particularly those you deem of lesser importance than yourself, will come back to haunt you. It doesn't matter what you do for a job as long as you do it to the best of your ability. Certainly, private hire drivers are low down on the scale of respected professions, albeit probably above estate agents, traffic wardens, prostitutes and, in these Brexit days, politicians.

So, very few punters had any idea that the geezer driving them was an educated sort, public school and Oxbridge, slightly down on his uppers perhaps. Maybe not particularly relevant as I was in their employ to transfer them from A to B. My private clients obviously knew who I was, and I drove many friends at reasonable rates to airports, weddings, Ascot and what have you. Others we drove included scores of architects from Foster + Partners (Prestige's best customer) who were all considerate, people connected with the Housing and Children's Social Services departments of Hammersmith & Fulham Council – some distressed souls there – once a young boy took advantage of a red traffic light to escape his escort, jump out of the car and career down an embankment to play on the railway line. I enjoyed taking little deaf Isla and Henry, with Polish D their escort, to and from their special school up near St Pancras station – that proved difficult on 7<sup>th</sup> July 2005 (the day of the bombing atrocities) but we all got home safely.

Celebs who I have driven were, on the whole, normal enough. Brian was Felicity Kendal's first choice as favoured driver but if he was unavailable, I tended to be sent – it was always a pleasure to drive her or her second husband Michael Rudman. We once went all the way from Chelsea to Malvern, Worcestershire, escaping harm when a pigeon flew into the windscreen on the M4. The music executives at Eagle Rock in Wandsworth were fun to take, less fun was one individual from 'The Brand New Heavies', more fun were all the band members from Travis, the Sugababes (Heidi in particular), and Bryan Adams, who signed little cards for my daughters. Sadly, Bob Geldof did not impress; indeed, I nearly stopped the car to ask him to leave as he was being so rude. A. J. Ayer, atheist philosopher and another Eton / Christ Church alumnus, was interesting – I told him he would assuredly appeal to God on his deathbed. Nigel Planer from the *Young Ones* TV show was a gas – he too had had a difficult divorce. I had that Rita Ora in the back of my cab when she heard on the requested Radio 1 that she was Number 1 in the pop charts. Sweetly she rang her mum with the news.

Other highlights included delivering a David Linley piece of carpentry to Buckingham Palace, driving in, and walking up the red carpet to the right-hand door. One of my favourite writers, William Boyd, was a regular customer from Greyhound Cars days in Fulham – he actually based one of his books, *Armadillo*, around his experiences. One job I did was to take a package from his Chelsea home to Joanna Lumley's place in Stockwell.

When the time came to cease work with Prestige it proved a difficult disengagement. In addition to the extra car checks that had been introduced, the Public Carriage Office demanded personal checks on all drivers. Fair dinkum I guess, and in order to continue for a few months doing private jobs for friends, mostly for Sandra and her fur business, I needed continued registration at Prestige. Initially, for some reason, they declined to help me out. Indeed, I suffered verbal abuse from some of their staff despite having worked for them for almost fifteen years and earning them thousands of pounds in commission on their allocated jobs. How petty – eventually, a manager broke with his superiors and allowed me some six weeks' grace until my hire and reward insurance came up for renewal.

Things got worse, much worse in my relationship with one of the company directors. Let me set the scene – over the years we had developed what I thought was a close friendship. It was he who introduced me to the Bounders cricket squad run by his mate Dave Higgins, who also became a close friend. Twice I gave him a week's free accommodation at the Austrian ski flat – we had fun times with Dave Higgins one year and again with his brother-in-law another year. He even had a dedicated pair of skis, with edges sharpened for him in our basement storage area. On countless occasions I drove him to cricket nets at the Oval and to cricket matches throughout the home counties. On cricket tours to places as diverse as the Cayman Islands,

Estonia and Malta we enjoyed much banter, booze and bonhomie.

So here is most of the email I sent him in mid-June 2013:

Subject: Business ethics

Morning,

I've had a little time to think of late which is nice, and I thought I would pass comment, not necessarily criticism, on the experience of leaving Prestige Cars and Couriers (remember them?!). I've copied our esteemed captain in because he may learn something about staff sensibilities (i.e. Dave Higgins).

Okay, so your drivers are effectively self-employed and perhaps merit no favours but I did work for you for nigh on fifteen years, probably clocking up some 25,000 jobs for which you received rather more money gross than I did net. *Not once, I repeat not once, has anyone ever said thank you, Jamie.* Indeed, all I have received of late is abuse ... my last email has not been answered, it was aimed at booking in my last few private jobs before I officially retire next month.

If you are Hampshire Hogging today, have a great day at backward square leg and I hope the rejuvenated Bounders squad triumphs, albeit sans Speno (Collard, star bowler for the Bounders).

No hard feelings because strangely I quite like you most of the time!                                      — Jamie

A pretty harmless email I thought. Ten days later, no reply had I received, so at a supper party in my Earlsfield garden with the two sent this email and my close friends Louise and Charlotte I had a bit of a go at him. Not wise, as it upset my female friends and as he left, he closed in on my face to almost spit the words ... "enjoy the rest of your life", spoken with spite and venom.

The worst, however, was yet to come. Less than a year later he was telephoned by Steve Hodder whose daughter, Emily, was desperately ill with an inoperable brain disorder. Steve was a regular at Malden Golf Club and had had many conversations regarding Emily's health with a fellow member, who shared a small office with his fellow director at Prestige. In the phone call Steve said that he would like to contact his old friend Jamie once again. Steve had moved on in the chauffeuring world and was earning good money driving BBC people, often Phil Tufnell and Clare Balding. We had lost touch and he assumed the man he telephoned would know how to contact me. He was told that I no longer played cricket (actually I had left the Bounders to play for the less aggressive LJs) and he had no contact details for me. Somewhat economical with the truth. My numbers and address would have been easy to find, probably in the contacts zone of his mobile. Steve persevered, knowing I lived in Earlsfield, and soon tracked me down via Cound & Co. estate agents – thank God he did, for I was then able to visit Emily in Great Ormond Street Hospital and pray at her bedside.

Steve recognised the spiritual side of his friend and was keen to seek me out once more. Dear Emily was being wonderfully cared for in the hospital but her remaining days were few. It was an honour to be asked to say some words at her funeral in Old Malden that September – I chose a passage from *The Broken Body* by Jean Vanier for Emily's young body was indeed broken. Her fellow schoolfriends gave beautiful testimonies in the packed church and it was special that Phil Tufnell attended to support his long-term driver and friend. Steve and I remain good friends to this day.

As a Christian I am expected to forgive those who sin against me – it's in the Lord's Prayer. I often have trouble with forgiveness, preferring to pass the buck and the judgement to Him upstairs. I cannot forget the iniquitous actions of this man – particularly denying grace to someone whose child was dying. Whether in time I will be able to forgive him, I do not know. About a year later we met again at a church in The Boltons, South Kensington for Dave Higgins' wedding where he breezed up to me exhorting me to conversation, as if nothing had transpired. Reader, I cut him dead and walked on by.

The Zafira I kept on, now paying way less in insurance, for it proved adept as a builder's van. There now followed a couple of years as a property developer – with my children now through school and university there was no need to own a three-bedroomed house. Its value had soared six-fold over the years and I sought to capitalise on these London property prices. In order to increase its value even more I decided to add a clever en-suite shower, basin and loo into a corner of the main bedroom.

Tomasz, my trusty Polish builder and friend enlisted the help of Dominic, a skilled carpenter who travelled over from Gdansk and our team of three set to work. Tomasz is 6 foot 4 inches at least, Dominic still had a penchant for smoking weed, so it was tall Pole and stoned Pole. Judiciously, we joined our outlet pipes to the main drain and built a solid little plastered room reached by a sliding panel door from the bedroom. All in all, it probably cost £15,000 in parts and labour but added perhaps £25,000 to the property price.

By now you will have realised that my attitude to money is a bit cavalier – budgeting is not a strong point. I had been funding this renovation project via an overdraft on my current account and credit card. There came the day when both cards were refused at a 'hole in the wall' – ooh, I was just considering using my joint Austrian Raiffeisen Bank card to withdraw some funds when my mobile rang. It was Simon Foster (Christ Church room-mate) over on Vancouver Island who, with no prompting, understanding my predicament, immediately volunteered to loan me some 20,000 Canadian dollars which he dispatched that very day. Wow, that's a true friend and one of those God-incidence moments.

These were moving times – through Craigie & Co. I sold the Earlsfield house and downsized to a lovely flat, the first floor of an 1832 house overlooking Wandsworth Common. Dominic stayed on to construct a wardrobe from IKEA remnants for me – there was now a chunk of money to invest in further property deals and so I spent some £200,000 buying a flat in central Farnham which was 'ripe for improvement'. Once again, my Poles and I did quite a bit of work – new flooring, new bathroom and new kitchen units. They were happy to stay 'on site' and after some £20,000 of improvements the place was sold for £240,000, netting me a reasonable return, although legal fees and hassle with all that conveyancing palaver ate into my profit. Still, I was now financially buoyant, fit from all the building work and ready to move on to other projects. Additionally, the sale of the Lillie Road properties, inherited from my mother, was progressing – Anthony Bonsor, our negotiator, had engineered a clever deal with Metsup, prospective purchasers, whereby penalty payments started to come through. Because I hadn't factored in that these were liable for tax, I felt richer than I actually was … poor financial management again.

One of the churches that I was attending was a rather special building in the middle of the Wandsworth gyratory system – huge but easily missed, surrounded as it is by larger buildings. This was All Saints Church, home to Henry Smith's memorial and grave – he being the 17th century philanthropist who gave his fortune to alleviate poverty. His benefaction still continues, The Henry Smith Charity now gives away over £30 million a year in grants, the thirteeenth largest largesse from a charitable trust. There has been a church on this site since the 13th century but the current structure mostly dates from 1810 when the galleried oak interior with gilded inscriptions was installed. The memorials to Henry and to Susannah Powell have been there since the early 1600s along with a plaque detailing his bequests of

£1,000 to the Surrey towns of Reigate, Guildford, Kingston, Dorking, Farnham and Croydon. Wandsworth, where he was born, was given £500, about £130,000 in today's money but this was clearly wisely invested.

Services there were a bit sporadic, it being part of a benefice that included the lavishly refurbished Holy Trinity next to the Royal Hospital for Neuro-disability on West Hill. I used to attend the Tuesday lunchtime Bible study talks and occasionally a Sunday evening service. Greg Cushing, the curate, was wise beyond his years and it was here that I met Geoff Coyne, the vicar of the RHN who sometimes took the Sunday evening service. Anyway, the place was depressingly moribund and 'ripe for renovation' – here was me with time on my hands and money in the bank. Most depressing I think, was the disrespect to Henry Smith himself, his gravestone obscured by the large piano and masses of black cabling. The whole church was filthy and unloved. So, I addressed the following letter to the vicar, Greg Pryor and all the people concerned with the church's fabric and faculty:

## PROPOSAL FOR ALL SAINTS CHURCH, WANDSWORTH

For some time, it has bothered me that such a fine church should be in such a decrepit state with peeling plaster and flaking paint mocking the intentions of the original benefactors whose names and beneficence are so beautifully inscribed on the gallery fascia.

The areas around the organ and to the side of the steps to the chancel are of particular concern. I propose that all flaking and crumbly sections are removed, the plasterwork in the main body of the church be repaired, re-skimmed where necessary with multi-finish plaster and the areas suffering from mild damp treated with a proprietary undercoat before applying a suitable brilliant white paint to all walls and columns up to the cornice level approximately 18 foot above the ground. We would also clean and renovate the outside porch and, if required the memorial tablets inside.

To address the holes and fading paint in the vaulted ceiling would need copious scaffolding and is beyond our capabilities at present.

That which is proposed could be achieved with two or three workers within two weeks using ladders and a small manoeuvrable scaffolding tower. I have worked with Tomasz Lukowski over many years on projects in Wandsworth and Farnham. He is an excellent hard-working craftsman and is available to start work from Thursday 11th December 2014. One might add that he is meticulous in leaving his workspace tidy after each day's work.

All material costs (plaster, fillers, equipment rental, paints etc.) and the workers' wages will be covered by myself as a gift to the church. I estimate that the sum involved will be less than £3,000. Obviously, times of work will not interfere with any services being conducted.

I hope that all concerned with the welfare of All Saints will welcome this initiative.

This was accepted without the need for faculty (i.e. permission from higher church authorities) but subject to health and safety requirements. Trouble was, there was a bit of a delay and by the time things were ready to start in early January 2015, Tomasz was busy on other work. So, I called upon the services of my Christ Church, Oxford pal Phil Butler who was able to start work with himself and a team of two or three others on the required date. They didn't come cheap, at about £1,000 cash per day, and drove up from outside Oxford for five days' work fuelled by plenty of tea, tabloid newspapers and Radio 2, ostensibly working from 8 a.m. to 3.30 p.m.

We rigged up copious amounts of scaffolding, sourced gallons of limewash for the damper walls and good paint to cover the 'tympanum' at the back of the church. Having mended holes in the lower ceilings, further painting of the upper chancel followed – at one stage we had to down tools for over half a day while a protracted funeral service took place. That cost me over £500 in lost time – my original costings had gone for a Burton and overall the project probably cost me £8,000. Once Phil and squad departed after their week, Tomasz became free again and together we completed the task using long ladders and less scaffolding.

Each pillar was freshly painted white, with gold spray paint embellishing the Doric and Corinthian tops. Up near Leicester Square I bought some gold leaf and special glue with which I made an amateur attempt to spruce up the pillars above the altar. Fiddly stuff to handle I can assure you, but it does give the richest gold colour. We repaired various wooden columns, floors and plasterwork – new carpets were fitted up to the galleries and the pulpit, every wooden surface was painted with woodstain, every pew was polished – memorials were sympathetically touched up with metallic paints. Outside, the porch got a facelift and its vegetation a prune. Tomasz and I continued for several weeks before being encouraged to finish by the church secretary.

The vast vaulted ceiling area was beyond the reach of our ladders and remains unimproved, one of the mended pillars needs repair and the porch could do with major reconstruction and refurbishment. But this is five years on from our efforts. I tried to encourage the vicar and his team to finish tidying up their inheritance but sadly there appeared to be little interest. The CEO of The Henry Smith Charity, to whom I wrote, would have been keen to fund further work – a cherry picker could have sorted that high ceiling. One day perhaps.

This church work was contemporaneous with other 'charitable' work that I was doing. My chairmanship of Being Alongside, the new name of the Association for Pastoral Care in Mental Health (APCMH) had commenced in May 2013 and consumed many hours over the following three years. I worked on our information leaflets, updating the main blue trifold one with Suzanne Heneghan, the effervescent vice-chair, and tweaking other ones explaining how to start a drop-in, how to combat stigma and so on. I produced a codicil document should people wish to bequeath us money in their wills.

I made a point of visiting all groups and drop-ins mentioned

in our newsletter and encouraging other churches and people to start projects – Burgess Hill was an example I visited a few times – I think they did start something but chose not to link in with our national body. I made visits to the CRE (Christian Resources Exhibition) up in the Trafford Centre, Manchester and then to a southern event at the Hampshire cricket ground outside Southampton. This networking brought me in touch with some wonderful people ... Tessie Cooling, calligraphy suprema, Sam Richardson of SPCK, the Barnabas Fund up at Manchester and Jo Swinney, then working for *Preach* magazine, at the Southampton event. This encouraged me to insist upon BA / APCMH's participation in two London events in subsequent years where we took small stands to spread our word. People might question whether the effort and expense (approaching £1,000 for three days) merited us turning up, but to me

it was important that mental health and spirituality got an airing at these massive Christian events.

Following the death of Bishop Stephen Sykes, one of our Patrons, in September 2014 I enlisted Canon Roger Royle to take his place. Roger had been one of the vicars at school and we had re-met during his time at Southwark Cathedral. I love his style, his honesty and his theology – always making mild jokes at the expense of Methodists but I'm sure God doesn't object. Our other Patron was and is Professor Andrew Sims, one of those rarities, a Christian psychiatrist. I had the pleasure of interviewing him at his home in the Midlands when researching my first book on pastoral care in mental health. Roger has recently asked to be relieved of his Patron duties and the search is on for his replacement.

Wherever I went in the world I would be handing out BA / APCMH leaflets and magazines. Mary Wright (Hillier) and I started work on a leaflet that would go to every church in the land but as I write this, that is still frustratingly unfulfilled. Committee meetings we held in my flat which saved money – we had a weekend away at Turvey Abbey, Bedford, in the early days of my chairmanship. Marlene, the company secretary and treasurer brought excellent cakes, but it cannot be left unsaid … relationships amongst the officers and committee were never easy. Feathers were ruffled by my no-nonsense style and keenness to motivate this charity out of its dormancy into more activities. Three years at its helm was tiring but I remain an interested member who wishes it to flourish.

When Steve Press resigned from his role as editor of the *Being Alongside* magazine, Suzanne and I edited one issue before we employed Trevor Parsons. His work for other charity magazines and knowledge of modern-day production and printing has transformed the quality of the issues. They can be viewed, along with many earlier ones, on the website www.beingalongside.org.uk. Oh, that this charity thrives in the years to come. Its message is crucial.

Another string to Marlene's bow was her co-ordination of the Robes Project for Southwark Cathedral. This project used seven different churches and halls across the diocese to feed a group of about twenty homeless individuals, giving them beds for the night and breakfast the following morning. From January 2016 through to early March 2017, this meant these people went from one warm venue to another each night over the worst winter weather. I volunteered to help out at Christ Church, Blackfriars where I did the night sleeping rota. The showers there weren't working so Tomasz, also an excellent plumber, came over to sort them out.

Marlene's fellow co-ordinator, indeed the chair of Robes, was George Martin whose day job was running the Queen's cinema room in the basement of Buckingham Palace. George kindly said that I took to these people like a duck to water, they were my kind of people. Indeed, they were good people, down on their luck to be homeless and I hope their lives have improved. One lady said that all of us were just two pay-cheques away from becoming homeless – so true. I enjoyed this work – it is encouraging that many churches throughout the UK do similar enterprises. My only qualm was that when in the summer there was an event to celebrate all the volunteers' roles at the Dragon Project venue by Borough tube, those we had helped were not invited.

My main volunteering role by this time was up at the Royal Hospital for Neuro-disability where Wandsworth meets Putney Heath and Wimbledon Common. This enormous building used to cower behind high palisade fencing when it was called The Royal Hospital and Home for Incurables. Geoff Coyne, the hospital's extraordinary chaplain – he knows just about all the patients, their families and all staff members too – had told me they were always looking for fresh volunteers. After a bit of form-filling, reference-seeking, DBS checks and so forth, I enrolled in the spring of 2015, helping Geoff out at his 11 a.m. Thursday quiz service and the larger Sunday morning services. There is a small squad of us volunteers who bring patients from their wards and return them afterwards. Others, including ace nonagenarian Margaret Rainbird, organise hymn sheets and look after people as they arrive in the hall.

The love and care exhibited here are marvellous. Most of the 400 patients are wheelchair-bound, some can only move an eyelid in communication, but staff work wonders in giving them as much help as possible. Huntingdon's Disease has afflicted some, others have suffered brain injuries and very few stand any chance of recovery. Yet each has character and Geoff is adept at reaching them all and brightening their days. Nowadays my scope for attendance has diminished what with living the other side of Oxford – whether I travel by train or car it's a five- or six-hour return journey for a couple of hours' volunteering so I'm down to about one visit a month.

What other work have I done recently? In December 2014 I started writing a book on the beach loungers at the lovely Mövenpick Hotel in Aqaba – this was *The Least of Mine – Pastoral Care in Mental Health* which I was encouraged to start by Sam Richardson of SPCK publishers, as they hadn't addressed the subject since 1984, when Canon John Foskett wrote *Meaning in Madness* for them. Dear John set the standard for mental health chaplaincy during his years at the Maudsley Hospital in South London but sadly died in July 2017 – I interviewed him down at his Dorset home when his lungs were weak but his heart, humour and compassion remained strong. He was super-helpful as I strove to get this book nearer to the shelves. Others too I sought counsel from – Canon Mike Law up at Ely who worked many years at Fulbourn Hospital outside Cambridge and the aforementioned Andrew Sims.

I love writing in old libraries and the Maxwell Library at the Royal Hospital became my default writing environment where I finished that first book after some six months. Regrettably, no publisher wanted it – maybe one day. This book, the one you are reading, was started in the library at La Ferme de Trosly, Jean Vanier's place near Compiègne, France. Interruptions are infrequent and the quiet is inspiring.

It was Jean who encouraged me on my next venture which is ongoing – the formation of a Faith & Light gathering in the Oxford area. But before trying to set up this group I did some paid work over the winter months of 2016 / 17 for local gardener Mark Waters. Very good for soul and body is gardening and I learn much from Mark. He has a tired old Toyota pick-up in which we travelled to local Cotswold properties, a score of which he serves. One day I am sure I shall become his slave again but at present this writing lark and the learning disabilities people of Faith and Light are my priorities. A long-term dream is to start a L'Arche Oxford … there are so few L'Arches in England. Recently I have started volunteering for another homeless initiative, the Gatehouse project in Oxford, which does great things for some of the many homeless souls who inhabit so many of the city's doorways. I pitch up most Monday evenings for two or three hours.

So, there we are then – my different career path evolved from being a Wall Street banker and City slicker via whole-sale baking and minicab driving to property spivvery and gardening. Idle rich? Perhaps not, as I've mostly done six days' toil a week – lumpenproletariat, no. Downwardly mobile – I'll accept that.

# 13

## Loose ends

What have I left out of this account of my years from birth to sixty-two or so? Let's have a quick look at literature. Earliest reading memories were the Beatrix Potter stories and some A. A. Milne poems and his Winnie the Pooh works. Cruelly, we used to call our father Eeyore, and it is said I have metamorphosed into a Pooh or a Tigger. I progressed onto a wonderful series of books (whose titles and authors I have forgotten) which followed the lives of children in different cultures and countries all around the world. Perhaps they inspired my later love of travel.

The books I hated were the 'cautionary tale' variety – okay, on rereading Hilaire Belloc's one, only Matilda stands out as particularly nasty … she told such dreadful lies so nobody believed her when her house did burn down, with her inside. It was the Struwwelpeter (Shock-Headed Peter) stories of Heinrich Hoffman that frightened me most – Little Suck-a-Thumb gets his thumbs cut off by the tailor's scissors, Kaspar didn't eat his soup and died within five days, Johnny Head-in-Air doesn't look where he's going thus falls into a river and Fidgety Philip gets buried under the table. The pictures were gruesome. Dad thought these books were funny, I didn't.

Another slightly odd aspect of growing up which bothered me was nanny's insistence that pulling a face, grimacing or whatever would cause one permanent disfigurement if 'the wind changed'. "Don't do that, the wind might change."

At prep school my main diet was 'war mags'. These were A6-size flick-through little magazines on cheap paper telling tales of brave soldiers, sailors and airmen in World War II. I also loved the Babar stories, Tintin books and later Asterix the Gaul with sidekicks Obelix and Idéfix the dog. Great way to learn a bit of French. At Eton one started getting 'set books' for O-level – always a Shakespeare, plus we had *Cider with Rosie* by Laurie Lee and Thomas Hardy's *Mayor of Casterbridge*. Textbooks varied in quality – some had been written by Eton masters themselves … D. P. Simpson's Latin Primer was a standard, he himself was a very difficult tortured soul dismissing class members regularly for not tying their little white ties correctly. I grew to like W. G. Hoskins books in Geography, but the Economics ones were pretty dire although John Maynard Keynes talked a lot of sense. *Future Shock* by Alvin Toffler came out in 1970, trying to make us fear rapid change but we seem to have coped fairly well in the technological age.

For fun I read the entire collection of Dick Francis novels which I used to love – horse-racing and skulduggery, great stuff and well written. I moved on to Evelyn Waugh's books at university, part modelling myself on that Sebastian Flyte fellow in *Brideshead Revisited*. Subsequent years have seen me enjoying Gabriel García Márquez's *One Hundred Years of Solitude*, magic realism in mystical Colombia, anything by A. N. Wilson with my favourites being *Jesus*, and the one on Betjeman. Did you know John Betjeman was treated very poorly by C. S. Lewis when at Oxford? – most unpleasant. I've read pretty much every book written by William Boyd, who I rate as the greatest modern novelist.

Like many, I always have four or five books on the go, dipping into them at night before falling asleep. Having discovered a firm called PostScript, virtually every month I am ordering books from their catalogue. Charity shops provide much of my reading matter – just recently I got *Him & Me* by Jack and Michael Whitehall which was terrific. How they got away with being so rude about so many people I know not. Biographies I favour, some religious tracts, exposés of dodgy dictators and double-dealing politicians. There was brave journalist Luke Harding's *Mafia State*, an excoriation of Vladimir Putin's dangerous reign and rise to riches. Works by Tom Bower on the likes of Robert Maxwell, Mohamed Fayed, Branson and now Corbyn are meticulously researched and well written. Whilst on the subject of communists like Putin and Corbyn, I bring to your attention again the book written by my grandfather on his return from Moscow duties, *Hammer and Sickle*, which lambasted early Bolshevism as a busted flush. Sadly, like a bad smell, it lingers to this day in Venezuela, Cuba, numerous African states and of course Russia and China. Oh for monarchies and even benevolent dictatorships.

If you want to experience quality English, exquisite grammar and punctuation and also be royally entertained I recommend you revisit anything by A. A. Milne.

As for newspapers and magazines, at Eton I used to read *The Times*, *The Economist*, the excellent *Ecologist* magazine, dipping into *Paris Match*. *The Times* was half price for students, a good idea to foster loyalty. *Private Eye* was and is always pertinent and fun. In the *Sunday Times* I used to like articles by Jilly Cooper which appalled housemaster Robert Hardy, who I imagine found her frivolous. My favourite columnists these days are Boris Johnson in *The Telegraph*, Peter Hitchens in *The Mail on Sunday*, recently discovered Johnny Grimond in *The Oldie* and past pieces by Jeremy Clarkson – chacun à son goût as the French would say.

Television programmes and films should get an outing. Of the former, one of my favourites was *Now Get Out of That*, hosted by Bernard Falk in 1981; the format pitted contestants from Oxford against ones from Cambridge in outdoor adventures solving puzzles and problems as they toiled. Early 'reality TV'. Man landing on the moon on 20th July 1969 was great TV, along with the World Cup Final three years before. Nowadays I tend to concentrate on the news from Channel 4 or the BBC although Radio 4 might be more informative. Radio doesn't feature enough in my life. Way back, Kitten and I would *Listen with Mother* in the North Rye nursery on the Home Programme or was it the Light Programme. Bill and Ben the Flowerpot Men, Andy Pandy, Muffin the Mule – innocent days. We had this huge brown radio, 3 foot by 2 foot, with crackly short-wave and dials featuring Hilversum and others, before the likes of Radio Caroline.

In my minicab days I always enjoyed Nick Ferrari's show on LBC but would change station when James O'Brien came on after Nick – too left-wing for me. In the afternoons Fi Glover did a good job and then Simon Mayo. Sunday mornings on Radio 4 with its religious hours can be illuminating and there was the superb *I'm Sorry I'll Read That Again* with Humphrey Lyttelton and talented comedy guests on a weekday evening.

But television is a wonderful invention, thank you Mr Baird, bringing delight to billions of people. Films do the same – in no particular order my picks would be:

*Z* by Costa-Gavras in 1969 on the Greek colonels' takeover.
*About Time* – "whatever you do, marry somebody nice."
*Love Actually* – "just in cases."
*The Sound of Music*
*Three Billboards Outside Ebbing, Missouri*
*Butch Cassidy and the Sundance Kid*
I quite like *Downhill Racer*, Robert Redford again, and *On Her Majesty's Secret Service*, the George Lazenby Bond movie but those are mostly for the skiing scenes.

Mustn't forget some other great films …

> *E.T.* and the ever so moving *Schindler's List* from Steven
> Spielberg – "I could have got more."
> The Marx Brothers' *Day at the Races.*
> Peter Greenaway's *The Draughtsman's Contract* – this
> was filmed at Jacobean Groombridge Place close to
> Burrswood, Dorothy Kerin's home in Kent mentioned in
> Chapter 15, where she moved in 1948.
> *Walking the Camino* – produced by friend Hilary Bach's
> goddaughter.
> *Life of Brian* – "he's not the Messiah, he's a very naughty
> boy."
> *One Flew Over the Cuckoo's Nest.*

At Cothill, we had occasional films shown in the main hall
– *North West Frontier* and was it there that we saw *Monsieur
Hulot's Holiday* with Jacques Tati? Charming – the way he
served when playing tennis. Let's move on from movies to
theatre – as an actor I was pretty rubbish. At prep school, I
was some sort of shepherd in *Elijah*, written and directed by
Mr Armitage, one of the teachers. At Eton, performances to
forget included Claudius in *The Marowitz Hamlet*, a priest

in *Luther* – slight improvement as Ratty in *Toad of Toad Hall* ... Julian Hill as Toad, Philip Remnant as Mole, Dave Profumo as Badger and Bob Spencer-Churchill as Chief Weasel. Enthusiastically directed by Tom Wheare. Having to sing the ditty, 'Up tails, down tails' was embarrassing and mocked many years later at a reunion dinner with Mr Hardy. Acting is not my forte.

Visits to the theatre from home were sporadic. We were no 'culture vultures'. Up in London we enjoyed *Jorrocks* ... "Hunting is the king of sports, the sport of Kings" – the best bit for me was the buffet supper downstairs at the Savoy with cold baked beans amongst the antipasto misto. There were no theatres in the North Cotswolds – just a fleapit cinema in Chipping Norton where I remember young Hayley Mills in *Castaways*. But when married to S, with her sister married to *The Times*' theatre critic, visits multiplied, often with a meal afterwards at Joe Allen's, that mecca for luvvies on Exeter Street. We saw an array of Pinter productions, some Shakespeare ... *The Merchant of Venice* with neighbour Geraldine James, a superb panto-style Offenbach's *Orpheus in the Underworld* at the Lyric Hammersmith, the fabulous Peter Shaffer play *Amadeus*, which set me off as a Mozart junkie, *Guys and Dolls* (my wife loved musicals), Victoria Wood, Spike Milligan, Barry Humphries as Dame Edna and Sir Les, *The Mousetrap* I'm sure ... now in its nth year, the classy *Sleuth* with Peter Bowles – masses of good stuff, some dross.

The evenings I enjoyed most were in slightly 'off Broadway' venues where The National Theatre of Brent performed *Zulu!!*, *The Black Hole of Calcutta* and *The Messiah*. Patrick Barlow and Jim Broadbent as his sidekick in those days were just brilliant, using the audience as extras to their two-man company. Patrick deserves more acclaim than he gets, Jim Broadbent has gone on to have a great career in more important roles than he was given by his mentor then. Such is life, but thanks guys for your wonderful shows. Absolutely hilarious they were.

Lately my attendance at plays has diminished. I enjoyed Nigel Hawthorne at the National Theatre proper (not Brent) in *The Madness of George III* by Alan Bennett. Also there I saw Griff Rhys Jones in *The Wind in the Willows* and Simon Russell Beale in *Collatorators*.

Concerts over the years have featured little – there was that great one in Atlanta, Georgia with J. J. Cale. And on an earlier trip to the USA, Bill Withers singing 'Lean on Me' at a Madison Square Garden concert in New York. Terrific song. Other memorables were Genesis in Earl's Court, Steve Winwood outside Cirencester, the Beach Boys and the Eagles at Wembley where I left before Elton John appeared. I've never been to a festival … don't fancy the tent element! A few classical concerts yes – Handel's *Messiah* in the Royal Festival Hall, Fauré's *Requiem* and Mozart pieces in Southwark Cathedral. My children are much more adventurous concert and festival goers.

Hope I'm not boring you. Just a few words on my physical health – no more frightening mental health moments. Generally sound of body – Asian flu at the age of four led to a week's convalescence up in Trearddur Bay on Anglesey at nanny Phil's cottage by the sea with blackberry bushes behind I remember. Chickenpox one Christmas aged eleven

or so – broken leg just above Les Ruinettes in Verbier, Switzerland aged fifteen … back at school within five days, hobble hobble on crutches. Annoying mole just above my upper lip that was removed (at BUPA's expense for just the once) by a Mr Volkers in Hans Place in 1980 – I often used to nick it when shaving so I'm pleased it has gone. A bout of mumps in the early nineties … always worrying for older men as it can cause impotence. There was a bit of a disquieting time early in the noughties when GP Michael encouraged me to get a melanoma-type blemish on my chest checked out. Expertly removed under local anaesthetic at the Royal Marsden in South Kensington. Tests later showed it wasn't a cancerous melanoma but a benign naevus. No real problems until very recently when I suffered a detached retina (not recommended) with consequent cataract surgery from which I slowly recover. Diabetes is an issue as my blood sugar readings are at 6.7, now three times in a row. But, and this may astonish you, I have never taken a course of antibiotics in my life. Just had to administer quite a few antibiotic eye drops into the left eye. I am still the proud owner of all my tonsils, adenoids and appendix. Teeth got filled with that mercury amalgam on London childhood visits to super-expensive Mr Simon on Park Street, Mayfair – filled too often probably, but that was what happened in those days. Sister Anne visited the practice for many subsequent years – I've long since migrated to NHS dentists on Webb's Road, Battersea who said I needed some dental hygienist attention. It's cheaper down Witney way, so I have just moved allegiances to a place on Corn Street.

Foibles or idiosyncrasies in childhood years included not stepping on the cracks in paving stones (mostly up in London as Stow-on-the-Wold and Moreton-in-Marsh were light on such slabs), a somewhat unusual trait of lining up man-made features when travelling by train or car … sort of eyesight ley-lines joining say telegraph poles with church spires, and when at Cothill I used to experiment with balancing acts. This involved twirling a golf club resting atop another golf club poised on a finger – and those diabolos were fun too, a large spinning rubber egg-cup launched into the air from two wooden batons joined by string, the idea being to catch the thing on taut string as it returned towards earth.

Hobbies can be a bit embarrassing – Rod Stewart not too bad with his model trains. King Abdullah of Jordan is a *Star Trek* 'Trekkie'. Angelina Jolie collects daggers. Mine started with toy soldiers on the cork-tiled nursery floor at North Rye, which I would align on the battlements of my fort and then shoot down with bits of matches shoved into the barrels of my artillery guns. There was a garage too, with a ramp to its upper level, and I had a great assortment of vehicles – the best were the Corgi ones with their sophisticated suspension, bestest of all was the James Bond Aston Martin DB5 with its ejector seat – these we hurtled down the corridors at Cothill. There was a bit of stamp collecting, more of Triang train set action on the pull-down table top at home and Scalextric – but these latter two often suffered mechanical breakdowns. In my first years at Eton I became a nerdy plane spotter – easy to note registrations of incoming Heathrow aeroplanes as we were on the flight path. One crossed off sightings in an Ian Allen Civil Aircraft book. In the holidays I might demand to spend time at Oxford Airport or even at the Queen's Building by Terminal 2 at Heathrow. Sad innit.

In the seventies and eighties handling one of those two-string Peter Powell kites was always fun and challenging. Oh, for a blustery day in the New Forest or on Clapham Common. Since the early nineties I have become a very amateur picture framer, carpenting my own frames, cutting my own glass (not easy I can assure you), securing prints with nails or staples and sticky brown tape. It's a skill I have yet to master.

Food – we haven't mentioned food. Mum was a very talented cook and she has passed on her skills to Anne, Carole, Kitten and a bit to me. Anne has done many thousands of meals for her children and grandchildren and evening entrées for her B&B guests. Carole too – she has recipes published in Hugh Fearnley-Whittingstall's mother's cookbook. Kitten produces a lavish meal every night for her husband Mickey and whoever pops in.

Mum often gave dinner parties – her specialities were Russian salad (a macédoine of vegetables with mayonnaise), jellied consommés, the ubiquitous egg mousse of the sixties, little 'oeufs en cocottes', poached in those ceramic containers with metal screw-tops and endive salads (that's chicory) – masses of vegetables and soft fruits came from the well-tended (by Dad) quarter-acre patch close to the house. I spent many hours in the fruit cage gorging on succulent gooseberries, tart red and blackcurrants, raspberries, loganberries and strawberries. There was rhubarb, earthed-up potatoes, rows of carrots, spinach, lettuces, a crab-apple tree and a much-used incinerator. He loved his horticulture. For family meals there was usually cooked cold meat in the larder, scrambled eggs with chives (when we had chickens un-slaughtered by the ghastly foxes), home-baked cakes – a beautiful raspberry cream sponge would come my way for my birthday spent at Cothill. Because Mum was busy busy exercising horses and what have you, lunch would often be delegated to our cook, Mrs White, the wife of handyman Mr White, Brian I think his name was. He was a rough diamond. The jobs came with free accommodation in a bungalow by the covered riding school. She made a fabulous barley pudding that I have never quite replicated. When the Whites left, Rose and Percy Lisseman took their places.

Picnics were assembled when we headed off to some horse event far and wide – there was cold Vichyssoise soup, that yummy leek and potato concoction kept cool in thermoses, sandwiches, scotch eggs, hard-boiled eggs with Knorr Aromat and celery salt, bread rolls with Anchor butter, Cox's apples and cheese. The Humber Super Snipe, which we had before an assortment of Ford Zephyrs and Volvo Estates, was my favourite (although the Commer horsebox with its secret sleeping slot above the front seats was rather fun). It had fold-down varnished wood little shelves for back-seat passengers. For picnics we had comfortable tiger-skin patterned rugs. Apple cores were always appreciated by our horses and ponies, Mervyn, Fred, Cashla, Lady Astor or whoever.

Dad couldn't boil an egg which is actually quite hard to get right anyway. But every morning he did make the breakfast tray with perhaps a slice of melon or a segmented grapefruit which he carried upstairs to the master bedroom. He was rather pathetically proud of this service. They rose early – there is much to do on a 350-acre farm with horses, some livestock, and orders to be given to Len Clark and Roy Williams our farmworkers. Mrs Clark was our cleaner and great fun.

In my brief time in the Cadogan Square mews house, supper would be prepared by Helga on trays – she did her best with cottage pies and pots of yoghurt. Out in Portugal the fare was generally tomato and onion salad for lunch, warmed-up brown rolls and Castelões cheese with merme-lada, the firm quince jelly. Supper may have been grilled sardines and salad or perhaps a venture out to the excellent La Cigale restaurant in Olhos d'Agua for fresh tuna steaks and chocolate mousse.

During the day one could feast on the fabulous black and green figs, particularly on the third and fourth holes of the Vale do Lobo course. All for free … well, once you had paid the green fee. Silvina, our occasional cook and cleaner, sometimes walked over with one of her, dare I say it, unpleasant sponge cakes which used to contain a whole unpeeled egg!

Not that my early baking skills were much better – I once managed to make a Victoria sponge cake forgetting to include the flour – yuk, disgusting. Mum's cookery bible became mine too, that Katie Stewart one I have mentioned. These days I might also dip into Prue Leith and Caroline Waldegrave's comprehensive compendium. In my minicab days I once drove Caroline and once Mary Berry. Other chefs were also transported – thankfully not that Gordon Ramsay who I dislike.

When I moved out to my own flat at age eighteen, I installed a massive double gas oven in the tiny galley kitchen. Terrines and pizzas, chicken-brick chicken (that was a craze then, those terracotta receptacles from Habitat), crumbles and more tumbled out of these ovens. Then moving to Battersea in 1977 allowed more innovations – there was a useful internal barbecue housed in an old chimney flue in the kitchen where I could grill kebabs, burgers, steaks, whatever. Before growing marijuana in the garden one year we had a crop of globe artichokes which made good, if fart-inducing, soup.

Plenty of dinner parties took place there – most with joints being passed round afterwards. Quiche was always a good stand-by with baked potatoes and a salad. With my Magimix, I could rustle up pastry quickly – 8oz of half organic wholemeal bread flour and half unbleached white, 4oz nice unsalted butter, Wheelbarrow then, Président these days. Whizz whizz until crumbly, add cold water till it forms a ball round the blade. Leave 30 minutes in the fridge then roll out.

Puddings varied between plum and almond flan, apple strüdel, trifle, bread and butter pudding, lemon mousse ... all from Katie Stewart's book. I'm a big fan of cheese so there would probably be a large platter of say Roquefort,

Camembert, Brie and a slab of Cheddar with seedless grapes, oatcakes and if feeling rich, some Bath Olivers.

In later years, dinner parties continued at Atheldene Road – added to the repertoire was Hugh F-W's fish pie recipe, a bit long-winded but jolly good. Turns out that Hugh was one of Robert Hardy's last pupil intakes at Eton when I had been among the first. Always I would make some bread rolls, past my baking career now, usually half Granary flour half white. Pommes Lyonnaise was often on offer or Dauphinoise as I erroneously tend to call the dish – slices of organic potato (Eve Balfour variety), sliced onions, layered with herbs from the garden, salt and peppered, dotted with butter and then doused with mixed milk and cream before baking for nearly two hours in a medium oven. A summer starter might well have been cold cucumber and mint soup. More exotic was crab mousse (mostly white meat) made with leaf gelatine with an aspic top and trellised criss-cross chives set inside. A bit of a showstopper when and if one turned it out of the tin successfully.

When the girls came to stay on a Friday night, they liked pasta dishes and yoghurts with watery Ribena or similar. Sounds mean doesn't it, but they seem healthy enough these days. I seem to have avoided poisoning anyone over the years – only myself with the occasional overdose of alcohol. On moving up to Wandsworth Common my kitchen was 15 yards from the huge sitting room which wasn't ideal, but we had plenty of fun evenings there too. The wine always flowed.

A summer supper dish might be salad niçoise, always a pleasure to look at and eat. And a stock dish of mine is baked eggs … get a small Le Creuset or similar, chop some mush-rooms and smoked streaky bacon. Add a knob of butter and shove in the oven. When sizzling, add cooked spinach if you wish, then break two eggs into scooped holes, add double cream and pepper and bake for another five minutes or so. Good with oatcakes on the side.

I once held a large drinks party down at Atheldene Road, buying 120 IKEA glasses (cheaper and nicer than renting them), making six or seven types of canapé and helped by two friends' children who served the food and wine. We had red and white Viña Sol from Spain which proved very adequate on a sale or return basis from Sainsbury's. It was that evening that friends Bolla Denehy and Jimmy C-G expressed their appreciation of me in a kind way – affirming indeed.

I am running out of things to tell you. My clothes are a bit shabby, I loaf around in jeans, T-shirts and trainers, smartening up into a Charles Tyrwhitt shirt and jacket for Sunday church, the 11 a.m. at Swinbrook, where the Mitford sisters are buried and with its ancient reclining stone Fettiplace monuments in the nave. Great vicars, great congregation, great music: Hilary on keyboards, David on guitar. Sometimes we have a trumpeter and always at least two hymns that I know.

It is always a pleasure to be asked to do a reading – Swinbrook has a large-print Bible which helps. My own reading of Bible passages is limited nowadays to a daily dose of scripture guided by the wonderful quarterly booklet which comes from Carnforth in Lancashire, *Our Daily Bread*. Each day one is alerted to a little chunk from either Old or New Testaments with a relevant testimony from modern times appended.

As regards prayer, I am not the world's greatest adherent. Perhaps reliant too much on His words in Mark 12 verses 38–40 when He was actually referring to self-important people like lawyers … "Watch out for the teachers of the law. They like to walk around in flowing robes and be greeted with respect … and have the most important seats in the synagogue and the places of honour at banquets. For a show they make lengthy prayers." (NIV.) Okay, so don't overdo the praying methinks, but there again, "Ask and it shall be given" was His general advice. As a child I would kneel beside my bed at night and say my prayers – the power of prayer can be awesome, I should use it more.

I still drop in at Southwark Cathedral whenever I can, monthly or more to Geoff Coyne's Thursday quiz service at the Royal Hospital, sometimes to many friends connected to the thriving St Mary's Cogges in Witney and infrequently to the services at St Michael's, Leafield which we are hoping to rejuvenate by modernising its cavernous and cold interior. Back to Cogges briefly. There was another of those God-incidences not long ago. Andy McCullough, one of the curates, was studying up at St Mellitus College in London and had just been cogitating about me and my connection to Nicky Gumbel when wandering round Kensington Pond who should he run into. "You don't know me," he says, "but Jamie Summers I know in Witney." "Oh, Pippa and I are so fond of Jamie," says Nicky, a modern-day Billy Graham really, bringing 20 million souls to Christ. On holiday too I will seek out any Christian churches for a visit – it was at the Anglican church, St Peter and St Paul, in the back streets of Aqaba, Jordan where I first met vicar Adam Boulter, wife Beth and children Joseph, Hannah and recent arrival Benjamin. They then went to live in Ruffec, east of Bordeaux in France where Adam ministered to all Anglicans over a huge area. Now Adam is Area Dean in Toliara, Madagascar and teaching at the local Bible college.

How fascinating an upbringing for the children. It was young Joseph who coined my nickname for the title of this book. Thanks Joseph.

# 14

# WINE, WOMEN AND
# SONGS

We approach dangerous territory, at least with the first two words of this chapter heading, both of which have caused me grief over the years.

My first encounters with alcohol took place back in 1959 when we temporarily lived in Donnington village while North Rye House was being built a couple of miles away. Sister Kitten and I would find our parents' empty bottles put out for the dustbin-men and drink the dregs. Kids, eh. Sips of Mum's Dubonnet on early skiing holidays were nice, Dad preferred his Amontillado sherry in his especially capacious glass – when he moved in 1970 to Portugal his tipple became white port in the same generous measure. On reflection, one or two of these glasses full would render him squiffy and liable to slur his words. If only I had learned by observation as to how alcohol affects people.

The French apparently like to imbue their children gradually with the pleasures of wine, offering them watered-down versions from an early age. No such sense for the English – certainly not in our family. My first over-indulgence was a regrettable incident at the 100$^{th}$ anniversary of my prep school. Several of us had come from Eton on a bus – towards the end of the afternoon a couple of us discovered a stash of champagne at the back of the marquee set up on the main football pitch – we stole a bottle or two, shame shame and I recall being sick on the 'Burning Bush' plinth outside the library as soon as our bus returned to Eton. I am sure George Pike, Cothill's Headmaster, was aware of our crime, but he kindly chose to let it pass.

There was an amusing incident a few years later at school – each house at Eton had two tiers of prefects, 'debate' and 'library', effectively Junior and Senior Common Rooms. At the end of 1972, the 'library' of RHH (Robert Hardy's house) comprised unusually four members of Pop – Julian Hill, Philip Remnant, me and Dave Profumo plus a few others, Bob Spencer-Churchill among them. For some reason Julian's father had given him two bottles of Château Palmer 1934, a particularly good year for claret. A bottle of this Margaux these days would set you back over £500 and I believe it still 'drinks well'. There we were in our special room that evening – the room from where after lunch we used to dispatch 'fags' on various slave errands around the school buildings in our arrogant elitist way – when the door opens, and our housemaster, 'Boot' was his nickname, enters.

This is more than embarrassing for all concerned – he is newish in the role of housemaster, what we are doing is against the rules, indeed a felony meriting rustication (temporary expulsion) or even expulsion itself but he is confronted with several seventeen-year-olds at the top of Eton's tree. A very awkward silence ensues before graciously he says, "Well, aren't you going to offer me a glass?" He was a timid man with a weak voice remorselessly mimicked by the talented thespian Dave. RHH was a Latin master, educated at Winchester, recently married to a much younger lady, Penny. He later left to become Headmaster of Monkton Combe, a venerable institution deep in Dorset.

Anyhow, 'claret-gate' resolved itself amicably. I think Mr Hardy was proud of the achievements of his charges and had not wanted to upset the proverbial apple cart, or 'noli turbitur pupillam cart' as he might say.

Funnily enough Julian's future wife featured in my next brush with alcohol. Dad had moved to a mews house off Cadogan Square in London and to a villa on the Vale do Lobo golf course in Portugal's Algarve soon after my mother's death. The latter house was a great place to invite friends for holidays. There was plenty of other youth from our posh public-school-educated 'tribe' also holidaying in the area. Vale do Lobo was Portugal's equivalent of Rock in Cornwall.

One night we gathered on the beach to barbecue a chicken, drink Dão Grão Vasco and memorably a flagon of cheap Portuguese brandy. Janie Robinson, later Janie Hill, was one of the participants along with Sarah Harding (a Cheshire Wirral girl I fancied), my mate Charlie Phillips and I'm sure Caroline Farr and others. Tragically the roasted chicken got dropped in the sand and thus my stomach was unlined for the onslaught of brandy that came its way. Dangerous stuff is brandy, well at least when over-indulged, but thankfully Charlie was able to carry / drag the comatose / nigh-unconscious idiot back to the villa.

Back in my Oxford days I was drinking bottles of 1972 Pommard from the Christ Church buttery (bar by the Hogwarts dining hall) along with the House port, all of which I was able to sign for, to be paid at the end of each term by my Trustees – spoilt little rich kid again. At drinks parties or at golf clubs I favoured vodka and tonic or whatever was on offer really! Royal St George's had particularly good Mâcon-Villages which is still one of my favourite white wines – I love its slight roughness in contrast to the bland creaminess of other Chardonnays or the bland blandness of a Pinot Grigio. These days I might favour a crisp New Zealand white Sauvignon Blanc, Villa Maria is top of the tree. Aldi, I have discovered do a marvellous red Douro from Portugal for under £5.

Over time vodka has given way to gin, of which nowadays there are so many varieties – my favourites are Hortus from Lidl, Hendrick's and Cotswolds which are twice the price so rarely consumed. The tonic used is so important and after trying many options it seems those little cans produced by Double Dutch (Waitrose only) are best with a slice of lime and chunks of ice. If you can't get these with their hint of orange then Schweppes will do.

During my first marriage and for many subsequent years, alcohol did not play a significant role. A bottle of spirits could and did last for ages. Oops, I almost forgot a vodka-gate incident. Dave Higgins and I attended the wedding of fast bowler Speno Collard and his Polish fiancée, Domenica, in Wrocław near the German border in the west of Poland. Beware these Polish weddings. The ceremonies took place mostly in the Art Hotel in central Wrocław. At teatime there were full bottles of Wyborowa or Zubrowka vodka on tables and we were encouraged to dig in. Neat vodka may suit the Russians, but I overdid it and after supper but before the dancing I crept / staggered back to my room upstairs to be seriously sick. Strangely, the next morning I felt right as rain, but it was an embarrassing adventure. Since about 2015 I have overdone the booze on a few more occasions. Once, on the day a relationship ended, I overdosed on wine and swayed home some four miles from a lunch party in Balham. On another occasion worse happened…

My lovely friend Suzanne, my vice-chair at Being Alongside / APCMH, had been to Guernsey and returned with a gift for me – a large bottle of local gin. At the time I was unaware of the different potencies of gin, from the standard 37.5% proof through the white-labelled Bombay Sapphire at 42% to this Guernsey version which I believe was 58%. It was Christmas time 2015. A friend was holding his traditional drinks party at his house in the Tonsleys, a smart little enclave of Old Wandsworth above Old York Road where 2 up 2 downs sell for £1 million – ridiculous but true. Equally ridiculous was my approach to this event. Because its start time was late, 7.30 onwards, I did something foolish and 'tanked up' pre-event with a couple of strong Guernseys and tonic, before tottering down the hill to the party and quaffing one of the generous G and Ts. Quite soon I was completely gaga, oblivious to my actions. I do recall saying something inappropriate about my friend Caroline Williams to her friend Jo King... I know, I am not joking, her name is indeed Jo King and she is fun, she doesn't take me too seriously.

If only someone had taken me aside, shown me the door and pointed me uphill back towards my flat, things would have been okay. But in this unconscious-of-my-actions state I apparently goosed or worse the wife of a close friend. He made me aware of this by email and phone the following day. Despite apologising profusely via email to both him and his wife I feel I have not been forgiven. I abased myself, as I should, but sadly that friendship seems to have gone. Despite being kind to him over many years and he has been supportive of me too, the gin cost me dear.

So that's about it for the completely blotto times with alcohol – there have been quite a few instances when I have been sick in the middle of the night after over-imbibing, usually red wine being the cause, me being the culprit. As I said it is post-2015 that coincides with the majority of my alcoholic misdemeanours – I must rein in consumption, it's not good for the waistline either. Whisky I've never really liked, except in a pudding where you use it to soak ginger biscuits before topping the mess with whipped cream. That wonderful thick sweet sherry, Pedro Ximénez, I use to make Katie Stewart's trifle out of her 1972 *Times Cookery Book*, my cooking bible. Marsala, a fortified wine from Sicily, is a bit special – I love Pollo or Vitello alla Marsala which I first ate up near the Via Vittorio Veneto in Rome. Beer, I can do without, although Shepherd Neame in a pewter tankard is good. A nice vintage cider sometimes, a wee glass of port (too much brings headaches) or use it in a gravy. Right, that's enough on the wine front, let's hit the women – no, let's not hit women. I have never hit a woman – they have hit me, however, thrown things at me, even spat at me. La di da.

How to broach the subject of my love life has been bothering me – my plan is to simply list chronologically those I 'dated' or at least fancied in the innocent days before sexual intercourse intervened to complicate matters. Later loves will perhaps merit a line or two, perhaps a paragraph or three but if it is embarrassing for me it may be mortifying for them … So, way back we go – I think the first girl I kissed was Caroline Sheldon (now a well-respected literary agent) at the Bourton-on-the-Hill school. In the Heythrop Pony Club days and even before there was Dinah Nabarro, AC with the long blonde hair, Alice Parshall (we had a mini grope in a hay barn), Carey Graham whose sister Juliet I re-met recently, then in Eton days we have Carina Hacking, Louise Foottit, Camilla Fane, Mary O'Brien out in Portugal and an unrequited crush on Sarah Harding. Once my virginity was lost at Christ Church, there was briefly Janie Stevenson then Mary Rose Chichester for many years. On returning to the UK from South America, my near neighbour in Battersea, Kitty Barrell, became very much part of my life and that of my house-mates. It was Kitty who gave me the silver cross that I wear to this day.

Before meeting Liduina Beckers there were brief liaisons with three ladies – if all this sounds like a loose morals existence I suspect it was, influenced as it was by my marijuana consumption. Things settled somewhat with Lid's arrival.

Lid was of Dutch heritage, her dad running the Flixborough chemical works up near Scunthorpe, where an explosion in 1974 had killed twenty-eight people and injured over a hundred. Like Johnny, Lid had been involved with the Exegesis 'therapy cult' run by Robert D'Aubigny (real name Fuller) which enveloped Tubular Bells musician Mike Oldfield and even Cherie Blair's guru Carole Caplin. It ruined many lives – a faux 'messiah' who convinced many of the virtues of his Exegesis programme, and duped up to 5,000 members. Lid became a little over-dependent on me, never healthy, and cruelly I parted company with her just days after meeting the lady who would become my wife at a King's Road party given by Rupert Johnson.

S had been at Southampton University with Rupert's friend Jerry Hemans and I found her very attractive and suitably sporty – we honed our early relationship with games of tennis up in London and down at Lepe near Lymington, Hampshire where I was co-renter of a little cottage with Sue Gernaey and her dog, Rufus. S soon moved in to Altenburg Gardens from her flat in Sands End, Fulham and we were married some two and a half years after meeting. I think I have explored our time together enough, particularly the acrimonious ending, but it certainly wasn't all doom and gloom. Lots of holidays before marriage and before our two daughters arrived, honeymoon in Mexico, Belize and Guatemala, long-stay sojourns in Jamaica and Thailand, shorter ones in Portugal, Ireland and Cornwall.

Around the time of my divorce I had another relationship which didn't work out. A long period of abstinence followed as I slowly got my life together, working first at Consumer Forum and then as a minicab driver as you know. Tikka the greyhound became my best friend and I took the care of my children seriously whenever they came to stay or when we went on holiday, skiing, boating, Disney World, whatever. So, it must have been around late 2012 that I began to think it's time to smarten my act up, take an interest in perhaps finding a partner again – did I want to be alone in my dotage? Seclusion was verging on loneliness.

In the previous chapter I mentioned D who escorted the delightful deaf duo, Henry and Isla, to their St Pancras school. Her sweet way with them impressed me much and I made a futile attempt at developing our own relationship. Sometimes we would be able to spend time wandering round Regent's Park enjoying each other's company, as we passed the hours before taking the children back to Fulham. Polish D was a lesbian, however, and my efforts at converting her to heterosexuality came to naught. She did say that I was the nicest man she had ever met, which was encouraging.

I began to rely on mutual friends to introduce me to Mrs Right, perhaps at dinner parties, but it never panned out that way. I had taken a shine to zany Sandra, for whom I did much private driving and helping out, setting up her fur-selling rails at shows around town. My romantic interest never developed the way I had hoped. Her son I introduced to the LJs cricket side and took to play golf at Swinley – boo, this never got me any nearer his mother's charms.

Around this time too I took a massive shine to C who I'd met at a dinner party given by our mutual friend Sarah at her new house close to the Petersham Meadows. I have a tendency to fall in love too quickly and this time was no exception. C I then invited to supper at my place – next was a 'date' at PizzaExpress, East Sheen which led to her inviting me back to her Mortlake flat for 'coffee'.

It was early days in my efforts at self-improvement and I was still overweight and somewhat ashamed of my body shape. When the beautiful C launched herself at me as I moved to leave, I chose to parry her advances and make my excuses. This must have been a first for her and I probably did not explain the reason for my reticence. Our relation-ship stumbled on for a few more days – a picnic in Kew Gardens, an outing to see the film *One Day* (the book by David Nicholls is better) in Richmond and the whole thing went wrong after I took her down to my roots in Gloucestershire. We were shown round North Rye House and its gardens by the current owners, the Stoddart family who have nurtured it well. Lunch we had with Francis and Georgie Mander who have converted the old Ludlow farm buildings into their comfortable Heath Barn home. We walked with Frankie around Crowthorne Wood to the River Evenlode – a wallow in nostalgia for me, but all too much for C. The drive back to London was conducted in silence – I had moved too fast and she never spoke to or contacted me again. Even enlisting the help of my stepsister Hutchy in scripting a letter got us nowhere – no reply ever received. Very bright, she had been on the board of a big company and is now a successful therapist. It seemed to me that a mutual friend put an end to my reconciliation attempts – why I am not sure, but perhaps C and I were unlikely to have enough in common to survive as a couple. Enya's music she found mournful and gloomy for instance – not my take on it, I find it spiritually uplifting.

Quite a few of my past girlfriends have been educated at Heathfield School near Ascot where few alumnae reach Ivy League potential. There followed one such liaison before an altogether more serious adventure – one that I thought would lead to marriage. At an October 2013 drinks party given by Bristol University pal Anthony Daniell and his wife, Sarah, at that great venue the Chelsea Gardener on Sydney Street, there were many of my friends from university days. Danielli had invited most of his Bristol muckers … Piers F-A, Julian Hill, Rupert Johnson, Robin Eggar, Andrew Mitchell and there lurking in a verdant corner was S, looking good. We exchanged a few words, not having seen each other for years and I was brave enough to scribble my phone and email on a piece of paper in the hope of a lengthier meeting down the line. This was despite Robin Eggar telling her, "For God's sake don't give him your details" out of my earshot. Why he is so against me I know not – he has featured elsewhere in this book.

So, soonish, we arrange a date up in town at a slightly more salubrious venue than a PizzaExpress where we bonded nicely before parting company after bussing back to downtown Wandsworth – she giving me a soft kiss before heading to Putney to stay with a sister, me going south to Earlsfield. The following morning, I was at London Bridge station off for a day's pilgrimage to Canterbury with Southwark Cathedral people when a text pings in to say, "Good morning dear heart" and we are up and running.

By now I have stopped minicabbing and am into my property development phase. S's home town is Farnham where I spend much time, eventually buying a flat there to do up. S is highly intelligent, writes exceptionally well and held a high position on the *Observer*.

But we thrive for many months, holidaying in Sri Lanka, Austria and the South of France until pretty suddenly, a year into our affair, she decides, "It has run its course." Funnily enough it became obvious that curtains were drawing when we went to Anthony and Sarah Daniell's big fancy dress dance in Dorset, and it seemed to me that I was cold-shouldered most of the evening.

I was not making her happy and I was ditched. A few weeks later I return to take her out to lunch and to help in the garden. We go for a long walk in adjacent Farnham Park. "Jesus was a con-man, taking money from people … of course he didn't exist. The Bible is a fairy tale," she says. Strange that one so intelligent should have such erroneous ideas. I reminded her of Josephus the Roman historian who documented Jesus' exploits in Judea.

Crazily perhaps, I still wanted to be with this woman. I bided my time for six or seven months, towards the end of which time we were exchanging emails and texts. I decided to buy her a Mini Cooper to replace her ageing Golf and on return from a trip to Aqaba in Jordan I drove it down to Farnham. It soon became apparent that I had totally misread her signals and she firmly dismissed any notion of together-ness. Nearly two years later I get a text saying that it is time I took back 'our' car. This I do, eventually selling it below market value to someone in the neighbouring village – its sunroof was a noisy problem. Anyroads, mistake mistake to buy one's ex-girlfriend a car, however kind and generous you think you are being.

Freud said, "The great question that has never been answered and which I have not yet been able to answer, despite my thirty years of research into the feminine soul, is 'What does a woman want?'" My friend Peggy Brown at Southwark Cathedral, almost ninety-two years old said, "She doesn't know what's good for her."

Men are from Mars, women are from Venus is putting it strongly, but differences are often irreconcilable. I recently came across Richard Rohr's take on male and female charac-teristics, the inner King contrasting with the inner Queen. Our animus and our anima are not mutually exclusive but true meeting of minds and souls is hard to achieve. It was ever thus.

Post this saga, I guess I should fess up to another unre-quited effort with Wandsworth neighbour Caroline Wil-liams, who chose to concentrate on her daughters although we had some fun and close encounters. It seems she was a bit frightened by my 'religiousness', although I prefer to call it spirituality. It was time to try internet dating, the modern lonely-hearts column, and something I had spotted on a tube-train hoarding caught my attention ... christiancon-nection.com ... let's give that a go.

Right, it's time to change focus onto the songs element of this chapter.

Music never mattered much to my parents. They had one of those Hacker wooden boxes and would occasionally load it up with *Gigi, Stop the World, I Want to Get Off, Carousel, Camelot* or other big musical LPs. I enjoyed Tchaikovsky's '1812 Overture' and would leap around the furniture in conductor mode, but the first record I bought for myself (6 shillings and 8 pence I think it cost) was 'The Pied Piper' by Crispian St Peters in 1966.

I had hoped to include here the first verse of 'The Pied Piper' but Hal Leonard who owns the copyright wanted a minimum of $300 so I didn't think it was worthwhile. If you are curious, you can always Google the lyrics.

Or perhaps the first record I bought was 'Get Off of My Cloud' by the Rolling Stones, which I remember buying when staying with my Cothill friend Mike Barnard at his guardians' place at Westcliff-on-Sea, Essex as his parents lived on St Vincent in the Windward Islands.

Mum enjoyed 'The Windmills of Your Mind' by Noel Harrison from that film *The Thomas Crown Affair*. Dad preferred anything by Noël Coward but overall we were an atonal unmusical family, despite owning an 1813 Broadwood square piano that may have been played by Ludwig van Beethoven.

A quick word or two on hymns. Many have such evocative phrases set to fantastic tunes. Mum's favourite was 'There is a Green Hill Far Away' by Mrs C. F. Alexander, possibly because she had lived on that very hill off the Nablus Road in Jerusalem in World War II. My early favourites were 'Onward Christian soldiers / Marching as to war' and 'The day thou gavest Lord has ended / The darkness falls at thy behest'. Later I grew to love 'I vow to thee my country', the first verse encouraging us to be patriotic, the second bringing us closer to God. I must mention too 'Immortal Invisible' and the Cwm Rhondda classic, 'Guide me, O thou Great Redeemer / pilgrim through this barren land'.

At Eton I had a Decca turntable and speakers (cost me £70 which was almost my whole term's allowance) and would regularly visit the Audiocraft shop up the High Street where one could listen to an album before buying. Canned Heat, the Woodstock albums, *Aladdin Sane* by Bowie, Simon & Garfunkel, John Fahey, Donovan, Cat Stevens and some embarrassing purchases like 'Ernie (The Fastest Milkman in the West)' by Benny Hill. Sister Kitten at one stage was going out with Peter Schuster who had been at Charterhouse with the Genesis founder members, Peter Gabriel, Mike Rutherford, Tony Banks, Steve Hackett, Anthony Phillips and Chris Stewart. Peter had somehow given Kitten about fifty copies of their first album, 'From Genesis to Revelation' which were piled up in the Ebury Street flat. Not sure what happened to them – copies retail at £40 each these days.

Subsequently I have become a massive Genesis fan but in my Oxford days it was the Beach Boys – Simon Foster and I would blast out 'Good Vibrations' from our Peck Quad windows to entertain / annoy the tourists below. An 8-track player in my BMW limited the music on offer but I recall 'Close to the Edge' by Yes. When cassettes came along one could then record stuff to play and choice improved.

A while back I made lists of my Top Ten songs in 1980 and my Top Ten in 2011. So here goes…

1980
Peter Gabriel – Solsbury Hill
Beach Boys – Good Vibrations
Fleetwood Mac – Rhiannon
Neil Young – Out on the Weekend
Supertramp – Dreamer
T. Rex – Hot Love
J. J. Cale – Ride Me High
New Musik – Living by Numbers
Pretenders – Brass in Pocket
Allman Brothers – Jessica

Two others came close to making the grade…
Mungo Jerry – In the Summertime
Kraftwerk – Autobahn


2011:
Peter Gabriel – Solsbury Hill
Genesis – Carpet Crawlers
Genesis – No Son of Mine
Mozart – Piano Concerto No. 21
Enya – If I Could Be Where You Are
Enya – Caribbean Blue
Steve Winwood – High Life Again
Streets – Dry Your Eyes
Mike + The Mechanics – Taken In
Sinéad O'Connor – Nothing Compares 2U & This IS a
    Rebel Song (equal)
Close to the list were a few more:
Gabriel Fauré – Pie Jesu / Sanctus
Sting – Every Breath You Take
Fleetwood Mac – Rhiannon
Nicola Benedetti – Carmen Fantasie
Joan Osborne – One of Us
Genesis – Shipwrecked
Marianne Faithfull – Ballad of Lucy Jordan


I should explain some of my choices. Solsbury Hill I clearly
hold high, those lyrics speak to me, here they are in full:

>                Climbing up on Solsbury Hill
>                I could see the city light
>                Wind was blowing, time stood still
>                Eagle flew out of the night
>                He was something to observe
>                Came in close, I heard a voice
>                Standing, stretching every nerve

I had to listen, had no choice
I did not believe the information
Just had to trust imagination
My heart going boom, boom, boom
"Son", he said, "Grab your things
I've come to take you home." ... *April Fool*

To keep in silence, I resigned
My friends would think I was a nut
Turning water into wine
Open doors would soon be shut
So I went from day to day
Though my life was in a rut
'Til I thought of what I'd say
Which connection I should cut
I was feeling part of the scenery
I walked right out of the machinery
My heart going boom, boom, boom,
"Hey", he said, "Grab your things
I've come to take you home."
Hey, back home.

When illusion spin her net
I'm never where I want to be
And liberty she pirouette
When I think that I am free
Watched by empty silhouettes
Who close their eyes but still can see
No one taught them etiquette
I will show another me
Today I don't need a replacement
I'll tell them what the smile on my face meant
My heart going boom, boom, boom
"Hey", I said, "You can keep my things
They've come to take me home."

There are a couple of words he sings at the end of the first verse which sound like "April fool" but they don't appear on 'Googled' lyric versions. I have thus put them in italics. This song was Peter Gabriel's opening salvo in his solo career on leaving Genesis in 1975 – the lines, "I was feeling part of the scenery / I walked out of the machinery" apparently reflect his emotions of feeling trapped in the projected rut of planned gigs and tours for the band's next eighteen months. But, goodness me, what about the rest of the lyrics? To me they sound like his walk and talk with God – that 'April fool' bit questioning whether these auditory hallucinations (as psychiatry would have it) are just fleeting figments or the real McCoy.

"To keep in silence I resigned" mirrors my own advice to self and others when in a manic flow. Overt behaviour and speech are likely to result in a visit from the men in white coats so keep schtum, that German / Yiddish word for quiet. These wonderful words crafted as he climbed that hill outside Bath echo my thoughts and feelings as I set off that night to raise Mary Rose from the dead, explained in Chapter 8. That episode landed me in the Priory where I first heard the New Musik song and its lyric about counting the days but questioning whether it adds up to you.

Some of these selected songs are just happy bopalong numbers but I guess it's those with powerful lyrics that really hit my spot. This all links in with the next chapter talking about my spiritual journey – the depth of the Holy Spirit suffusing through Enya's compositions is awe-inspiring, Roma Ryan's lyrical librettos adding to Enya's mystical magistery. I wrote to Enya once back in 1992, just about my only letter to a celebrity, informing her that her music spoke to God.

Then I remember the hairs on the back of my neck ruffling up when I first heard Joan Osborne's extraordinary words in her 1995 'One of Us'. I was in the main room of that drop-in centre in Hammersmith … let's remind ourselves of some of that song:

> If God had a name what would it be?
> And would you call it to His face?
> If you were faced with Him in all His glory
> What would you ask if you had just one question?
> What if God was one of us?
> Just a slob like one of us
> Just a stranger on the bus
> Tryin' to make His way home?

Originally written and recorded by Eric Bazilian of the Hooters I learn, it calls us to stay alert in anticipation of Christ's return. Matthew 24 verse 44 (NIV)… "So you also must be ready, because the Son of Man will come at an hour when you do not expect him." He will come like a thief in the night – and consider this, would you recognise Him? Jesus warned us to be careful, to beware false messiahs, a.k.a. David Koresh, some of those American evangelists parodied in the Genesis track 'No Son of Mine', Robert D'Aubigny / Fuller and that Jonestown, Guyana creep … there are so many candidates. And when He comes again in 'glory' he's more likely to be down there with the downtrodden, and Heaven help him if he proclaims himself to be at God's right hand because they'd be after him with that syringe of anti-psychotic medication.

So, last updated in 2011, what other tracks might I add to the list some nine years on? Something by Guy Garvey's Elbow without doubt – perhaps 'The Birds' from the *Build a Rocket Boys!* album. He's a talented man; happens he was at school in Milnrow near Rochdale with friends of mine.

Other candidates would be:

Frightened Rabbit – Old Old Fashioned

Arcade Fire – Neon Bible
Editors – Nothing

I am grateful to daughter P who alerts me to these modern bands. C's taste in music is generally less my style, although we all like The National.

Anything by Mozart has risen up my chart, bits of Bach, less of Beethoven but I am a philistine as regards classical music. Supertramp's 'Child of Vision' I love, terrific piano playing ... but once again I cannot give you even one verse because despite months and months of trying to get permission from Universal Music I failed. It took their London office over three months to say they didn't hold the rights (and only after I had visited their post-room in the vaults of their fancy King's Cross place to leave a chaser to my original letter). Well actually they do hold the European rights but their US office simply don't answer emails so I have given up asking for worldwide coverage.

Leonard Cohen would get a slot in today's list – his superb last album offers a host of opportunities, perhaps I would choose 'Steer Your Way'. You can hear his quest to find Jesus from his Judaic roots – great gravelly voice and songs that many find depressing but most I find enlightening. Wow, listen to his 'Democracy' ... "is coming to the USA".

Have I bored you enough with my Desert Island Discs? Apologies, but isn't the English-speaking world brilliant at music and what a vital part of life it is. At home, in the car, on the beach or sun-lounger with CD player and headphones on, it sustains me, nourishes me. Those cassette tapes used to get mangled in machines, CDs get scratched and jump about, TV pictures get pixelated (certainly on our telly) but we should rejoice at this digital age. Pity those poor souls toiling under the Taliban or Wahhabiism doctrine who are denied the pleasure of music. It's 'haram' (forbidden) they assert.

I was hoping to close this chapter with lyrics from Emily Hodder's favourite song that framed her funeral. Sung so well by Ellie Goulding but which originally featured in Richard Curtis' great film *About Time* when sung by Sam Sweeney, Jon Boden and Ben Coleman, written by Mike Scott. But sadly my request to use the lyrics was turned down. So, if you want to read his words you will have to visit your preferred search engine. I termed the song a paean of praise to Jesus, but Mr Scott may have had someone else in mind.

# 15

# MY SPIRITUAL JOURNEY
– HE CHOSE ME

We come to probably the most important chapter of this book and I am writing these words in the library of La Ferme de Trosly, an oasis of peace, just yards from Jean Vanier's little home. Dear Jean had languished in a Paris hospital since November 2018 weakened by surgery and developing cancers and sadly passed away in early May 2019. The great man was an inspiration to millions over his ninety-plus years on earth. Recently a darker side to Jean's character has emerged following an internal L'Arche inquiry into his predatory sexual relationships with several women between 1970 and 2005. Sadly one has had to re-evaluate the man in the light of these revelations. But let us love the sinner and hate the sin.

As I've said before I love working in libraries – at Cothill I spent time reorganising the shelves, marking book spines in indelible ink with the first three letters of the authors' names – not a good idea, particularly with the quality of my script at the time. I am somewhat averse to writing inside books too, but it's probably okay if done in pencil. Sister Kitten once showed me a copy of some intractable philosophical tome in which Mum had chosen to make some comments in the margins – this Kitten claimed was evidence of Mum's mental illness. Maybe, maybe not. At Eton I revised for A level and university entrance exams in the tucked-away Provost's Library, another oasis of calm in the cloisters between College Chapel and the Headmaster's lodgings. Most of these pages were crafted in the bibliothèque at L'Arche, Trosly-Breuil, others took shape in the Maxwell Library at the Royal Hospital for Neuro-disability, yet more in the library / sitting room of Jane Taylor's Mill House Retreat at Westleigh near Tiverton in Devon. It's the smell of ageing paper, being in the presence of millions nay billions of carefully thought-out words in French, English, German and Spanish. 'Print is dead', declared that teletext TV company Oracle back in the eighties. It was they that died on New Year's Eve 1992, their screen stating, "… 00:00 THE END OF ORACLE, NOW THE NIGHTMARE BEGINS!" Oracle lasted about fourteen years, books have lasted over 2,000 and look likely to last until the end of time.

So, baptised in August 1954 at St Lawrence Church, Bourton-on-the-Hill above Moreton-in-Marsh yet not 'confirmed' until April 2015 in Southwark Cathedral – the reason for that will emerge later. Every Sunday the Summers family would take their pew in St Paul's Church, Broadwell dressed in their Sunday best. At Cothill it was the Sunday crocodile in grey flannels and maroon caps to St Helen's Church in Dry Sandford, at Eton first in Lower Chapel then for older boys in College Chapel there were often daily prayers as well as regular Sunday services. There we were blessed with charismatic priests, Peter Pilkington and Roger Royle prominent.

But it was at Cothill that my Christian journey really begins with those tears in the torchlight under the bedclothes aged seven in my first dormitory. It was reading Matthew 27 that choked me up with its powerful evocative words…

> They spit on him, and took the staff and struck him on the head again and again … "save yourself! … if you are the Son of God!" … the chief priests, the teachers of the law and the elders mocked him. "He trusts in God. Let God rescue him now" … From noon until three in the afternoon darkness came all over the land … "Eli, Eli, lama sabachtani…" [My God, my God, why have you forsaken me?] … he gave up his spirit … the curtain of the temple was torn in two from top to bottom. The earth shook, the rocks split and the tombs broke open. (NIV)

I used to play those games with God – "Okay God, if you exist I want you to prove it by … let's say, make that candle over there on the windowsill fall over." Pause, nothing happens does it! He chooses rather more subtle ways to let you know He's there.

At school, university and after there are no further revelatory incidences of the God-induced kind until we come to those extraordinary days in January 1980 that I described in

Chapter 8. That is not to say I didn't lead a Christian life – I hope I did with most of my words and actions between the ages of seven and twenty-seven. There were obviously lapses in behaviour – at age fifteen, I wrote a rude letter to Wallace Heaton, the fancy London photography people, who had sent me an invoice intended for my father. No excuses, and it cost me a beating from the lower master, 'Bush' Forrest and a second rather creepy examination from Anthony Chenevix-Trench, the Headmaster. Well, perhaps an excuse might be found in the fact that my mother had recently died but that wasn't factored in by anyone.

On the whole, I trust I acted kindly to all I encountered. There was that voluntary afternoon with the Thursday Club doing the hokey cokey with learning disabilities people in Slough – oops, I recall another slip-up when we rearranged the gnomes in nearby gardens one Thursday. There was generally behaving as an ambassador for Britain when travelling the world – did something in my genetic inheritance kick in? You will remember that my maternal grandfather, Mark Patrick, had passed out top in the Civil Service exams going on to be 'our man in Switzerland' at the age of twenty-nine and First Secretary in the Moscow Embassy in his early thirties. For sure sometimes I was an arrogant tosser, but I tempered this with genuine attempts at a more measured humble approach to situations.

But God came to me big time in early 1980 and fired me up. I was keen to do His work. Psychiatrists were keen to slow me down and marijuana was a false god to worship, a craven image. Perhaps I put God on the back-burner during my first marriage – certainly church-going dwindled in the years between 1982 and 1992 ... Christmas and Easter attendance and not much else.

It was probably in 1983 that I became interested in the hypothesis proposed in the early chapters of *The Holy Blood and the Holy Grail*, namely that Mary Magdalene had settled in the South of France with the child or children of Jesus. This was the book written by Michael Baigent, Richard Leigh and Henry Lincoln and its paperback version came out in 1983. Later Baigent and Leigh took that Dan Brown (*Da Vinci Code* author) to court for plagiarism but the judge threw out their claims.

These were certainly cataclysmic ideas which caused much consternation in church circles. Heresy, preposterous piffle, many shouted but to me the premise seemed logical – poor Mary Magdalene gets meagre mention in the Gospels but that was the lot of women in those days. Her closeness to Jesus is obvious and it was she who first met the resurrected Christ. "Rabboni (teacher)", she calls him in John 20 verse 16. Indeed, it is women who surrounded Him at His death and rising – Mary, Joanna, Salome, His mother and others are named.

In the 1890s Bérenger Saunière, the priest of Rennes-le-Château up in the hills in lovely Cathar country, definitely found some sort of treasure in his church or cemetery. Gold coins, perhaps a chalice, perhaps documents relating to Christ and Mary Magdalene. Whatever; he became immensely rich as a result. The mystery remains unsolved. I visited the area in the summer of 2012 and a year later on holiday near St Tropez thought perhaps that Mary Magdalene had landed in a bay near there before heading inland.

Top candidate for me is Pramousquier between Le Lavan-dou and Cavalière-sur-Mer. Or maybe somewhere near Per-pignan which is closer to Rennes-le-Château? And why not? Me being me also entertains the notion that Jesus did indeed come to England with his great-uncle Joseph of Arimathea on one or more of Joseph's Cornish tin-mining trades. "And did those feet…" as in William Blake's hymn. It is reckoned that Joseph went again to Britain after the resurrection with St Philip and others and died at Glastonbury.

Back to my story … while recovering my sanity during and after that last admission to Springfield, it was then that church attendance blossomed again. There was that 'magi-cal' moment in the St Peter and St Paul's Church at Spring-field when a sort of inside-style St Elmo's fire illuminated and arose from that funeral coffin I chanced upon. I think it is worth revisiting some of my correspondence with that church's vicar, the mental health chaplain of Springfield at the time, Tony Yeldham, about whom I wrote in Chapters 1 and 9. Tony and I met again in the Westminster Abbey café and he remembered a visit made by my wife and sister Carole, who he mistakenly recalled as my mother.

In my July 1993 letter to Tony questioning the outcome of

that meeting with S and Carole, I explained why I sought his assistance. You can find the relevant extracts in the middle of Chapter 9. It took two and a half years and a 'chaser' to get a reply from Tony in which he at least said, "For my part, I valued your presence & contribution to the life of the chaplaincy at Springfield." Damned by faint praise a tad – it seems Tony Kyriakides-Yeldham, as he names himself these days, saw no touch of grace in me. Others have and do – for example Martin Peppiatt, missionary in East Africa once playing host to Corrie ten Boom before becoming vicar at St Stephen's, Twickenham and retiring close to me in the Cotswolds, who sees me as 'filled with the Holy Spirit'.

Sad to say, but my detractors outnumber my supporters. Mild disdain has come from sister Kitten – 'You're not normal. You need to see a doctor,' when I was teasing someone for having gone to Cambridge, and from her husband who felt I shouldn't go to post-earthquake Nepal. Nastier vibes emanated from that director at Prestige. Then, in an email sent to over forty fellow cricketers in the LJs squad before the season started in 2016, their captain writes: "Strange award: Jamie S." I replied to him (not 'reply all') straight away, saying, "You are stranger. But then we are advised to welcome the stranger … but perhaps that message passes you by."

The beleaguered Dean of Christ Church, Martyn Percy, spoke to those leaving the vicar training centre at Cuddesdon in June 2012 when he was Principal there – "… look for the Christ in the odd, the alien, the stranger, the awkward and the unexpected." In 1 Corinthians 1 verse 27, Paul tells us, "But God chose the foolish things of the world to shame the wise; God chose the weak things of the world to shame the strong." (NIV) The New Living Translation puts it as "… God chose things the world considers foolish in order to shame those who think they are wise. And he chose things that are powerless to shame those who are powerful."

The good old King James Version I like too – "But God hath chosen the foolish things of the world to confound the wise; and God hath chosen the weak things of the world to confound the things which are mighty."

This passage featured at Jean Vanier's funeral service, specially selected by the man himself, and was read in three languages, French, English and Arabic.

But I digress; forgiveness for Tony Yeldham I offered at the time along with prayers for his family. I struggle with forgiveness, unlike Jean Vanier whose canonisation is probably now delayed. Much to learn, Jamie. The feelings of being close to, indeed chosen by, God intensified with the earlier admission to the loony bins in May 1990, portrayed at the beginning of Chapter 6. There was that oven-cleaning with its Holocaust overtones, the white crosses on the tiles, the prostrating on the pavements close to where I'd had the vision of the church on the hill, St Mark's, Battersea Rise suffused with surreal, nigh-supernatural light. Those whom God loves does He first make mentally unwell? Hebrews 12 verses 5–6: "… do not lose heart when He rebukes you, because the Lord disciplines the one he loves, and he chastens everyone he accepts as his son." (NIV)

That sure was a messy time. By this time, however, I had learned to keep quiet about the spiritual messages coursing through my cranium. Not so back in 1980, when I blurted out to two people that I was convinced I was one with God, so powerful were those feelings. That was to my mate Johnny Piper (Oxford golfer RIP), who promptly slapped me across the face in an attempt to knock some sense into me and to my long-suffering GP Michael Gormley, who merely noted my words in the medical records.

From the Hammersmith drop-in centre I would often take several people to choral evensongs at Southwark Cathedral, which was becoming my default church in the early nineties. I had re-engaged with my vicar from school, Roger Royle, who was a Canon there. Disagreements with Colin Slee, the then Dean, led to Roger leaving Southwark, to become an Emeritus Canon, but both were always wonderful speakers. Roger helped me in a mini-mission to help Mordecai Vanunu who had angered Israel and their security service Mossad with his true assertion that Israel had nuclear weapons. Agents kidnapped him in Rome in 1986 and, poor man, he spent the ensuing eighteen years in prison in Ashkelon, twelve of them in solitary confinement. He converted to Christianity from Judaism and was eventually given sanctuary in the confines of the Anglican Cathedral in Jerusalem, St George's where he remains to this day. Roger helped me approach George Carey, ex-Archbishop of Canterbury who became an ally in our futile quest to get Mordecai released. Those Israeli politicians are hard nuts to crack.

Around this time P and C were christened at Southwark – P was a Brownie and she wore her Brownie uniform, and we enjoyed tea and home-baked fruit cake after the service at the back of the Cathedral. Of the chosen godparents I think only Jamie Dallas was able to attend. The girls were baptised rather later than is customary, but better late than never as they say.

In the early nineties too, began my connection with The Association for the Pastoral Care of the Mentally Ill, as we were called in those days. Led by Jeremy Boutwood as chair, and Pam Freeman as co-ordinator, the ethos and approach of this charity to those with mental health problems echoed that of Jean Vanier's approach to those with 'mental handicaps' – early on in my APCMI days the three of us heard Jean speak at Quaker House off the Marylebone Road. Moving indeed … "do you love me?" his charges appeared to be saying. His message shines out of his book, *The Broken Body*, that I purchased that day and with his permission APCMH (mental health not mental illness now) uses a quote from that book in all its leaflets these days.

Here it is:

> If you enter into relationship
> with a lonely or suffering person
> you will discover something else:
> that it is you who are being healed.
> The broken person will reveal to you
> your own hurt
> and the hardness of your heart,
> but also how much you are loved.
> Thus the one you came to heal
> becomes your healer.

Henri Nouwen, or to give him his full Dutch name, Henri Jozef Machiel Nouwen, worked with Jean for nine months in 1985 at L'Arche, Trosly-Breuil before becoming pastor at L'Arche Daybreak in Toronto, Canada where he spent the last ten years of his life. A prolific writer and Catholic theologian, thirty-nine books to Jean's thirty, but who is quibbling or counting.

There are many of Henri's quotes that inspire people. How about:

Spiritual identity means we are not what we do or what people say about us. And we are not what we have. We are the beloved daughters and sons of God.

Or:

Did I offer peace today? Did I bring a smile to someone's face? Did I say words of healing? Did I let go of my anger and resentment? Did I forgive? Did I love? These are the real questions. I must trust that the little bit of love that I sow now will bear many fruits, here in this world and the life to come.

My favourite I found in one of his books in the library of the Abbey House Retreat in Glastonbury where I was staying – sadly, it is no longer a retreat house.

"How much did you earn during your lifetime?" or, "How many friends did you make?" or, "How much progress did you make on your career?" or, "How much influence did you have on people?" Were any of these to be the questions Christ will ask when he comes again in glory, many of us could approach the judgement day with great confidence.

But nobody is going to hear any of these questions. The question we are all going to face is the question we are least prepared for. It is the question: "What have you done for the least of mine?"

Jean and Henri first met at Harvard in the early eighties. I am sure that they are now together once more in Heaven.

My own long and winding road continued post-divorce with the five or so years running Consumer Forum. In those years, as outlined in the travel chapters, I made holiday forays to some troubled parts of the world – to Northern Ireland, where I visited the healing sanctuary of Corrymeela (Protestants mingling with Catholics) and then on my return attended a service in Portsmouth Cathedral celebrating their work. To Mostar, the bullet-ridden hilltop town in Bosnia-Herzegovina whose medieval arched bridge over the Neretva River effectively divided the Croats from the Muslim Bosniaks until it was destroyed in November 1993 shelling. Now rebuilt I believe, there was a temporary metal structure in place when I visited. Ethnic hatred was palpable in the 'occupied territories' of the West Bank in Israel / Palestine, most notably in Bethlehem, but also in Hebron, where I was shot at.

I often feel it is us Christians who are destined to heal these wounds. But we are persecuted in so many countries – worst offenders are North Korea, Afghanistan, Somalia, Libya and Pakistan. It is often too dangerous to proselytise in these countries. Wonderful work by Open Doors, the Barnabas Fund and Release International charities, all working on behalf of persecuted Christians and doing great things. God bless their efforts.

When I turned minicab driver in the late nineties my church attendance dropped again, mostly because sabbath Sunday tended to be my highest earning day, also the day when traffic volumes were lowest. Friday evening and much of Saturday became my time with my children before they got bored of old dad and started to spend more time with friends. Hoist by my own petard, because I often said that friends are usually preferable to family. Not always though, and it's marvellous when one sees a happy thriving family group like the Boulters or the Dallas clan. But somewhat reassuringly, Jesus seems to have had trouble with his own family. Philip Yancey wrote in *The Jesus I Never Knew*:

Jesus' life was *defined* by rejection. His neighbours laughed at him, his family questioned his sanity, his closest friends betrayed him, and his countrymen traded his life for that of a terrorist. Throughout his ministry, Jesus gravitated toward the poor and the rejected ones, the riffraff.

And here we are in the Gospel of Mark, Chapter 3 verse 21 (NIV) to start:

> When his family heard about this, they went to take charge of him, for they said, "He is out of his mind." [My heart goes out to you sir … here we go again with verses 31 to 35.] Then Jesus' mother and brothers arrived. Standing outside, they sent someone in to call him. A crowd was sitting round him, and they told him, "Your mother and brothers are outside looking for you."
> "Who are my mother and my brothers?" he asked.
> Then he looked at those seated in a circle around him and said, "Here are my mother and my brothers! Whoever does God's will is my brother and sister and mother."

The minicab years were drier than most in terms of the Holy Spirit making His presence felt. However, I never lost touch. One way was to dangle a sock in front of my feet – invariably it would point to the correct foot to put it on. Throwing a selection of clothes onto the bed would lead to similar convictions as to what to wear. I know this may sound a bit weird, but my GP Michael was doing parallel things with his pendulum in the Basil Street practice.

In the mid-nineties I was introduced to Burrswood, near Tunbridge Wells, by a friend who spent much healing time there. The incredible story of founder Dorothy Kerin needs retelling. In 1912 she was raised from her five-year deathbed by a vision of Jesus with miraculous immediate strengthening of her limbs and instruction to go and raid the fridge downstairs. This is well told by Dorothy herself in *Fulfilling* and by her biographer, Ruth Farr, in *Will You Go Back?*. Dorothy went on to adopt nine children and set up this wonderful Christian holistic healing centre, initially in Ealing and later in the Kent countryside. Special place, special lady; an undoubted saint who received the stigmata.

If you don't believe in God please read about Dorothy and I think you'll change your mind. If your faith is flagging her tale will reinvigorate your belief.

Once I had parked the driving job and its 87p per hour earning capacity, my life became freer and God took a firmer grip on me. The words of the Genesis song, 'No Son of Mine' became strangely relevant ... here I was hoping to include three or so verses from this song which talks about how to remain on the safe side of sanity. But, you guessed it, having approached Mike Rutherford's people in person in Chelsea and talked to others at his management company on the telephone who referred me on to Concord Music I still got nowhere. Despite filling in forms online no one at Concord ever got back to me. If you fancy seeing what Genesis felt was the key to one's survival you will have to use your internet search engine again.

I have talked about the spiritual impulses of a 'manic' or 'hypomanic' high being akin to the inspiration of the Holy Spirit, which has infused into so many saints and mystics through the centuries. Well, this intensification of emotion now permeated into me. To keep those 'men in white coats' at bay, though, it was important just to get on with life as 'normally' as possible.

God moves in mysterious ways – 'Immortal, invisible, God only wise. In light inaccessible hid from our eyes, Most blessèd, most glorious, the Ancient of Days, Almighty, victorious, Thy great name we praise.' (Walter Chalmers Smith 1867.)

I became a regular at the 9 a.m. service in the retro-choir at Southwark Cathedral. This was a sort of dress rehearsal for the main event at 11 a.m. when the preacher would deliver the same homily that he or she had tried out before the much smaller congregation earlier. And goodness me, the quality of the preaching from Dean Andrew Nunn, Sub-Dean Michael Rawson and Canons Leanne Roberts and Stephen Hance was exceptional. There were exceptional figures too in the congregation, doing great works in all sorts of pastoral and ecclesiastical fields.

One sermon early on set my pulse racing, when Leanne, who once described Jesus' mother as an early example of a single mother teenage pregnancy statistic, spoke about the Paraclete, παράκλητος in Greek. This was new to me – in John's Gospel where the word features most, it is translated as counsellor, helper, advocate or comforter. In John, Chapter 14 v. 16 Jesus tells us, "And I will ask the Father, and he will give you another advocate to help you and be with you for ever." (NIV) The early church, as does Jean Vanier, likened the Paraclete to the Holy Spirit, part of the Trinity, the three-in-one of the new covenant of Christianity. For me it brought back memories of advocating on behalf of others who came to the Consumer Forum drop-in, and work that Pam Freeman and I used to do for people seeking help from APCMH.

John, Chapter 14 verse 26 goes on to say, "But the Advocate, the Holy Spirit, whom the Father will send in my name, will teach you all things and will remind you of everything I have said to you." (NIV) That spirit of truth resides with us and is within us – reminds me of the cavorting Doukhobors in Georgia who have internalised the living spirit of God so it is revealed within each individual.

Another sermon almost brought me to tears. This time it was Michael Rawson basing his words on the book *Velveteen Rabbit* by Margery Williams …

"Real isn't how you are made," said the Skin Horse. "It's a thing that happens to you. When a child loves you for a long, long time, not just to play with, but REALLY loves you, then you become Real" … "It doesn't happen all at once," said the Skin Horse. "You become. It takes a long time. That's why it doesn't happen often to people who break easily, or have sharp edges, or who have to be carefully kept. Generally, by the time you are Real, most of your hair has been loved off, and your eyes drop out and you get loose in the joints and very shabby. But these things don't matter at all, because once you are Real you can't be ugly, except to people who don't understand."

Woof! Sounds like my journey – most of my hair remains but my eyes are dodgy after a detached retina and cataract surgery and shabby I am, not even shabby chic. For me this journey verges on predestination; God has ordained all that has, does and will happen – He is very much in charge, He knows and sees everything. As Enya sings in 'Pilgrim' ... goodness me, once more you will have to search for the first two verses that I was hoping to insert here. I wrote ages ago to Aigle Music in Dublin explaining that I wished to use a few lines written by Roma Ryan in this book. Roma's website has crashed and Enya's has no 'contact us' tag. I even tried inventing an email address for them, info@unity.enya.com to no avail. Having discovered the address of one of her houses I made one last effort but sadly never got a reply – it's a shame really, I think she might like to know how much her spiritual music charmed the dust particles and flora of Eilat and Jerusalem.

Back to the predestination thread ... Romans, Chapter 8 verses 29–30 reads: "For those God foreknew he also predestined to be conformed to the image of his Son, that he might be the firstborn among many brothers and sisters. And those he predestined, he also called; those he called, he also justified; those he justified, he also glorified." (NIV)

Over the winter months of 2014/2015 a mixed group of us took confirmation classes with Michael Rawson and Stephen Stavrou, then precentor at Southwark, now a vicar in Barnes. Over forty years previously I had resisted the urge to become confirmed at Eton. My friends who were being confirmed seemed to be doing so for reasons not very holy – like getting presents from godparents and enjoying a nice day out at St George's Chapel, Windsor Castle where the ceremony would take place. Okay so this precluded me, for the most part, from taking communion, the bread and wine, for all those years. Exceptions I occasionally made when I felt confident in the presence of supportive clergy but that was rarely the case. Rules and regulations regarding 'the host' are interesting – it irks me grievously that Anglicans and divorced people are refused communion in Catholic churches whereas reciprocally they are welcome to receive in Anglican churches.

So as dawn broke on Easter morning, 5.40 a.m. on the 5th April 2015, we were officially welcomed as communicants, taking our first bread and wine at the morning service and given a nice leather-bound liturgy book by Bishop Christopher. I hold no truck with the Catholic doctrine of transubstantiation as regards the Eucharist and am quite happy to take communion once a month or whenever it is offered. The words of the Eucharist service are special … "Thank you for feeding us with the body and blood of our Lord Jesus Christ" but a blessing at the altar rail can be equally wonderful.

E. F. Schumacher's seminal book was *Small is Beautiful* (one of my favourite Economics textbooks) but he also wrote *Good Work*. Never good to boast as St Paul told the Ephesians (Chapter 2 verses 8–9) but I would like to think 'boy done good' in those years with Consumer Forum and by now I was continuing that sort of work with Being Alongside / APCMH as they were now called, starting to volunteer on Thursdays and Sundays at the Royal Hospital for Neuro-disability and completing my efforts in the Wandsworth church. Money in the bank from the property dealings made this all possible but my ethos is to serve others. And as humbly as possible. Noblesse oblige as my father would have put it. His financial security from the steelworks inheritance allowed him to serve Gloucestershire County Council and the North Cotswolds Rural District

Council on a voluntary unpaid basis. At times he suffered verbal abuse from at least one council member – funny how doing something for no financial reward can lead others who dislike you to take umbrage, as happened to his son at times when chairing BA / APCMH.

My favourite New Testament book is James, written by Jesus' half-brother who became head of the early church in Jerusalem. Initially, he and fellow disciple Peter disagreed with Paul as to the inclusion of Gentiles in the new covenant but all was amicably resolved over time. James gives one hope – here in Chapter 1 verse 12: "Blessed is the one who perseveres under trial because, having stood the test, that person will receive the crown of life that the Lord has promised to those who love him." (NIV)

He continues in verse 22: "Do not merely listen to the word, and so deceive yourselves. Do what it says." (NIV) Faith without deeds is dead. Job persevered and finally found happiness with his 14,000 sheep, 6,000 camels, 2,000 cattle, 1,000 donkeys, three beautiful daughters, living to a ripe old age with grandchildren and great-grandchildren.

I hope you remember some of the God-incidences that I have mentioned in previous chapters – the farmworker's pocket contents in Warminster, the lady's gift in San Agustín, the sonic boom in the Garden Tomb grounds, the hail at Tabgha Primacy of Peter Church, the chest-to-chest with the lady on the Bethlehem pavement, the swirl of swifts and swallows at Bodbe, the Arab boy struggling up the Bethany hill or maybe the vision at the Battersea Rise crossroads.

Milder versions bless my to-ings and fro-ings virtually every day. Like just now here at La Ferme where I was talking about Gary Webb at lunch. He used to run a L'Arche house at nearby Cuise-la-Motte but now lives in retirement near Compiègne – at 4 p.m. I take a break from writing and there he is, here in Trosly-Breuil, showing some friends around. We laugh and joke and seek the possible translation

of 'Slightly Bonkers' into French – 'Tordu' they suggest ...
twisted. Perhaps 'Le Tortue Tordu' as it's been slow progress
– tortoise and hare stuff.

But what I am trying to get across is that these days
wherever I am is seemingly the place that God wants me
to be – He has something to show me, maybe a person to
meet, an inspiring piece of His creation, an encounter to
enjoy. There I was a while ago on the Circle & District line
platform at Victoria when Archbishop Justin Welby appears,
sporting purple frock and massive cross. I had written to
him ages before with no reply granted but I let that pass.
"Aha, Justin – you may remember me, Summers OS (for
he was a year below me at school)." I blurted out that I was
a friend of Jean Vanier, and was on Southwark Cathedral's
Anglo-Catholic reunification committee i.e. the 'be nice to
Catholics committee'. "Oh," he says, "I'm off to be nice to
Catholics too. I'm off to meet the Pope!"

I believe Justin found his faith and calling worshipping
at Holy Trinity Brompton. That church is Alpha course
central, Nicky Gumbel's domain. Nicky was my exact con-
temporary at school, in some of the same classes – funnily
enough his wife-to-be, Pippa Hislop, became a friend in the
early seventies. Her soft warm-heartedness inspired me.

Anyway, bless you Justin, and your talented daughter
Katharine. Not an easy job is it being Archbishop of Canterbury? ... up there with Prime Minister I imagine. Particularly when nutters accost you in public places! But this
feeling of being in the right place at the right time even
occurs in the Beatles song, 'All you need is Love' ... I par-
aphrase here, you can't be where you're not meant to be ...
love is all that's needed.

Kathryn Spink, biographer of Jean Vanier in 1990, captured him talking about the discovery of being chosen, of
being shaped in order to do God's work. I included his precise words in an earlier chapter. Jean must have been about

sixty years old at the time. I posted a comment on my 'blog' (www.shirtyletters.com) ... "Absolument, Jean, je suis en accord. Même chose pour moi. Nous sommes logés à la même enseigne (we are in the same boat)."

I do feel chosen by God – it's a real privilege, an honour. What His ultimate purpose in using me is, who knows? 'Lord make me an instrument of your peace' is the opening line of St Francis of Assisi's famous prayer. Now, interestingly, St Francis was born Giovanni di Pietro di Bernardone in the late 12th century to wealthy parents in Assisi. A 'boulevardier', man about town, horseman, swordsman before turning his back on fame and fortune. Jean Vanier's father Georges was Governor-General of Canada – the most important role in Commonwealth Canada – from 1959 to 1967. From these wealthy well-respected families come some of God's ambassadors. St Francis is known as Little Jesus – I'm sure Jean will in due course be elevated to sainthood, but this may now take longer than we anticipated.

How does the Spirit move me? Remember that odd escapade in the *Masquerade* chapter when I followed the brightest lights on a night-time walk across south-west London? Well, matters are a little more sophisticated these days – the dangling sock scenario I still use and it's a joy to be out on the streets of a town or out in the countryside when my path is outlined for me. My eyes will alight on the flutter of a bird's wing, on the raised hand of a child, on a bright reflection in a puddle, the rustle of leaves, the direction a twig on the ground is pointing, a blackbird in a field, the sun shining upon something – countless little affirmatory signals. Sometimes, to make a decision my gaze will settle on something white or silver as confirmation that it's a correct choice – alternatively if my gaze falls on something black or red perhaps it's a course of action to avoid. Almost like that colour code which at times plagued me back in the early nineties. Might sound crazy to you but that's how it works for me and has done now for ten years-plus in this height-ened awareness heyday, a blossoming florescence of my mental faculties. If only my language, the words I use day to day, would follow such a peaceful path – but I am aware of oft overstepping boundaries in speech, certainly after a gin or two. Words can do lasting damage. It is rarely my inten-tion to bruise another person's ego – may God grant me the correct words to use in any particular situation. Amen.

Another wacky theory, of which I have yet to disavow myself, concerns the genealogical lines that God has given us. One of my favourite places is the gift shop at the Garden Tomb in Jerusalem, close to both the American Colony Hotel and St George's Cathedral. Over the years I have bought many maps and charts there. Many of these framed maps etc. now adorn the walls of SEITE (The South East Institute of Theological Education) off Borough High Street, who graciously thanked me for their donation. One of them is a large A3 chart depicting the line from Adam through Abraham and Jacob, through David all the way down to Joseph His stepfather. Who is to say these lines did not con-tinue? Particularly if one accepts the supposition that Jesus and Mary Magdalene were, if not married, perhaps had at least brought a child into this world?

Could some of the great Christians over the centuries have

inherited traits on this Davidic line? People like St Francis, Leonardo da Vinci, William Shakespeare and Wolfgang Amadeus Mozart? Distant relatives of all the apostles must be around today. Could the extraordinary Mozart, who was composing symphonies at the age of five and whose original scores bear precious few scratched-through mistakes ... could that genetic genome have divine inheritance? I fancy that a sort of 'Buggins' turn' might be in operation.

But my raised awareness, 'mindfulness' it might be called, could well be diagnosed as a symptom of mental illness, according to psychiatrists. Three of us siblings trained from Euston to Holyhead on Anglesey in late September 2013 for the memorial service of our splendid nanny / governess Phil who had been part of each of our lives. The memorial service in a small chapel was remarkable – attending were most of the Church of Wales hierarchy, including one scurrilous thief whom she had held in high regard when he was at St Paul's Cathedral. He was the subject of my letter to Justin Welby when his crimes near Barnsley in Yorkshire were exposed during his tenure at Farnham in Surrey. I think he's still on the run from justice.

I'm not on the run anywhere – just biding my time awaiting God's further instructions. Helping to start up Faith and Light Oxford is a current priority – a group in formation to foster community among those with learning disabilities and their families. As I have said in the longer term it would be wonderful to start a L'Arche community near Oxford, but this will require much help to overcome the bureaucratic hurdles of the modern world. What He wants me to do He will make clear. More work as gardener's assistant to Mark Waters would be good – to earn money while attempting to direct nature's exuberance is a bonus, outdoor work good for body and soul. More writing? Who knows? He knows.

Bottom line is that I have a heart for the dispossessed, the lonely, the fragility of the broken. Jesus sent the poor and the frail to confound the wealthy and wise. He is hidden in the weak and the small. I used to say that those diagnosed mentally ill were the most vilified in society – The Least of Mine – but there are other potential candidates ... refugees, prisoners, the physically handicapped, addicts, those with dementia or Alzheimer's. We need to befriend the marginalised. Paul's words in 2 Corinthians 12 verse 10 are particularly relevant, "... I delight in weaknesses, in insults, in hardships, in persecutions, in difficulties. For when I am weak, then I am strong." (NIV) Each of us has work to do.

The penultimate verse of the Bible, part of Revelation Chapter 22 verse 20 reads, "Come, Lord Jesus." (NIV) Amen to that.

# EPILOGUE

Thus far it's been a good life – long may it continue. Some people who have read draft versions of this book have commented that my life has been tough and tenebrous but I guess I have 'bouncebackability' because I remain optimistic. This is no epinikion, no song of victory – indeed one person condemns my words as bizarre verbal diarrhoea, a stream of manic ramblings.

As we near its end, I want to reinforce the reasons why I wrote this book. First off, it has been a cathartic exercise to tell the truth about my life – quite a few people have chosen not to be included and I have respected their wishes. Next off, and I truly hope this has come across in spades, is to warn everyone about the dangers of marijuana and the way it can cause psychosis. There is pretty much a sole voice in the print media alerting the world to this, Peter Hitchens in the *Mail on Sunday*. He has rightly said that the perpetrators of all those high school shootings in America have long histories of cannabis use, often allied to taking the prescription drug Ritalin. This simply never gets mentioned in other press reports. To me it is frightening that so many American states and countries around the world have legalised dope – millions are being made by astute businessmen but beware the sequential consequence of millions more admissions to already crowded mental institutions. And here in the UK, the Liberal Democrats in their last manifesto said they would legalise cannabis and spend more on mental health. Yes, but they underestimated the latter several-fold. Another reason for this book is to highlight the effect of head injuries on one's health and persona. I am no expert here but volunteering at the Royal Hospital for Neuro-disability has shown me the results of cataclysmic brain injuries. My elder daughter tells me that *all* serial killers have suffered damaging head traumas before the age of two. Wow.

My final reason for doing this book is a selfish one – to get my name sufficiently known and the way I write enough respected so a publisher will take a second look at my book on *Pastoral Care in Mental Health*.

The last words of the Bible are: Revelations 21 verse 22 – "The grace of the Lord Jesus be with God's people. Amen." (NIV) Apostle John the Evangelist wrote those words in a cave on the island of Patmos in the Sporades, or were they written by John of Patmos in exile from Roman persecutor, Domitian? The man was allegedly plunged into boiling oil in Rome and did not suffer one jot – all who witnessed this miracle in the Colosseum were converted to Christianity. He died in Ephesus, modern Turkey, around AD 100.

My last words shall be, echoing Jean Vanier ... be free to be a little silly, being slightly bonkers is okay. Be child-like not childish. "Power is made perfect in weakness," says God to Paul. He comes, hidden deep within the marginalised.

Yes, come, Lord Jesus, come...

# Acknowledgements

Thanks go to my favourite artist, Kit Williams, for graciously allowing me to insert pictures of his paintings into the *Masquerade* chapter.

I am also grateful to Sarah Sharp at Warner Chappell Music for permission to use lyrics from 'One of Us' by Eric Bazilian covered by Joan Osborne. Special thanks must go to Beth Marshall at Sony/ATV who tried hard to secure permissions from Enya and Mike Scott for 'Pilgrim' and 'How Long Will I Love You' – no reply and no respectively. We had success with the 'Solsbury Hill' lyrics from an enthusiastic Rob Bozas at Peter Gabriel's studios.

Max Goodwin Brown (occasional barista to Guy Garvey) deserves a medal for deciphering my handwritten chapters and turning them into computer documents.

Without Sam Carter, my editor, this book might never have seen the light of day – Sam is a talented wordsmith with an eye for grammatical detail, sentence structure, libel issues and people's sensibilities, and he put in many hours honing this memoir into shape, when not disappearing on exotic holidays. Bless you Sam.

I would also like to thank various people who read parts of earlier versions or even whole book drafts and came up with sensible ideas for improvements – Ali, Vole, Joy, Alex, Steve, Chris, Mark & Josie, Wease, Simon & Nicky, Margaret, Sally & Brendan, Tessie, Michael & Mary Clare, Matt, Andrew & Sue, and others I may have forgotten.

# Appendix

Saturday 28<sup>th</sup> December 1991

from Springfield Hospital
61 Glenburnie Road
London
SW17 7DJ

Dear Mrs. Bottomley,
Allow me to introduce myself. My name is Jamie Summers, age 37½, educated Eton College and Christ Church, Oxford (14 'O' levels, 3 A grade 'A' levels, 2 S levels). I believe we have a connection – my brother-in-law, Andrew Ingram is I think godfather to one of your children (very good choice!).

Firstly, a brief summary of my personal predicament. Nearly three weeks ago I voluntarily admitted myself to the above establishment on the instigation of my wife, S, in order to ease the pressure on her mind caused by my somewhat restless and sleepless behaviour. Armed with a prescription from my G.P., Michael Gormley, I presented myself at Bluebell Ward under the auspices of my allocated NHS doctor, a man called Jonathan Hillum. Without my knowledge or consent, Michael's prescription dosage was immediately almost tripled and administered – this being that favourite toy of the psychiatric profession, namely Largactyl now called Chlorpromazine. Two days later, when this cosh was not having (in their eyes) a sufficiently stultifying effect on yours truly's brain a second doctor, one Dr. Vince, without even consulting Dr. Hillum, who was absent, decided to give me 80 mg of Droperidol liquid – I would here like to point out that the <u>maximum</u> dose given by Desmond Kelly and his team at the lovely Priory in Roehampton Lane is 5 mg at any one time ... I was pole-axed for ten hours, stiff as a floorboard from the neck down. Anyway, blood had been taken (yet again) and glory be, when the analysis came back, I was told by a member of the night nursing staff that they were worried because my white blood cell count had increased dramatically and that I was to be given no drugs at all for two days (yippee!). This white blood cell problem is usually due to some infection but in my case had clearly been caused by massive over-prescription of these dangerous drugs, as I am not a sick person by nature and have never taken antibiotics in my life.

Two days off these substances gave me sufficient breathing space to recover my senses and to assert my rights in refusing to take them. Thus for the past 12 days or so I have simply taken 800 mg of Lithium Carbonate (Priadel) at night as I have done religiously for the past 19 months. I have been able to view the system dispassionately ever since.

Enough of my story. I understand your friend Kenneth Clarke doesn't visit many schools although I am sure my cricketing friend Tim Eggar makes up for him. I hope, nay I am convinced that you are of a compassionate nature and will take it upon yourself to come and see some of the evils that are masquerading as care in the rotten apple that is psychiatric medicine in the National Health Service. Perhaps you and your boss, Mr. Waldegrave and your underlings have been concentrating your energies on the normal hospitals, but your eyes and ears are needed here.

Let us start with the quality (sic) of the food. Perhaps Caroline Waldegrave could take an interest here – I hear she knows her onions! When I arrived the cupboards were nigh bare – oh, the staff have their cosy little locked cupboards full of reasonable things but us patients/animals for our hungrier moments had little. For ten days there was no sugar, no butter – only the lowest form of 'spread' – then the cheapo powdered coffee and the teabags ran out and were not replenished. The bread was the pappiest form of white trash available – any salad left over from 'supper' (at 6 p.m.) is generally thrown away vindictively by the staff.

Fruit? There might sometimes be 5 bananas or oranges between twenty-eight of us.

As for the regular meals dished out from the kitchens ¼ mile away I would not deign to feed pigs or rats on the stuff. The mashed potatoes look tainted, the vegetables are boiled dry of nutrients, the meat if any is poor, poor quality and our boiled eggs at breakfast are regularly done to a turn of 17 minutes – marvellous for everyone's bowels! Since I arrived I have done my utmost to upgrade this miserable diet with injections of fruit, butter, cheese, mayonnaise, marmite and loaves of my own bread – you see I am a wholesale baker by trade. We are what we eat after all.

Secondly, one must comment on the nursing. As in all things there is good and bad, but regretfully I have to report that predominantly the curtain falls on the distaff side. People crying in pain for help are left smirkingly to flounder on the floor, pleas for aid go unheard … "no, I'm busy" is a favourite excuse. Vomit, shit and urine are left to be smeared around the ward. There is little love and care here. Petty rules abound; the kitchen, bathroom & washing/utility room are almost permanently locked and out of bounds to the 'loonies' – smoking is confined to a sauna (the radiator is jammed on) and the dining/play area, and yet the staff and doctors flaunt their own no smoking sign in their office, the hypocrites. Us patients do 90 per cent of the nursing of our elderly co-sufferers – the incontinent ones often awash in their own urine and faeces slumped on their soiled and never-changed sheets. I am not over-painting my canvas.

As for the doctors here I shall name names. I can only speak about those I have met here on the ward and compare them with the doctors I met almost 12 years ago in the Priory and more recently briefly 19 months ago before the money ran out (it's £400 per night now privately) and BUPA, bless their little cotton socks, won't pay for my stays in these places. But I digress. The chief rottweiler in the pack of Wandsworth hounds is a man called Greville

Gundy who has been in this game for many years (he featured in Jonathan Miller's recent madness series). Nearly retired now, he has been pushing drugs down people's throats with relish for ages – not long ago he gleefully told me that he has prescribed 2 grams per diem of Largactyl to some patients. Let us take this in context – Desmond Kelly probably wouldn't give anybody more than 300mg per day possibly half that – so we are talking seven or eight times the doses meted out under the private system. It is like taking ten paracetamol or aspirin at a go – not good for the liver or the arteries as I am sure you will agree. Does he want the animals to become vegetables?

Second in command are his lieutenants Hillum, Dr. Vince and Potter. Of these only Dr. Vince incurs my wrath, probably because of his spiteful treatment of yours truly not to mention others under his 'care'. If only the doses of these terrible body-shaking drugs, which I believe are desperately expensive anyway, were reduced to a palatable level or better still switched to more natural remedies available then the money saved could be reallocated to give more nursing staff, better wheelchairs etc. Excuse my Bernard Levin length sentence!

One last gripe concerns the lamentable cleaning staff – a cursory wipe here and there simply ain't good enough – new brooms are needed.

Please let me know your views.

Yours faithfully and sincerely,

Jamie Summers

\*\*\*

And then:

Thursday 16th January 1992

from Springfield Hospital
61 Glenburnie Road
London SW17 7DJ

Dear Mrs. Bottomley,

I wrote to you 19 days ago on matters of great import concerning your department and have not received a reply, not even a cursory "Mrs X thanks you for your letter and has noted its contents." Perhaps you dismissed my words as the ramblings of a mental asylum inmate and binned them? A brief phone call to Carole and Andrew, your friends, would have sufficed to allay your doubts, but no, you chose to ignore my letter. Well, I have more to say – should you require a copy of my earlier epistle please do not hesitate to ask.

My comments of 19 days ago still hold true and far from improving, the general situation has indeed deteriorated since then. Just to mention some individual cases which must come under your aegis as number 2 in your department. The most horrifying was the man at Springfield who around New Year's Day started getting severe chest pains – an ambulance was called and he was driven down to the nearby St. George's Hospital, I hope you know the one, it's your showpiece NHS hospital for South West London – you've closed most of the other ones. On arrival he was turned away because the doctors there don't want the loonies from Springfield on their wards. I have to report that he died in the ambulance on the way back. I quote your boss speaking on the 14th January ... "more and better care is being extracted from the resources available and in a more efficient manner." Oh yes, Mr. Waldegrave? One expects more from Eton/Christ Church men, let alone fellows of

All Souls. Why does he tell such porkies and massage his facts? We all remember there are lies, damned lies and statistics … his reforms are working well are they, not here they aren't.

Let us move to the private system. BUPA not only won't pay for my stays in mental hospitals but I understand now they won't pay for any psychiatric care whatsoever. I assume private hospitals do come under your remit as well? Being connected to health as they are, although I am told extracting money from them for treatments received often causes more anguish than the illness itself. I have another medical case to bring to your attention and the name may well ring a bell with your husband. A close friend of mine called Mark Faber, who was about your husband's vintage at university and played cricket for Sussex in Tony Greig's era, undertook a fairly routine operation to remove a varicose vein that had troubled him for some years. This was about 12 days ago, something obviously went wrong in the operation, Mark screamed in agony but <u>no doctor came for one hour</u> and he died. And that is the private sector.

Back to Springfield – why is it that these human beings are denied access to non-psychiatric doctors? They suffer from physical ailments just like you and I and yet their GPs become non-persons once they have crossed this threshold. There is a lady here who is 64 but looks 94 (you should see the cocktail of drugs swilled down her throat every night), she is incontinent at both ends, she slobbers continuously, her clothes stink permanently, she has a gout-like swelling on one ankle and her lungs are feeble. This is long-term care under your blessed NHS. She has no teeth and consequently is nigh impossible to understand, she can't even eat a sandwich without spewing it out. There is a dentist on site, some 300 yards away who could fix her up with some dentures but does he move? No. She needs a doctor badly, not a shrink, or she will die soon.

I reckon someone could present a good case against your department for gross negligence or at the very least driving without due care and attention. I am sure it is now possible to sue the government; there is that wise man who is currently tackling Norman Lamont and his team at the Treasury. He followed government advice regarding small businesses for 11 years and eventually went broke – well I could have told him a thing or two about your counterpart at the Treasury, John Patten, who came as a supply teacher to Eton in my time. I well remember his lectures on the economics of imports/exports which were so nonsensical they were almost farcical. What a dismal science it is. And if that man has reached such an exalted position in government, God help the rest of us! My apologies for being somewhat rude but one can't help becoming angry in a place like this.

By the time you get this letter you will have had three weeks to muse over the first one and had it been an electricity bill you probably would have been cut off by now. I want to see some action, and I want to hear some truths from you and Mr. Waldegrave – no political double-dutch, no side-stepping the facts. None of this "the NHS is safe in our hands" lark because very clearly at the moment it isn't.

This is my last time of asking. I want answers.

Yours etc.

Jamie Summers

***

POH (2) 1701/418
Mr J Summers
79 Altenburg Gardens
London SW11 1JQ

Dear Mr Summers,
Thanks you for your letter of 28 December 1991 about the treatment you are receiving at Springfield Hospital.

I am sorry to hear that you feel this is unsatisfactory.

You have raised an important matter that essentially concerns the local provision of health services in Wandsworth Health Authority.

As you know, the reforms of the NHS have centred upon the importance of establishing the role of district health and family health authorities as the purchasers of hospital, community health and primary care services and prevention. They have important functions in translating patients, needs and concerns into improved services. A major aid to them in developing the quality of care is the Government's initiative on citizen's (sic) rights. The Patient's (sic) Charter introduces national standards but more importantly the concept of local standards to be incorporated into local health charters. At the same time the reforms have sought to delegate management decisions to the level of service provision

So that you may receive an answer to your specific query about the treatment you are receiving at Springfield Hospital, I am copying your letter to Dr. Enid Vincent, Chairman of Wandsworth HA, together with a request that she reply to you direct at the same time as reporting to me.

Thank you for bringing this matter to my attention.

Yours sincerely,

Virginia Bottomley

*** 

Your ref: POH (2) 1701/418
Altenburg Gardens
London SW11 7th March 1992

Dear Mrs. Bottomley,
Thank you for your letter of the 27th January replying to mine of the 28th December and I presume my 'chaser' of the 16th January although you made no reference to this second letter.

Whilst I accept your comments that decentralisation of the NHS has transferred power from Government to the local health authorities I regret this seems to have done little to speed the wheels of reform. You promised to send a copy of my first letter to the Chairman of Wandsworth Health Authority, Dr. Enid Vincent and I am sure you did so, but I have to inform you that after some 6 weeks I have yet to receive any comments from her. Perhaps a reminder from you might hurry her up? I would very much like to meet her personally to air my grievances, and those of current patients at Springfield.

I am currently preparing an article which has been promised national newspaper coverage highlighting the heinous practices of 'megadosing' and 'polypharmacy' so much in vogue at Springfield, together with the disgraceful lack of care and respect exhibited by the majority of doctors and nurses. One suspects this is a nationwide phenomenon and I hope you will devote more of your time in the future (re-election permitting) to improving conditions for these downtrodden and forgotten human beings.

Looking forward to receiving Dr. Vincent's reply,
I remain, yours sincerely
Jamie Summers

\*\*\*

Our ref: EH/LL449
Harewood House
61 Glenburnie Road
London SW17 7DJ
13th April 1992

Dear Mr. Summers,
I am writing in reply to your letter to Virginia Bottomley

dated 28th December 1991 which was received here at the end of January. I apologise for the delay in replying but you raised a number of issues which required a comprehensive investigation.

You are correct in saying that your medication was increased at the time of your admission to Bluebell Ward. The dose which you received was prescribed by a doctor in the light of your clinical condition at that time. There is nothing to suggest that your white blood cell count was affected but your medication was stopped temporarily once the sedation due to droperidol began to take effect. This is common practice. I am unable to comment on treatment given to other patients but Dr. Gundy prescribes medication in accordance with the British National Formulary guidelines.

I am sorry that you were not happy with the standard of food provided. The quality of catering is regularly reviewed by the Mental Health Unit and comments as to how this might be improved are welcomed. There is a problem with maintaining adequate provisions in the cupboards. It is difficult to maintain a balance between allowing full access to provisions for all patients and rationing, to ensure supplies remain, which does involve less freedom of use. Staff have to use their discretion to ensure everyone has a fair share. I'm sorry if stocks were temporarily exhausted on the day you arrived. Any food which remains after a meal is thrown away to comply with environmental legislation.

Bluebell Ward does have rules with regard to smoking and non-smoking areas. These were agreed by the patients and staff in the light of the Health Authority's smoking policy. Staff are equally bound by the ward policy and if any of them are seen to flaunt it, this would be taken very seriously. As you are not specific about the incidents you describe the managers in the Unit are unable to take further action in respect of this now. The bathroom and utility room are locked at times when nursing staff believe that they are unable to give adequate supervision of these areas but if at any of these times a patient wishes to avail themselves of these facilities they would not be denied access unreasonably.

I understand your concern with regard to incontinence experienced by elderly patients on the ward. Staff do make every effort to maintain a high standard of hygiene and certainly are expected to change sheets as necessary. Without information about a specific incident the Managers have been unable to identify a specific instance that matched your description. With regard to the overall cleanliness of the ward there is a specification which the domestic staff follow and I understand that monitoring on Bluebell Ward shows they do this particularly well.

I am sorry that you perceived a lack of love and care on the ward as the staff there regularly demonstrate their commitment to a caring and sensitive approach to the treatment of their patients. I apologise if you feel the service was not offered to you in an acceptable manner.

I regret that overall your experience of admission to Bluebell Ward was such an unhappy one. I do however appreciate your bringing these concerns to my attention and believe that the Mental Health Unit will continue to keep the standards of care they provide under review.

Yours sincerely,

Dr. Enid Vincent

Chairman

Wandsworth Health Authority

\*\*\*

Your ref: EH/LL449
Altenburg Gardens
18th May 1992
London SW11


Dear Dr. Vincent,

Thank you for your letter of the 13th April. There are several inaccuracies in the information you have gleaned. I would like to concentrate on the second paragraph.

Yes, I accept that my prescription was increased at the time of my admission due to my clinical condition. Shortly thereafter, in addition to the daily 800 mg of Largactyl, I was prescribed 80 mg of Droperidol. My registrar, Dr. Hillum, had gone away on holiday and the additional dose was recommended by Dr. Vince alone on the basis of my 'increased state of agitation', namely opening the ward windows because the internal temperature was about 90°F. It is the unnecessarily large doses and particularly the mixing of these drugs that I object to. I repeat my allegation that in the private sector such practices are considered obscene.

You say there was nothing to suggest my white blood cell count was affected but the relevant blood test showed a level of 77.3 per cent of neutrophils in the total. As my medical notes stated this is "considerably raised". It was when the results of that test came through that I was informed by Ray, the duty nurse, that I quote, "your white blood cell count has gone bananas and we are stopping your medication for a day or two." There was never any suggestion that my drugs were stopped because the Droperidol had taken effect.

You say that Dr. Gundy prescribes medication in accordance with the British National Formulary guidelines. Although he was away on holiday for most of my time at Springfield I cannot let such a statement pass. As regards

Largactyl, the BNF states that 'up to 1 gram daily may be required in psychoses'. Dr. Gundy admits to giving up to 2 grams daily. Furthermore, the BNF states that 'prescribing of more than one antipsychotic at the same time is not recommended'. I suppose I was lucky to only get two, many patients get a 'polypharmacy' cocktail of three or 4 of these drugs.

About your other points, most patients and ex-patients would concur with my views on the lack of love and care shown by the staff, particularly on the acute wards. Naturally there are exceptions and on Bluebell I would nominate Simon Lancaster, Sheila and many of the night staff for praise. As regards smoking in the staff room, the chief perpetrator was Dr. Vince and although you say this would be taken seriously I somehow doubt it.

Yours sincerely,
Jamie Summers

\*\*\*

20 May, 1992

Dear Mr. Summers,
Thank you for your letter dated 18 May 1992 referring to my letter to you dated 13 April 1992.

I have asked for the additional points you have raised to be looked into and will reply more fully as soon as possible.

Yours sincerely,
Dr. Enid C. Vincent

\*\*\*

17 June 1992

Dear Mr. Summers,

I am writing in response to your letter of 18 May 1992. I am sorry that you were not happy with all the points made in my previous reply to you. I understand, however, that when you last attended the outpatient clinic Dr. Gundy went through your case notes with you and answered all your queries on medication.

Whilst I note your praise of certain staff on Bluebell Ward, and will pass your comments on, I feel that we have already investigated your complaints thoroughly and that I have nothing further to add.

Dr. Gundy has assured me that he would be happy to discuss the question of your medication with you again at your next appointment should you so wish.

Yours sincerely
Dr. Enid Vincent